CAMPAIGN FOR PRESIDENT

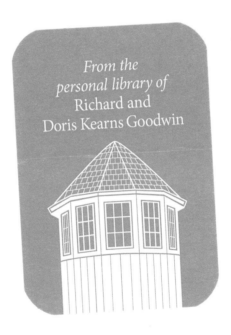

Campaigning American Style

Series Editors
Daniel M. Shea and F. Christopher Arterton

Few areas of American politics have changed as dramatically in recent times as the way in which we choose public officials. Students of politics and political communications are struggling to keep abreast of these developments—and the 2000 and 2004 elections only fed the confusion and concern. Campaigning American Style is a new series of books devoted to both the theory and practice of American electoral politics. It offers high-quality work on the conduct of new-style electioneering and how it is transforming our electoral system. Scholars, practitioners, and students of campaigns and elections need new resources to keep pace with the rapid rate of electoral change, and we are pleased to help provide them in this exciting series.

Books in the Series

CAMPAIGN FOR PRESIDENT

The Managers Look at 2008

THE INSTITUTE OF POLITICS
JOHN F. KENNEDY SCHOOL OF GOVERNMENT
HARVARD UNIVERSITY

ROWMAN & LITTLEFIELD PUBLISHERS, INC.
Lanham • Boulder • New York • Toronto • Plymouth, UK

Published by Rowman & Littlefield Publishers, Inc.
A wholly owned subsidiary of The Rowman & Littlefield Publishing Group, Inc.
4501 Forbes Boulevard, Suite 200, Lanham, Maryland 20706
http://www.rowmanlittlefield.com

Estover Road, Plymouth PL6 7PY, United Kingdom

British Library Cataloguing in Publication Information Available

Library of Congress Cataloging-in-Publication Data
Campaign for president : the managers look at 2008 / The Institute of Politics,
John F. Kennedy School of Government, Harvard University.
    p.   cm. — (Campaigning American style)
  Includes index.
    ISBN 978-0-7425-7046-7 (cloth : alk. paper) — ISBN 978-0-7425-7047-4
(pbk. : alk. paper) — ISBN 978-0-7425-7048-1 (electronic)
    1. Presidents—United States—Election—2008—Congresses. 2. Political
campaigns—United States—Congresses. 3. Campaign management—United
States—Congresses. 4. United States—Politics and government—2001— —
Congresses. I. John F. Kennedy School of Government. Institute of Politics.
  E906.C36 2009
  324.70973—dc22
                                                                    2009008161

∞™ The paper used in this publication meets the minimum requirements of
American National Standard for Information Sciences—Permanence of Paper
for Printed Library Materials, ANSI/NISO Z39.48-1992.

Printed in the United States of America

CONTENTS

THE PARTICIPANTS

Marc Ambinder
Associate Editor
The Atlantic

David Axelrod
Chief Strategist
Obama-Biden

Joel Benenson
Chief Pollster
Obama-Biden

Rick Berke
Assistant Managing Editor
The New York Times
Member, Institute of Politics Senior
  Advisory Committee

Valerie Biden-Owens
National Campaign Chairperson
Joe Biden

Guy Cecil
National Political and Field Director
Hillary Clinton

Chris Cillizza
Author
The Fix, WashingtonPost.com

Sheryl Cohen
Campaign Manager
Christopher Dodd

Jeanne Cummings
Chief Lobbying and Influence
  Writer
The Politico

Fred Davis
Media Strategist
McCain-Palin

Rick Davis
Campaign Manager
McCain-Palin

Frank Fahrenkopf
Co-Chair
Commission on Presidential
  Debates

Christian Ferry
Deputy Campaign Manager
McCain-Palin

Steve Grubbs
Iowa Campaign Manager
Tommy Thompson

Mark Halperin
Editor-at-Large and Senior Political
   Analyst
Time

Sydney Hay
Campaign Manager
Duncan Hunter

Gwen Ifill
Managing Editor
Washington Week
Member, Institute of Politics Senior
   Advisory Committee

John King
Chief National Correspondent
CNN

Bill Lacy
Campaign Chairman
Fred Thompson

Alyssa Mastromonaco
Director, Scheduling and
   Advance
Obama-Biden

Bill McInturff
Chief Pollster
McCain-Palin

Lew Moore
Campaign Manager
Ron Paul

Beth Myers
Campaign Manager
Mitt Romney

Luis Navarro
Campaign Manager
Joe Biden

Susan Page
Washington Bureau Chief
USA Today

David Plouffe
Campaign Manager
Obama-Biden

Trevor Potter
General Counsel
McCain-Palin

Ryan Price
Deputy Political Director
McCain-Palin

Jonathan Prince
Deputy Campaign Manager
John Edwards

Mark Putnam
Media Consultant
Bill Richardson

Ed Rollins
Campaign Chairman
Mike Huckabee

Lois Romano
Political Reporter
The Washington Post

Joe Rospars
New Media Director
Obama-Biden

Chip Saltsman
Campaign Manager
Mike Huckabee

Brent Seaborn
Director of Strategy
Rudy Giuliani

Sarah Simmons
Director of Strategy
McCain-Palin

Joe Trippi
Senior Adviser
John Edwards

Howard Wolfson
Communications Director
Hillary Clinton

THE OBSERVERS

Niels Aaboe
Executive Editor for Political
    Science, American History, and
    Communication
Rowman & Littlefield Publishers

Anne Aaron
Director of the Profiles in Courage
    and New Frontier Award
    Programs
John F. Kennedy Library
    Foundation

Iris Adler
Executive Editor
New England Cable News

Graham Allison
Director, Belfer Center for Science
    and International Affairs
Harvard Kennedy School

Eric Andersen
Fellows Program Manager
Institute of Politics

Dan Balz
National Political Correspondent
The Washington Post

Joseph Bower
Baker Foundation Professor of
    Business Administration
Harvard Business School

Sheila Burke
Adjunct Lecturer in Public Policy,
    Malcolm Wiener Center for
    Social Policy
Harvard Kennedy School

Alex Burns
Reporter
The Politico

Chuck Campion
Principal and Founder
Dewey Square Group

Heather Campion
Member
Institute of Politics Senior Advisory
    Committee

Alex Castellanos
Consultant, National Media,
    Inc.
Fellow, Institute of Politics (Fall
    2008)

David Chalian
Political Director
ABC News

Daniel Chew
Intern
McCain-Palin

Charles Cook
Publisher
"The Cook Report"

Mark Dalhouse
Director, Office of Active
    Citizenship & Service
Vanderbilt University

John Della Volpe
Director of Polling
Institute of Politics

David Ellwood
Dean
Harvard Kennedy School

Sam Feist
Political Director
CNN

Daniel Fenn
Lecturer
Harvard Kennedy School

Christian Flynn
Director of Conferences and Special
    Projects
Institute of Politics

Amanda Fuchs Miller
Editor
*Campaign for President: The
    Managers Look at 2008*

Marshall Ganz
Lecturer in Public Policy
Harvard Kennedy School

David Gergen
Professor of Public Service, Harvard
    Kennedy School
Fellow, Institute of Politics (Spring
    1984)

Craig Gilbert
Political Reporter
Milwaukee Journal Sentinel

Bob Giles
Curator, Nieman Foundation
Harvard University

Brian Goldsmith
Producer
CBS Nightly News with Katie Couric

Jim Gray
Associate Vice President of Harvard
    Real Estate Services
Harvard University

Marcia Hale
Managing Director
McKenna, Long & Aldridge

Tony Halmos
Director of Public Relations
City of London Corporation

John Heilemann
Contributing Editor
New York Magazine

Fred Hochberg
Alumnus
Harvard Kennedy School

Edie Holway
Fellows Coordinator, Shorenstein
    Center
Harvard Kennedy School

Maxine Isaacs
Adjunct Lecturer in Public
    Policy
Harvard Kennedy School

Elaine Kamarck
Lecturer
Harvard Kennedy School

Kathy Kendall
Research Professor
University of Maryland

Alexander Keyssar
Matthew W. Stirling, Jr., Professor
    of History and Social Policy
Harvard Kennedy School

Dotty Lynch
Executive in Residence in the
    School of Communication,
    American University
Fellow, Institute of Politics (Spring
    2006)

Sandy Maisel
William R. Kenan, Jr., Professor of
    Government
Colby College

Charles Mathesian
National Politics Editor
The Politico

Alex Maurice
Harvard College Class of
    2009

Tom McClimon
Assistant Executive Director
U.S. Conference of Mayors

Catherine McLaughlin
Executive Director
Institute of Politics

Nicco Mele
Visiting Lecturer in the Murrow
    Chair, Harvard Kennedy
    School
President, EchoDitto
Fellow, Institute of Politics (Fall
    2008)

Mark Merritt
President and CEO, The
    Pharmaceutical Care
    Management Association
Fellow, Institute of Politics (Fall
    1996)

Adam Nagourney
Chief Political Correspondent
The New York Times
Fellow, Institute of Politics (Fall
    2005)

Nancy Palmer
Executive Director, Shorenstein
    Center
Harvard Kennedy School

Cathey Park
Women in Leadership
    Coordinator
Institute of Politics

Esten Perez
Communications Director
Institute of Politics

Julia Piscitelli
Assistant Director, Women &
    Politics Institute
American University

Roger Porter
IBM Professor of Business and
    Government
Harvard Kennedy School

Noelia Rodriguez
John F. Kennedy, Jr., Forum
    Director, Institute of
    Politics
Fellow, Institute of Politics (Fall
    2007)

Bill Rubenstein
Professor of Law
Harvard Law School

Michael Scherer
White House Correspondent
Time

Thaleia Schlesinger
Schlesinger & Associates

Julie Schroeder
Executive Assistant
Institute of Politics

Maralee Schwartz
Fellow, Shorenstein Center,
    Harvard Kennedy School
Fellow, Institute of Politics (Fall
    2007)

Walter Shapiro
Political Writer

Laura Simolaris
National Programs Director
Institute of Politics

Roger Simon
Chief Political Columnist
The Politico

Ben Smith
Blogger
Politico.com

Lynn Sweet
Washington, D.C., Bureau Chief
Chicago Sun-Times
Fellow, Institute of Politics (Spring
    2004)

Lisa Taddeo
Writer
Esquire

Ryan Taney
Harvard College Class of 2009

Kristin Unruh
Harvard College Class of 2010

Greg Wilson
New Media Manager
Institute of Politics

Jeff Zeleny
Writer
The New York Times

Peter Zimmerman
Senior Associate Dean for Strategic
    Program Development
Harvard Kennedy School

INTRODUCTION

S INCE 1972, THE INSTITUTE OF POLITICS at the Harvard Kennedy School
has gathered managers and senior advisers to presidential campaigns in
Cambridge immediately following the election. We provide a rare opportunity for them to engage in an exchange of views about their strategies
and tactics during the course of the campaign. We have published a lightly
edited transcript of these discussions every four years so that future candidates, managers, journalists and scholars can better understand the nature
of modern presidential campaigns as they appear to the participants at the
time.

There are several factors that make this election distinct from all we have
covered before. The Obama campaign was able to use new technology as
an organizing tool that surpassed every other campaign's expectations and
abilities for fundraising and grassroots mobilization. The candidates also
represented the diversity of America as never before. For the Institute, the
most exciting part of this election cycle was how young people got involved
in politics like never before. They also changed their views about public and
political service.

The Institute of Politics is a memorial to President John F. Kennedy and
our mission is to stimulate and nurture student interest in public service and
leadership. Our *15th Biannual Youth Survey on Politics and Public Service*
taken prior to the election found that a majority of eighteen- to twenty-four-
year-olds are personally interested in some form of public service to help the
country. Many in this group will consider careers in federal, state or local
government and a smaller, yet significant, group think they will consider
running for office.

Equally interesting, our survey found an increase in the number of young
people who see the effectiveness of political engagement. They also increasingly see politics as an effective way of solving our nation's problems and
running for office and getting involved in politics as an honorable thing

to do. These are changes from our past surveys. There is great anticipation among our constituents for the change this election promised. Young people are anxious for a working grassroots government that allows them to participate in their own future. This campaign set expectations high.

With the presidential campaign of 2008 now concluded and the editing of these proceedings complete, we turn to study and analyze the political and policy decisions that follow. Those results will become the foundation for the next presidential campaign, which may start any day now. For Harvard students and all students of democracy, it is most important that the premises and promises of a successful campaign result in a successful administration. They will be watching and, more importantly, weighing in.

The conference and this book could not have happened without the hard work of our staff at the Institute. Christian Flynn managed the complex logistics of the conference and the production of this book with Cathey Park. Catherine McLaughlin and Amanda Fuchs Miller edited the transcript, which you are about to read. Harvard students Ryan Taney, Alex Maurice and Kristin Unruh compiled the timeline of campaign events. My great thanks to them for all their hard work. Special thanks to the managers and journalists who participated in *Campaign for President: The Managers Look at 2008*. They are at the center of this work as they are in the success of our electoral process.

Bill Purcell, Director, Institute of Politics
February 2009

EDITOR'S NOTE

O<small>N</small> D<small>ECEMBER</small> 11 <small>AND</small> 12, 2008, the Institute of Politics brought campaign managers, senior advisers, political analysts and journalists to Harvard University to discuss the 2008 presidential campaign. The following is a transcript of the five sections of the conference. The transcript has been slightly edited to make it easier to follow but, for the most part, the text is a verbatim transcript so that readers can place themselves at the table of these conversations and hear about what happened in the voices of the campaign decisionmakers. At the end of the book, there is an abridged timeline of key events from the 2008 election cycle. For a more in-depth timeline, as well as a video of the forum, "War Stories: Inside Campaign 2008," please visit the Institute of Politics website at www.iop.harvard.edu.

The 2008 election was truly a historic one. We hope that as you read the transcript of the conference, you will appreciate the behind-the-curtain look at the key events that occurred throughout the election cycle—from making the decision to run to, for some, making the decision to drop out; from the candidates' announcements to their participation in the debates; from raising dollars and building a volunteer base to counting votes.

Despite the negative ads and the attacks in debate after debate, the people behind the candidates share a love of politics and a desire to make the world a better place. Regardless of what they believe is the best way to reach that goal, they recognize that they can share and learn from each other—and their willingness to do that with us is greatly appreciated.

Amanda Fuchs Miller

The Decision to Run for President

BILL PURCELL: It is my very special privilege and pleasure to welcome each and every one of you here today to what is our tenth such event, *Campaign for President: The Managers Look at 2008*. These proceedings began in 1972 and have run every four years since. It's my pleasure to introduce Rick Berke, the assistant managing editor of the *New York Times*. Rick serves as a member of our Senior Advisory Committee and, in the spring of 1997, was a fellow at the Institute of Politics.

RICK BERKE: I was going to start by saying the juiciest political story of the year was this guy in Chicago named Obama. But it's really not—his name is not Obama, and I'm really excited to see that people are still here, given all

IOP Director Bill Purcell (left) and The New York Times' *Rick Berke (right) kick off the two-day conference looking back at the 2008 presidential campaign cycle.*

that's unfolding in Chicago as we speak.[1] [*laughter*] This part of the program gives us a chance to catch our breath and reminds us how fast the world changes. When you think about it, two and a half years ago, if we were all sitting around here, the question might have been, will [former Pennsylvania Senator] Rick Santorum run for president? There were questions about will [former Virginia Governor] Jim Gilmore run for president? Will John Kerry try again? Will Al Gore run again? Will Fred Thompson, with all his star power, dominate the field and come in here and just be our next president? Just think about how the world has changed since that period. And, when I was looking back at some of the clips, I saw that right around this time two years ago, the two people Hillary Clinton made a point to reach out to, to get their support and public endorsement for her to run for president, were Charlie Rangel and a guy named Eliot Spitzer, who was the governor of New York at that time. She made a big deal of having a two-hour brunch with Governor Spitzer. Do you think if you were running for president now, you would even go near Eliot Spitzer[2] or Charlie Rangel?[3] It just shows you how the world has changed.

I want to hear from all the campaigns about what you were thinking two years ago, three years ago, four years ago. Let's start with the first person who announced seriously—Duncan Hunter.

• DUNCAN HUNTER •

SYDNEY HAY: Early on, I looked at that adage that has been attributed to Bill Clinton—Democrats fall in love and Republicans fall in line. I do think that that is very true. Looking at the upcoming presidential race, back in about 2006 and 2007, I looked at, who is the one that now all my Republican buddies in the party and around the country are going to anoint as the person whose turn it is? That, of course, was John McCain, in my view. I'm from Arizona and I've known John McCain a very long time. I viewed this as an opportunity for another candidate. I'm a conservative and thought I would see who else might get into this race and be a potential nominee.

---

1. On December 9, 2008, Illinois Governor Rod Blagojevich was arrested as part of a long-running corruption investigation.

2. On March 12, 2008, former New York Governor Eliot Spitzer resigned from office after getting caught in a call-girl scandal.

3. In September 2008, the House Ethics Committee began an investigation into New York Congressman Rangel for his reported failure to properly report income taxes on a Caribbean villa in the Dominican Republic, his use of four rent-controlled apartments in Harlem, questions about an offshore firm asking Rangel for special tax exemptions, and whether he improperly used House stationery to solicit donations for a school of public affairs named after him at City College of New York.

I wrote a memo called "Arizona on the Road to the White House," and I got it into the hands of several potential presidential candidates—some of whom ran, some of whom didn't run. Duncan Hunter was one of the people who got my memo. It laid out an opportunity for a conservative, alternative candidate to surprise. One of those ways was we orchestrated a straw poll in Arizona that would be held early on. We tried to be a cactus call version of the Iowa cattle call—because everyone would expect that John McCain would win that hands down. In January of 2007, Duncan Hunter announced an exploratory committee and, a couple of weeks later, made an official announcement. In between there, there was an Arizona straw poll. Duncan Hunter followed the advice laid out in my memo and he won that straw poll.

RICK BERKE: Did you or he really think he could win the nomination, or was it to make a statement? What was really your goal here?

SYDNEY HAY: My goal was to lay out a potential strategy where lightning could strike—try to catapult Duncan Hunter, who no one thought could win, and elevate him to a second-tier candidate. From there, we went into a South Carolina strategy. We thought, with limited resources, we should focus on one place where he was perfect—a fair trader, not a free trader, in

Duncan Hunter's campaign manager, Sydney Hay, explains her
search for an alternative conservative candidate.

a state that's lost textile industry overseas, for military veterans, a person of deep religious faith, the type of conservative Republican that could catch fire in South Carolina where you have small straw polls that don't take a lot of resources to compete in versus the giant Iowa cattle call that now takes so many resources that there is no possibility for a candidate like Duncan Hunter to compete.

RICK BERKE: What is the special thing about Duncan Hunter that you thought would work? What did he have that no other Republican offered?

SYDNEY HAY: Other candidates offered it as well, but I felt that he was a great communicator. Our next hope was the opportunity to break through in the debates, where he did well but not well enough. The debates were our other opportunity to see if lightning could strike—which, of course, it didn't. We would then be prepared with all the potential things in place to be able to capture the momentum, with the Internet and the Web things. We did have a tech deficit and were without the resources to do better at that, but we tried to have our own channel on YouTube and do all these things like the social networking stuff, hoping that lightning would strike. Lastly, we worked the affinity groups in the hope that the folks who really care about the gun issue would realize here's the real deal—he's a real hunter, not just Duncan Hunter—the type of things like that in the taxpayer groups with the fair tax or the pro-life groups, and just seeing if it was possible for him to break through.

One last thing. It wasn't about a cabinet post. People say, well, he was just running because he wanted to be Secretary of Defense or whatever. If that were the case, when we had our exit strategy, he would have left the race and endorsed John McCain. He had endorsed John McCain in 2000 but, in 2008, he instead went with what he thought was the more principled choice. He endorsed Mike Huckabee and left the race that way.

• JOHN MCCAIN •

RICK BERKE: At this point two years ago, McCain, your campaign went to the RGA meeting in Florida[4] and spent fifty thousand dollars with three open bars, shrimp, the works, to upstage Mitt Romney. It showed a certain confidence that you all thought, we're the one to beat, we're the front-runner, we are going to win this and there is no doubt about that. Was that what you were thinking in staging that event?

---

4. On November 30, 2006, John McCain hosted an elaborate reception at the annual meeting of the Republican Governors Association at the Doral Golf Resort and Spa in Florida.

John McCain's campaign manager, Rick Davis, talks about launching McCain's presidential campaign.

RICK DAVIS: Absolutely, Rick, we were the "let's get drunk" campaign. There's no question that was the master strategy from day one. When the alcohol ran out, that's when our support dwindled away. [*laughter*]

First, I would like to take the opportunity to congratulate my colleagues—David Plouffe and the entire Obama campaign. They did a spectacular job.

As a snapshot, I'm going to do exactly what we've tried to do for the last two years—ignore the questions from the *New York Times*. [*laughter*]

RICK BERKE: I was waiting for the *New York Times* attack. If that's the best you can do today, then that's fine with me.

RICK DAVIS: No, it's been good. The last five weeks had no investigations, nothing. [*laughter*]

The campaign at the get-go was, to some degree, a reaction to the campaign in 2000.[5] We ran a totally different campaign in 2000 and it lost, so the idea was, we like running campaigns, John McCain is a great candidate, he loves being on the campaign trail, but we would much prefer to win this time. The win quotient was probably the strongest motivator for our design and strategy. Therefore, we looked at the Bush successes in both 2000 and

---

5. John McCain ran in the Republican primaries in 2000 against George W. Bush.

2004. We believed bigger was better and we designed the campaign to start early. We actually had a debate—do you get in late or do you get in early? We did both. [*laughter*] We just couldn't decide. So the idea was get big—the Bush model—and we had a lot of people, who had gravitated toward the campaign, who understood that pretty well. That was the design. Unfortunately, what we didn't really take into consideration—because we started the exploratory committee a couple of weeks after the election—was the devastating effect from the 2006 election on the Republican party. It was historic losses in virtually every state—governors, senators, and state legislators turned over. New Hampshire was a classic example—there were more losses in New Hampshire than since the party began. We were looking forward and really not evaluating what that meant for the campaign. What it meant was less money, less support, less activism, a bifurcated party and one that really—even though there was a great primary going on with lots of good recruitment and lots of good activity—never fixed itself. By the time we emerged victorious in a primary, we had a relatively hollow franchise which had very little enthusiasm and very little money. There was nowhere near the excitement, through the course of the primaries, that there was in the Democratic primaries.

RICK BERKE: In your private conversations two years ago at this time, who were you expecting your biggest competition to be?

RICK DAVIS: We thought Mitt Romney was a formidable candidate. We knew he had been moving around and had the backbone of the Governors Association on his side.

I think John McCain had some peculiar hurdles that other candidates really didn't have, and that is, he had to overcome the image that he had in 2000. Even though maverick became a very important symbol for him later in the campaign, it was not a symbol that was particularly embraced by party regulars and activists who play an inordinately important role in the primary process. There were a lot of definitional issues that we had to deal with. So events like the RGA meeting that may seem meaningless in a general perspective played an important role for us because we had to get back into the party cycle. Contrary to some of the debate that occurred during the course of the campaign, McCain had spent a significant amount of time in the eight years running up to the Republican primary bucking the party. Who would have thought immigration reform[6] and the surge[7]—things that really were just beginning to emerge as major political issues—would play such a huge role in the Republican primary?

---

6. Senator McCain and Senator Edward Kennedy (D-MA) sponsored a bill to overhaul the nation's immigration laws. The measure was opposed by conservative Republicans because of provisions that would have allowed undocumented immigrants to become U.S. citizens.

7. John McCain was a vocal proponent of, and took credit for, President Bush's surge policy to increase the number of troops in Iraq.

RICK BERKE: Was there a consensus in your campaign about who the Democratic nominee would be?

RICK DAVIS: Hillary. Just like everybody else in the Democratic Party. [*laughter*]

RICK BERKE: Given your confidence about McCain and the nomination, how much were you thinking at that point about a race against Hillary—how you had to position yourself and how that might play into the primary?

RICK DAVIS: Not much. We made a lot of mistakes, but that wasn't one of them. We knew that the central focus of our activities for 2007 needed to be winning the nomination and we thought it would be nice to have a vigorous Democratic primary. In 2007, 2006, we weren't sure there was going to be much of a Democratic primary. There wasn't the emergence of the Obama candidacy at that point—they really hadn't shown up on the radar screen. The other candidates, certainly by most commentators' perspectives and maybe like our own, just didn't seem like they had the infrastructure to fight off the Clinton armada, politically. And so our view was wow, it would be nice for them to get tied up a while. We sure don't want the Hillary campaign wrapping up a nomination early and then turning their guns on us. Thank you David for taking care of that part of it. [*laughter*]

RICK BERKE: You mentioned plenty of mistakes. What was, in 2006, your biggest mistake, if you could redo it?

RICK DAVIS: Well, I think, gee, the list is so long. [*laughter*]

RICK BERKE: Not 2007, but 2006.

RICK DAVIS: I think the whole idea that somehow you needed to come out with a big battleship of a campaign that was going to sort of dominate the field. The lesson we learned is it's very hard to dominate a field and stay dominant for that long. McCain is a natural insurgent, he is only happy when he is behind and he is the best candidate when he is behind, and so it's just a matter of who your candidate is and what they like to do when they run. I'll tell you something that everybody here knows and that is presidential campaigns are intensely personal campaigns, unlike governors' races, Senate races or anything else. Your campaign needs to reflect the candidate. You can't run separate campaigns. The campaign can't say one thing and not reflect the views and personality and interests of the candidate. Our campaign may be a model of how that works and doesn't. One of the admonitions I would say going forward is regardless of what kind of campaign you want to run, that you think is winnable in a cycle, it has to reflect the personality, the likes, dislikes, issues and attitudes of the candidate.

• TOMMY THOMPSON •

STEVE GRUBBS: In the summer of 2006, I thought I would be working for Senator Allen. I had been in talks during that time with his pollster and his lead consultant, who I had previous relationships with, and we thought we were going to be putting that together in Iowa just as soon as the fall campaign was over. But, of course, "macaca" happens,[8] and the campaign ended up falling apart there. After the election, I got a call from an old friend of mine, Governor Thompson from Wisconsin. When Governor Thompson called, we looked at where he was positioned within the party and there were essentially three front-runners at that point—Mayor Giuliani, Senator McCain and Governor Romney. We considered all three of those as having significant problems with the base. There were some of the positions Governor Romney had taken in Massachusetts, Senator McCain had spent a lot of time fighting the party, and Mayor Giuliani was just way far away from the base, at least in Iowa. We looked at Governor Thompson as a very successful governor, a reformer, had more experience than anybody we considered in either party running, having served as a very successful governor and as Secretary of Health and Human Services. He was positioned as a social conservative but, at the same time, had governed in the mainstream, so we thought he was positioned both to pull together the party base as well as winning throughout the campaign in New Hampshire and beyond. Unfortunately, his ability to raise money did not come to fruition—the first million dollars that was supposed to come in ultimately never came in. After he was in the campaign for almost a year, we just barely broke the million dollar mark when he dropped out.

RICK BERKE: When you were sitting in the room with the governor privately, did he really think he had a clear shot at the nomination?

STEVE GRUBBS: Absolutely, absolutely. Having been through enough campaigns in Iowa, more on the Democrat side than the Republican side, you see enough dark horses move to the front. In 1980, George Bush was

---

8. On August 11, 2006, at a campaign rally in southwest Virginia, Senator George Allen (R-VA) repeatedly called a twenty-year-old volunteer of Indian descent from his opponent Democrat Jim Webb's campaign "macaca." Depending on how it is spelled, the word *macaca* could mean either a monkey that inhabits the Eastern Hemisphere or a town in South Africa. In some European cultures, "macaca" is considered a racial slur against African immigrants. The exchange was videotaped and posted on YouTube.

Steve Grubbs, Tommy Thompson's campaign manager, explains why he thought Thompson could do well in Iowa.

certainly not considered a front-runner when he won the Iowa caucuses, which propelled him to later become president. Jimmy Carter in 1976, and on and on. The dark horse candidates can do well in Iowa. We felt there was no strong front-runner in this race. We were definitely a second-tier candidate but we were well positioned to become a surprise in the Iowa caucuses. We felt like we were gaining momentum; things were going well on the ground in Iowa. Fundraising wasn't going well but, nevertheless, building the grassroots was. Unfortunately, at the Reagan Library debate, Governor Thompson got the question about whether he thought employers should be able to fire homosexuals. He failed on that question.[9] Then, in the following week, he said his hearing aid was not working and he was sick and he had to go to the bathroom.[10] [*laughter*] Those comments just

---

9. During the May 3, 2007, presidential debate, Governor Thompson was asked, "If a private employer finds homosexuality immoral, should he be allowed to fire a gay worker?" Thompson responded, "I think that is left up to the individual business." When the moderator followed up and asked if the answer was yes, Thompson replied, "Yes."

10. The day after the debate, Thompson apologized for saying that it would be okay for employers who oppose homosexuality to fire workers, saying he misinterpreted the question. On May 12, Governor Thompson expanded on his reason for his debate answer, saying, "I was very sick the day of the debate. I had all of the problems with the flu and bronchitis that you have, including running to the bathroom." Thompson, who has lost hearing in one ear, then said his hearing-aid battery for the other ear had died.

continued to mount. From the Reagan Library debate on, the campaign really was unrecoverable.

RICK BERKE: Was it more from how he handled the question, how he tried to recover from the answer, or the whole combination?

STEVE GRUBBS: He said that yes, he felt employers should be able to fire homosexuals and that there essentially should be no legal protections there. Other candidates who might have felt the same way avoided the question, but Governor Thompson did not. Two of his close staff members and aides are gay, so it was ironic that he sort of missed handling this question. That didn't help because he got a lot of bad publicity, but that probably wouldn't have hurt him in the caucuses. It was the follow-up that did.

• FRED THOMPSON •

BILL LACY: I was a recovering political operative until last July. I fell off the wagon when I got a call late in the month from Fred. I had done his 1994 and 1996 Senate campaigns. He called me at the end of July and said, "Bill, my campaign is in horrible shape—we haven't worked together since 1996 but I need you to come in and take over." When I got to the campaign, the first thing I realized was that the way the campaign had been set up, the campaign actually thought, and maybe had deceived the candidate into believing, that you could do a few Internet videos, place a few op-ed pieces in a variety of places, do a couple of speeches and be elected president. It doesn't work quite that way. When I got to the campaign, I knew there was trouble. There was no campaign plan, there was no strategy and no polling had been done. This was August of 2007, five months before the Iowa caucuses. There were some personnel in place, some extremely good although our communication shop, in all honesty, had zero experience in political campaigns—not presidential campaigns but political campaigns—so we had to make changes. What we wound up doing for the whole campaign was triage. We made changes. I found out when I arrived in early August that an announcement was set for September 6. I asked to see the announcement plan and was told, "We don't have one." I asked to see the draft of the speech and was told, "We haven't done that yet." Well, where are we going to go? "Well, we really don't know." Can I meet with our advance team? "Well, we don't have an advance team." [*laughter*] So we literally were doing triage, putting things together the whole time, starting in early August.

The reason that we thought Fred had a chance was that he had a record of true reform from his Watergate days[11] and from the Blanton pardon and

---

11. Fred Thompson worked as a counsel for the Senate Watergate Committee.

*Fred Thompson's campaign manager, Bill Lacy, talks
about the downside of being a celebrity candidate.*

parole scandal in Tennessee.[12] We felt we could sell him as the genuine conservative in the race, based upon his credentials. We found in our early polling, what room we had at the time to do it, that his strength obviously would be in the South but also in the Mountain States. Our basic strategy became, at that point, to try to do well enough in Iowa to keep us alive and to keep us rolling so that we could go into South Carolina, and that would be where we would ultimately put down our marker and succeed.

RICK BERKE: How important was the celebrity element in your thinking that he could win the nomination?

BILL LACY: There were two reasons that we ultimately did not win the nomination, and one of the reasons actually is the celebrity thing. In the 1994 Senate race, Fred was already a celebrity, but he did a variety of roles in movies and TV and never had one role. In retrospect, the fact that millions of Americans had seen him as Arthur Branch for years on two TV series on NBC worked to our detriment because Fred Thompson is not Arthur

---

12. As a lawyer in Tennessee, Fred Thompson represented Marie Ragghianti, chairwoman of the Tennessee Parole Board, who sued then Governor Blanton for selling paroles and pardons. The suit resulted in Blanton going to jail.

Branch.[13] They didn't get Arthur Branch and they were disappointed. So I think that actually cut against us. Fred is a very different person than that personality. The other reason that I think we failed is we simply didn't have the time. We literally had five months to put it together. As late as April, I was telling journalists that Fred will never run for president.

RICK BERKE: When you were in the room with Fred, how much fire in the belly was there? Was he saying, "I want to be president. I will be president."?

BILL LACY: Absolutely. Fred definitely had fire in the belly. He wanted to be president. He wasn't a hundred percent pleased with the way that we pick our presidents. He really did buy in early on to the notion that you could do a campaign in a different kind of way. But by late July, he understood that wasn't working and that he needed to go back and do it the way that the Obama campaign and everybody else tried to do it in this election cycle.

RICK BERKE: How fired up was his wife?

BILL LACY: She was very fired up.

RICK BERKE: I mean compared to him. [*laughter*] Did she understand what it took?

BILL LACY: I think she understood it from a communications point of view because that's her specialty, and Jeri [Thompson] was actually a delightful lady to work with. There's been a lot of very unfair stuff written about her. She really did not get in my way. She did not create any problems after I came on the scene. But I think there was a real misconception of how presidential campaigns are won.

RICK BERKE: If she had not been so enthusiastic, and I mean this in a good way, would he have run for president?

BILL LACY: It's something that we seriously considered doing in 2000, and he ultimately decided not to run in 2000 because he was very close to Senator McCain. So that was toyed with, very carefully considered, then discarded, and that was before he and [his wife] Jeri ever met. I think the answer is yes, I think he would have made the race. I think that she was very excited about him making the race and gave him some very good advice during the course of the campaign.

---

13. After serving in the U.S. Senate, Fred Thompson played prosecutor Arthur Branch in NBC's television show *Law & Order*.

RICK BERKE: We could not resist running on the front page of the *New York Times* a picture of Thompson at an event with someone in the audience in the front row with a big yawn. When you see that, was that like, oh my God, or not really, or you don't care what the printed newspapers say?

BILL LACY: Well, we didn't read the *New York Times.* [*laughter*] I'm joking. Fred had not served in the U.S. Senate for several years. He had not run a campaign since 1996. There was a lot of preparation involved and a lot of it involved with him. In the 1994 Senate race, we started fifteen months before the general election and we found that, over the course of time, in the summer of 1994, he really hit his stride and he was the best candidate that I've ever worked with, short of Ronald Reagan. He didn't hit his stride in this campaign perfectly until that *Des Moines Register* debate, when he took on the editor who was moderating the debate on the hand show thing.[14] I think he was outstanding from then on, but I think he had lost the voters by that point.

RICK BERKE: Why did people, when we interviewed them at events, say, "The guy is boring," "I can't listen to him," "There is no charisma there."? For a guy who is a movie star, what happened to him?

BILL LACY: Again, I think that there was a conflict between the person they saw on TV for years and who Fred actually is. He's a pretty low-key person. And, I think it's an issue of preparation and an issue of time. I think everybody in this room would agree you don't run for president in a few months—it's a long, hard path.

• RUDY GIULIANI •

RICK BERKE: Let's just start in the room with Giuliani. What did he say? Did he think he would be the Republican nominee early on, and when did he actually decide that he would definitely do it?

BRENT SEABORN: The decision came reasonably late. He looked at it for a long time in 2006. In 2007, he finally decided he was going to go and scrambled to put together a campaign staff. The McCain people were hiring up virtually everybody and it became very difficult to find competent staff, especially when we were also trying to replicate a little bit of their organization.

---

14. On December 12, 2007, at a debate in Johnston, Iowa, the moderator Carolyn Washburn, editor of the *Des Moines Register*, asked all the candidates to raise their hands if they thought global warming was a serious threat caused by human behavior. Thompson replied, "I'm not doing hand shows today."

Rudy Giuliani's director of strategy, Brent Seaborn, talks about how they thought the compressed primary calendar would benefit their campaign.

When you looked at how massive their organization was going to be, you thought you needed to replicate, at least in part, what they were going to do. In the end, we were probably bigger than we needed to be, part of it in response to how big the initial McCain campaign was. But we put together an organization as quickly as we could and ultimately leveled off the growth—but probably bigger than what we wanted to be.

RICK BERKE: Was McCain the biggest rival?

BRENT SEABORN: Early on, yes. John McCain was clearly the establishment candidate at that time who we were most focused on as the closest competitor. He was also someone who Rudy Giuliani had tremendous respect for and really considered a close, personal friend. Rudy really looked at this as running against one of his good friends, which makes the whole campaign dynamic very interesting. All of the complimentary things he says about John McCain at the debate before he takes a little swipe at him are all true. He is not up there trying to butter him up before he lands a punch—he really means all those very nice things he says about him.

RICK BERKE: As you suggested, there was a lack of clarity in his own mind, it seems, about whether he would run or whether he wanted to be president. The same thing happened when he was going to run for Senate and then didn't run for Senate.[15] What's your sense of him and the extent of his desire to be president and to go through the process?

BRENT SEABORN: There was never any question about his desire to do this or his willingness to do this. He was incredibly accommodating. I think he always wants to be in a position where he knows he can win. That is probably the biggest obstacle—he wants to know that he has an excellent chance of winning. He is a Yankees fan and, if you look at the Yankees, the Yankees go into every season expecting to win the World Series. I think he has some of the same attitude. He is not going to get into a race to make a statement or to take a position. He would get into a race only if he thinks he has a clear opportunity to win.

RICK BERKE: What was his biggest concern—that he wasn't sufficiently conservative to win the nomination?

BRENT SEABORN: He knew that he had a number of positions over the years that weren't exactly in line with the Republican electorate, at least the early Republican electorate. When you talk about a Republican nomination process, we are talking about Iowa, New Hampshire, South Carolina and then a bunch of other states. Where Rudy saw an opportunity was that there was a lot of movement going on. We had a lot of states moving to that February 5 date. Florida was looking at moving forward. When Rudy saw that was going to happen, he thought that probably would be the opportunity we had. We all agreed that the traditional calendar—where you go to Iowa, you wait a couple weeks and New Hampshire happens, there is a very slow burn at the beginning, and then the primary calendar is much more expanded—was probably not a calendar that Rudy could ever win in. But, in a more compressed calendar, there was at least a shot and with Florida moving forward, that was very helpful.

The candidates running posed their own challenge. We had John McCain and Governor Romney running. That made it very difficult in a state like New Hampshire, where typically Rudy would feel he'd have an excellent chance of winning. There was no easy opportunity to win there. What we would have expected there, or would have hoped for, is that it would have turned very ugly, very bloody. The two of them would have engaged in hand-to-hand combat, believing that both of them had to win, and that, in the end, we would be able to come up the middle. It never quite happened the way that Rudy would have liked it to happen or the way that we had hoped it would happen. South Carolina and Iowa are states that Rudy is

---

15. Mayor Giuliani dropped a U.S. Senate bid in New York in 2000 after being diagnosed with cancer.

probably never going to win. He might make a good showing, he may be able to do well enough, but you can't count on winning those two states in a traditional primary. Michigan moving up its primary date presented yet another challenge—it was another obstacle before we got to Florida.

RICK BERKE: Do you see similarities with Fred Thompson in terms of two celebrity candidates who kind of thought they didn't have to do it the traditional way?

BRENT SEABORN: Maybe, but I think it was for a different reason. Rudy and the entire campaign saw that with his positions on social issues or on guns and a number of things, a traditional candidacy or a traditional campaign calendar wouldn't allow him to make it through. The other thing that maybe we didn't do well enough is he was essentially the 9/11 candidate, and I don't think he ever wanted to be that. He certainly is proud of how he handled things on what was probably the toughest day of his life, but I think he is equally proud of what he did as mayor of New York. I think that was part of the story that we never were able to get through as well as we would like to have.

• MITT ROMNEY •

RICK BERKE: At this RGA meeting in Florida that I keep obsessing over, what was your state of mind when you saw the McCain people swoop in?

BETH MYERS: We had a very natural constituency in the RGA at that point and we decided not to try to go neck and neck with the McCain campaign at that particular venue.

RICK BERKE: In the private rooms in that hotel, when you were talking to Mitt Romney, were you thinking McCain is the one we've got to watch out for and we've got to get these governors behind us before he picks them off?

BETH MYERS: In any campaign, I think that the campaign reflects the candidate, and Mitt is a very analytical guy. We had been looking at how to run this race for a while. We had looked at what we were seeing as "Battleship McCain"—that's precisely what we saw happening. We also looked at the Giuliani campaign as another juggernaut. Our challenge, at that point, was not to be relegated into second- or third-tier status. What we were focusing on, at that point, was ways in which, very quickly, in the calendar year, when people talked about the race, they talked about, instead of two candidates—Giuliani and McCain—three really prominent candidates—Giuliani, McCain and Romney. At that point, we were putting together our Call Day, which was an event we had in the first week of January where we wanted to raise a big amount of money. We raised $6.5 million in one day. Most of that came in credit card receipts, so we had cash on hand immediately. I think that changed the way reporters looked at our campaign.

RICK BERKE: What year did you all first start talking about Mitt Romney's presidential campaign?

BETH MYERS: He bowed out of the running for re-election in December of 2005, so at that point, he had decided that he wanted to keep the option open.

RICK BERKE: When did you have your first official, serious meeting to plot strategy for this presidential campaign?

BETH MYERS: I was chief of staff and I left that role in August of 2006, so probably right about then.

RICK BERKE: Why did he think he would be elected?

BETH MYERS: I think he took a look at the electorate and where the country was. Our two themes that we ran on in the primary were America needs change—obviously we got a little outshouted on that—and a need for a strong America. We felt that Mitt was uniquely qualified. In the primary, Mayor Giuliani had a good line on the strength brand and Senator McCain on the maverick brand, but we felt that Mitt Romney, with his turnaround reputation and his ability to communicate, was uniquely qualified.

RICK BERKE: What early conversations did you have in 2006 about his Massachusetts record and whether he would have to move to the right from that and how that would play?

BETH MYERS: We felt that there were a couple of problems. We looked at the fact that he was from Massachusetts, a Mormon and a millionaire as three problems that we had to overcome. I'm not sure which order we put those in. [*laughter*] All of them were two-edged swords. The governor was able to infuse cash into his campaign because of his personal wealth and that was a positive thing about being a millionaire, but there is a perception out there that there is this rich guy from a liberal state who's got a funny religion.

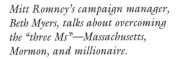

Mitt Romney's campaign manager, Beth Myers, talks about overcoming the "three Ms"—Massachusetts, Mormon, and millionaire.

RICK BERKE: Were you more worried early on, at the beginning, about Giuliani or McCain?

BETH MYERS: We were worried about both of them. But we were also very concerned about an insurgent candidate rising on the right and that was something that we looked at at all times. Governor Huckabee's campaign was always sort of lurking in the background as something that we had to be worried about.

RICK BERKE: If we had Mitt Romney in this room three years ago, and he was telling the truth, and we asked him, "Who is the one candidate you are most worried about?" who would he have said?

BETH MYERS: Probably McCain.

• MIKE HUCKABEE •

CHIP SALTSMAN: I got a call from Governor Huckabee late in December and he wanted me to come to Little Rock, and I said no. He said, "Why?" And I said, "Because I might like you." When I got there, I found out I had been to Iowa more than Governor Huckabee had. I had been to New Hampshire and South Carolina more than he had. My first meeting with his senior staff, we spent the first thirty minutes talking about what are we going to do if Florida moves up the primary. I raised my hand and

Chip Saltsman, Mike Huckabee's campaign manager, talks about running a campaign on a shoestring budget.

said, "Have we thought about, I don't know, opening an office?" [*laughter*] "Or maybe having a website or maybe get some people to work for us? Maybe have a fundraiser, that would be something we should do." [*laughter*] "Maybe we should announce, that would be good." [*laughter*] So, after we got all the basics covered, we went to work. We raised $330,000 in the first quarter—which is a slow Tuesday afternoon for Obama—and we were in the mode of survival. We didn't have an infrastructure, we didn't have a staff, we didn't have a team, we were going at it day by day. It was twelve months before and we were still trying to figure out what to do.

RICK BERKE: You make it seem like he just kind of decided out of the blue, but he had written that book.[16] He must have been thinking about national office.

CHIP SALTSMAN: There is no doubt. He was chairman of the National Governors Association. He felt like he was a national spokesman on a lot of issues, which he was on health care and health and wellness. But there was absolutely no evidence that I could find that he had been plotting and planning and strategizing. His mailing list was 3,700 names of a Christmas card list that wasn't mailed the last Christmas. [*laughter*] We had zero e-mail addresses.

---

16. In 2006, shortly before leaving office due to term limits and announcing his presidential bid, Governor Huckabee published a memoir titled *From Hope to Higher Ground*, which offered a preview of his policy proposals on areas ranging from taxes to education.

RICK BERKE: What led him to decide, at that point, that he wanted to move ahead?

CHIP SALTSMAN: Sometime in December of two years ago, he had gone through that process and talked with his family, and they were very supportive and encouraging of him to run for president. I think ultimately it was him and his family that sat together, probably around Christmas, and said we are going to run.

RICK BERKE: Didn't people say it's too late?

CHIP SALTSMAN: At that point, it's two years away, it's a year to Iowa, you can say you can put it together. In the room, he absolutely believed he had a chance to win if he could get out there in front of enough people. Of course, every campaign does or you wouldn't run. In his world, it was like, I'm the right guy at the right time and I can do this. If I announce, they will come. That's not how it works.

RICK BERKE: What was he thinking—that a small state, Arkansas governor—

CHIP SALTSMAN: Yeah, a guy from Hope, Arkansas, being president? That's crazy. [*laughter*]

RICK BERKE: In private conversations, would he mention Bill Clinton?

CHIP SALTSMAN: There was some talk about that. He and Clinton were friends and they had a good relationship. He has been the longest-serving governor, he had done some pretty interesting things in Arkansas—especially with health care and health and wellness and obesity. There were some pretty interesting issues there that were dynamic and they were different, but yet, he did still have the core base of the Republican Party with him. As he looked at the field, just like everybody else in the field looked at everybody else, he said, "Yeah, I can beat those guys."

RICK BERKE: Why? Would he talk about the celebrity factor at all, how he was sort of a smooth guy?

CHIP SALTSMAN: Did he talk about how he was smooth? No. I would have laughed at him. [*laughter*] He's from Hope, Arkansas. He is not smooth. He really did not see himself as this dynamic speaker. He felt like he could compete in the debates. He felt like he was a good speaker. But he didn't see himself as the guy that, give me 10,000 people and I will line them up and they will follow me. That's not how he saw himself. But he did think, with the field, as the primary was in place, that he had a chance. I had always pitched this Iowa–South Carolina strategy, and I said, "You've got to be true to it because we don't have enough money to do anything else." The nice thing about my job, as compared to Beth's or Rick's or anybody else's—they had decisions because they had options. They could do other things. [*laughter*] What are we going to do? We are going to get on Southwest and fly to Des Moines and stay there for a week because we can't afford to fly out of Des Moines. [*laughter*] That's a pretty simple decision as a campaign manager. [*laughter*] Every decision in a campaign, when you are raising seven thousand dollars or eight thousand dollars a day, could be your last, and so every decision becomes that much more amplified.

RICK BERKE: Who was he most worried about?

CHIP SALTSMAN: Probably himself.

RICK BERKE: No, which other candidate?

CHIP SALTSMAN: McCain.

• RON PAUL •

LEW MOORE: In November of 2006, a few of us thought he should run for president and he was mortified at the idea of being the head of the largest

Lew Moore, Ron Paul's campaign manager, discusses using the Internet to raise money and mobilize supporters.

governmental agency in the world, since he doesn't like government very well. We talked him into running and he started that in January 2007. Our strategy was, try to knit together some traditional coalition groups that were dissatisfied with the Republican party, with the large number of libertarians who are floating around all over the place—a lot of them on the Internet. We did not have the kind of success, initially or ever, with some of the traditional Republican coalition groups. But, at some point, it caught fire on the Internet and we were able to start raising money. We were able to start building an organization through Meetup.[17] Before the end of the campaign, we had seventy-five thousand people in Meetup groups and we raised thirty-five million dollars. We just couldn't convince a lot of people to vote for Dr. Paul—that was the one problem that we had. I think it was an election year where people were looking for somebody genuine and there is a growing number of people who believe in free market economics and believe in a noninterventionist foreign policy, and it played out in his campaign.

RICK BERKE: Did he see himself more as a message guy and just running to push his cause?

LEW MOORE: Very much so. We couldn't get him for six months to say that he wanted to be president. Finally he would say, "Oh, yes, I want to be president," but initially, no.

• JOE BIDEN •

RICK BERKE: I know that there was no scheme on Joe Biden's part to run for president so he would be picked as vice president because on the day that he announced, he praised Obama as the first African American who is articulate and bright and clean and a nice-looking guy.[18] So we know that he wasn't angling for anything with Obama. [*laughter*] But look what happened. It all worked out well.

LUIS NAVARRO: Yes, it did. It worked out very well. Where we were at the beginning of 2007, prior to the *New York Observer* story coming out, was the rationale for the campaign was Senator Biden was someone who had a long history of bipartisan cooperation with folks like Senator Dick Lugar, Senator Chuck Hagel and others, and someone who had a plan for

---

17. Meetup is an online network of local groups that is designed to make it easier to organize or find groups meeting face to face.
18. In a January 2007 interview with the *New York Observer*, Biden, talking about Barack Obama, said, "I mean, you got the first mainstream African American who is articulate and bright and clean and a nice-looking guy. I mean, that's a storybook, man."

Joe Biden's campaign manager, Luis Navarro, and national campaign chairperson, Valerie Biden-Owens, talk about their plan to win.

Iraq, which he believed, and which we all believed and still believe, is the most pressing issue for American foreign policy. The question was, now we are there, how do we get out? The third element was that, as a combination of his experience and his vision for ending the war in Iraq and the lessons learned from 2004, we would have the ability to argue that our viability would allow us to expand the map of electoral possibilities in the fall. With the *New York Observer* story, we went into a period of dormancy until April, when the senator's famous one-word response at the South Carolina debate refocused people on what his good qualities were.[19] By that point, we had made a decision, as a result of what we saw as the financial juggernauts of the Obama and Clinton campaigns coming out of the first quarter, that our real opportunity to win was predicated on doing a surprising showing in Iowa. From April on, we focused all of our energies on Iowa. We racked up a considerable number of state legislative endorsements. We thought that we might have a shot at the *Des Moines Register* endorsement. That was the

19. In an April 26, 2007, debate in Orangeburg, South Carolina, moderator Brian Williams asked, "Senator Biden, words have, in the past, gotten you in trouble, words that were borrowed and words that some found hateful. An editorial in the *Los Angeles Times* said, 'In addition to his uncontrolled verbosity, Biden is a gaffe machine.' Can you reassure voters in this country that you would have the discipline you would need on the world stage, Senator?" Biden answered, "Yes."

essence of what we thought would help to launch us in a momentum candidacy, not unlike Gary Hart's presidential campaign model in 1984 against better-known and better-funded opponents.

RICK BERKE: Who were you most worried about?

LUIS NAVARRO: For us, it was actually a two-part problem. We knew that either Obama or Hillary would end up as the leading candidate, based on their financial resources. We also knew that we had to first get past the Edwards campaign in Iowa if we were going to have a surprise showing because of Edwards's residual strength coming off of the 2004 campaign. So where we hoped, ultimately, we would be matched up against one of the two top-tier folks, we knew we had to get past Edwards first.

RICK BERKE: How about Chris Dodd? They are similar, in some ways, in terms of Senate experience and so forth. Was he a factor at all?

LUIS NAVARRO: No, not in our calculations. We thought that by dominating the dialogue around national security and foreign policy, hopefully setting the pace for the rest of the candidates in that area, we would own that part of the real estate, and we didn't see Dodd as competing with us for that. Frankly, Bill Richardson was more competition for that than anyone else.

RICK BERKE: When you were in these private meetings with the senator, how seriously did he take Obama?

LUIS NAVARRO: After the first quarter, very seriously. [*laughter*] When you post, I think it was twenty-six million dollars after the first quarter, I would say that settles any question about whether or not someone is serious.

RICK BERKE: Was he surprised at how well Obama was doing?

LUIS NAVARRO: It demonstrated to him that the challenge in making an argument that through experience you could achieve change was going to be that much more complicated by a candidate who had a historical narrative that was more tangibly representative of change. I would also point out that because of the senator's consistent performance in the debates, a lot of folks and a number of columnists, especially at the end of the race—despite the fact that throughout our entire campaign, we spent only ten million dollars—talked about the surprise that Biden was going to show in Iowa. That is a testament, first and foremost, to the candidate. Second, because we had a really good earned media operation. And third, because of our continual endorsements in Iowa, we demonstrated organizational strength that people didn't expect.

RICK BERKE: If you were to ask Joe Biden in December of 2006 who the Democratic nominee would be, what would he have said?

LUIS NAVARRO: I think in December 2006, it would have been Hillary Clinton, just like everyone else.

RICK BERKE: That day he announced, getting back to the *Observer* story, what was it like in the bunker? Was he ever saying this campaign is not going to fly?

LUIS NAVARRO: No. In fact, I think the great thing for us on that day was by serendipity. We had always planned on ending the day's events on *The Daily Show* with Jon Stewart. So rather than having Jon Stewart pummel us and thereby create this notion of a cacophony of a concern about his candidacy, I think his ability to play well to an audience that would have been susceptible to a different interpretation of those events allowed him to stay in the race.

BIDEN-OWENS: Immediately after the *Observer* story, Biden had validators, including Senator Obama, speak out because for thirty-six years, he walked the walk—his record, his legislation, his person. When we first got in this in August of 2006, we were not faced with the Hillary/Obama juggernaut. He ran and got in the race because he thought that he was the most qualified to be president and he thought that he had what the American people wanted. And after the seven years of Bush, what he believed is that the world wanted an American leader that they could trust. The American people wanted a leader who had the depth and breadth of knowledge of national and foreign policy and national security, which meant Katrina[20] and jobs and Iraq. We had the great luxury of running a campaign that was honest to what he wanted to do, what he thought the country needed and what he had to say.

• BILL RICHARDSON •

RICK BERKE: Was he running for president, vice president or Secretary of Commerce? What was his goal two years ago?

---

20. In August 2005, Hurricane Katrina hit the Gulf coast and caused devastating damage in Louisiana, Alabama and Mississippi.

Mark Putnam, Bill Richardson's media consultant, explains why Richardson's resume uniquely qualified him to run for president.

MARK PUTNAM: Governor Richardson was looking at this for a while. To paraphrase one of our TV ads—fourteen years in Congress, Secretary of Energy, UN Ambassador, governor of New Mexico, negotiated with six or eight dictators, nominated for the Nobel Peace Prize. Clearly, he thought he was prepared for the job. We were hired to work on his 2006 gubernatorial re-election with an eye towards running. He saw that he occupied a unique place in the Democratic primary field. On the Republican side, you had a glut of governors running. On the Democratic side, you had Iowa Governor Vilsack and Indiana Senator Bayh, who had gubernatorial experience. Both of them were out of the race very early. So the combination of foreign policy experience and gubernatorial experience seemed like a natural place for him in the race. We knew that we were in the second tier. You can't be running against Hillary Clinton. And the thing about the Obama campaign—it's a little bit of revisionist history to say he was an underdog from the beginning. He really wasn't. A lot of us on the Democratic side saw that he was going to be a very formidable candidate, based upon a lot of factors. We saw that our imperative was to get past one of those top three candidates. We had a game plan that was fairly straightforward. First, we wanted to do well at the

DNC winter meeting speech.[21] We didn't expect to do what Howard Dean did in 2004 and launch our campaign there, but we wanted to be credible there. Secondly, we wanted to lead in that second-tier fundraising in each quarter. We wanted to get on the air early. We didn't think that an end-game advertising campaign would work in this sort of dynamic, so we were actually one of the first presidential campaigns on the air, along with Governor Romney's campaign. Third, we wanted to do well in the debates. That didn't quite happen at the outset. Governor Richardson, by his own admission, didn't do his best in the early debates. From our perspective, the media was looking for a way to winnow down the field, and they saw not a great debate performance and immediately relegated him to a lower stature. We wanted to do well on *Meet the Press*. If you go back and watch Richardson's *Meet the Press* interview from Memorial Day of 2007, he did very well in the first half when it was on substance, but he wasn't really prepared for the extreme adversarial nature of the interview. He should have been a little better prepared in expecting that, but it was an onslaught of questions—every one of which we had rehearsed except whether or not he supported the Red Sox or the Yankees, that was the one that we didn't anticipate.

RICK BERKE: Did he talk early on about his close relationship with Bill Clinton and Hillary Clinton and what it would mean to run against her?

MARK PUTNAM: That really was not a factor in his thinking about the race. He saw her as an able candidate, but he was running his own campaign and it really was not part of his calculations at all. We saw her as a very strong candidate, perhaps the nominee, but that wasn't something that he was going to run away from.

• BARACK OBAMA •

RICK BERKE: Could you pinpoint for us your first meeting with Obama to discuss his running for president?

DAVID PLOUFFE: It was the day after the 2006 elections and, at that point, most of us believed that we would go through the process and he would not run because most people spend a lot of time in Iowa, New Hampshire and South Carolina, building up a finance network. It was a very unusual way to get into the race and was very challenging and, in many respects, it served us well because we didn't have a stagnant playbook on the

---

21. Governor Richardson gave a speech at the Democratic National Committee's winter meeting on February 3, 2007.

Barack Obama's campaign manager, David Plouffe, talks about the candidate's decision to run.

shelf. We had to be agile and move very quickly. That was our first meaningful discussion.

RICK BERKE: What was his sense of, and your sense of, his prospects at that point?

DAVID PLOUFFE: First of all, I would like to thank Rick for his comments. He and his team went through something that only those of us on the other side of the fence can really appreciate the grueling nature of. They caused us to have five sleepless months and kept us on our toes.

From a political standpoint, it was obviously worrying about Senator Clinton. From the very beginning, and really through the whole primary, we understood what a distinct underdog we were and what a formidable front-runner she was. One of my mantras during the general election was that we wanted multiple avenues to the presidency. We wanted to be able to win—to reach 270 electoral votes—in a lot of different ways. In the primary, the opposite was true. We had a very narrow path and if we fell off that path, she was going to win. So from a political standpoint, it was oriented about her. We thought that Edwards was going to be very formidable in Iowa, so in the beginning, our sense was we had to beat Hillary Clinton in Iowa. That might have meant coming in second because Edwards was so big. Our first survey in Iowa had Edwards at 32, Clinton at 26 and us at 16. So we knew we had a hole to dig out of. From a voter standpoint, our sense was the country was hungry for change. We had just seen that the day before in the 2006 elections. We had a candidate who potentially could tap into that in a very effective way, could try and suggest that the country could be more united under his leadership—pushing off against the kind of politics that people had soured on in Washington. We knew that we had a lot of hurdles for people to see him as a potential president and nominee.

RICK BERKE: When you had that first meeting with him, had he decided at that point to run?

DAVID PLOUFFE: Not at all. We had a lot of remedial discussions about what this was like, what a caucus was, what the calendar was. Most importantly, what it would mean to him and his family. A lot of discussions about whether there was a way to do this differently that would allow a lot of time at home.

RICK BERKE: Did you leave that meeting thinking he would end up doing it or not?

DAVID PLOUFFE: I figured at that point it was less than fifty-fifty. History is littered with people who get right up to the line and don't do it—particularly people that get into it this way. He had been to Iowa once in his life for politics, never New Hampshire, never South Carolina. Because he did not have a competitive 2004 general election for the Senate, he did not have a big, national fundraising base. He had maybe ten thousand e-mail addresses. We didn't have much organizationally. You had to assume eight out of ten times you run the race, you don't win.

RICK BERKE: What was his biggest fear about running?

DAVID PLOUFFE: I think he had a high degree of confidence, as I did. I thought he had the potential to be a terrific president. The question was, could you be a great presidential candidate and mount a campaign? The first thing was whether we could put this together in enough time to really be competitive. The second thing for him was the grueling nature of it. He's got young kids and he's very close to them. That was really the biggest hurdle—could he reconcile his desire to see his family a lot? In the summer, he was able to spend a lot of time with them in Iowa, but it was hard. That was the biggest challenge.

RICK BERKE: Was he worried that he had this great, quick rise and that a losing campaign would ruin his whole trajectory and future?

DAVID PLOUFFE: No. I know there has been some suggestion that he had this master plan going back to kindergarten—which was a helpful moment in the campaign[22]—but no. This was not something he had a pathological hunger for, and so if he ran and lost, he'd go do something else.

RICK BERKE: Did you talk at all at that meeting or at other meetings about his pledge not to run for president?[23]

DAVID PLOUFFE: We had to talk about that back in the fall. He was going on *Meet the Press* and we knew he was going to be getting the question. At that point, I put the odds at fairly low that he would run, but it was possible, so he felt the best approach was to be honest about it and say, "I'm gong to take a look at this." That's always something that's somewhat of a fascination in the media—someone who says they weren't going to run and runs—but, generally, it doesn't have much impact with voters.

RICK BERKE: Beyond Hillary, was there another candidate he was worried about?

DAVID PLOUFFE: We wanted to winnow this down to a two-person race, so we were worried about anybody that was going to come out of Iowa with any kind of energy. Our sense was that even if Edwards were to come out of Iowa with a win or a number two, he would have a harder time transacting the whole calendar. New Hampshire was always challenging to Edwards, although I think if Edwards came in third in Iowa, we might have won New Hampshire. Coming in second, he got 16 or 17 percent of the vote. If he had come in third, he might have gotten 10 or 11 percent, and most of that was ours. Hillary was the real challenge and we had to execute that obstacle course. We had to finish ahead of her in Iowa. By the fall, it became clear that didn't mean coming in second—that meant winning. She wins Iowa, she is the nominee by February 5, at the latest. The big surprise was that we were able to win the nomination without winning the New Hampshire primary. We thought the New Hampshire primary was necessary to give us the velocity to survive February 5. Febru-

---

22. During the Democratic primary, Hillary Clinton's campaign drew ridicule when her aides criticized Barack Obama for having written a kindergarten essay saying he wanted to be president.

23. On January 22, 2006, Senator Obama said on NBC's *Meet the Press*, "I will serve out my full six-year term." Asked by Tim Russert, "So you will not run for president or vice president in 2008?" Obama replied, "I will not."

ary 5 was always a day that scared the living daylights out of us. All these big states where she is well known and we are going to have ten days to campaign there between South Carolina and February 5. The big surprise was that South Carolina gave us a surprising amount of velocity because heading into that weekend, there was some sense in the press that we could lose South Carolina. So, to win it by twenty-eight points and to do better with white voters than people thought, thanks to a bad NBC poll. Third, there was some backlash to the Clinton tactics that week.[24] The way we won, and the margin that we won, gave us a boost out of South Carolina that we couldn't have expected because we assumed all along that we were going to lose February 5. We won more states and won more delegates. At 3:00 a.m. on February 6 was the first time I thought we were going to win this thing because I thought they missed their opportunity to put us away.

RICK BERKE: Could you take us from that moment that you left that meeting, when it was fifty-fifty that he would run, to the decision—when you went home saying this is it, he is doing it. When was that?

DAVID PLOUFFE: It really wasn't until January. He went to Hawaii for a family vacation at the end of December, leaving with the belief that he was going to run but hadn't signed the contract.

RICK BERKE: How did we get to that point?

DAVID PLOUFFE: We had a lot of discussions, a lot of it being personal. What is this going to mean? How often will he be in Chicago? How many weekends will he be home? Then it was how do we put this together—just put it together, much less win? And then, third, was the strategy for how we were going to win. We spent a lot of time working on budgeting, fund-raising and strategic assumptions. When he left for his family vacation, I personally thought that sort of glimpse of normalcy may keep him from running. We've seen this many times before, you are on the precipice and then someone says, at the last minute, "I'm just not going to do this." I think he came back from Hawaii and he still wrestled with it a little bit. Then, by the end of the first week of January, he decided to go.

RICK BERKE: So, you left that first meeting fifty-fifty in November, after the election. He went to Hawaii in December and you were thinking he

---

24. After Barack Obama won the South Carolina primary, Bill Clinton was accused of injecting race into the election results when he said, "Jesse Jackson won South Carolina in '84 and '88. Jackson ran a good campaign. And Obama ran a good campaign here."

is going to do it. What happened between election day and that vacation? What changed? Did anything turn or change? Did he tell you or Axelrod, "Something has changed, I think now I'm going to do it."? Something must have changed.

DAVID PLOUFFE: The most important thing is he and Michelle had a lot of conversations about it and I think they got comfortable.

RICK BERKE: What was that moment when you knew that they got comfortable?

DAVID PLOUFFE: There was no moment. It's as you go through it that I think he got more comfortable with the notion that he had something unique to offer the country. He may not win the election but he had to answer the question, do I have something that's unique enough from the rest of the field to put my family through this and put myself out there? He's a very reflective person. He spent a lot of time thinking about that—I think more time thinking about that than how we were going to organize Cerro Gordo County in Iowa.

RICK BERKE: How critical was Michelle's initial reluctance in that decision?

DAVID PLOUFFE: I wouldn't term it reluctance. I think that this wasn't her idea of how they were going to spend the next year. At that point, he had to look at it as a year, not two. But I think she was very supportive of the process to think about it. And, as time went on, she got more energized by it and was looking forward to campaigning herself. So I wouldn't term it as reluctance. I think she just needed to have a lot of questions answered about how destructive this would be to their family.

RICK BERKE: What about the notion that this would be the only time he would run? She had said publicly, if he doesn't do it this time, he is never going to run again. Was that discussed in the conversation—this is your one shot at doing it?

DAVID PLOUFFE: The sense was if they ran and lost, in all likelihood—nothing is ever a hundred percent certainty—they wouldn't run again. So it was not run this time or not. But we talked a lot about how you don't choose your timing in these things. There is no doubt that the political playbook of how to run for president would have had him wait to spend more time in these states, get more familiar, get more legislative accomplishments, and build up the fundraising network. There's no doubt about that. But the timing seemed that the people were so hungry for change, and something new and different, where lack of Washington tenure was probably going to be an advantage. There are elections for president where that's not the case. But this was. So the sense was also you really can't fight the timing. It may not be yours to choose. The time might have chosen him.

RICK BERKE: Who was the most reluctant within the inner circle of his running?

DAVID PLOUFFE: One thing I'm proud of is we were all very sober about it and laid out the worst-case scenario—how grueling it would be, taxing on the family, your odds of winning certainly are not great and then you cast your chips and you are no longer the bright star on the horizon, your star has faded. I feel good about how we did that. There weren't any cheerleaders for this internally. None of us were looking to do this for the next two years. So I think we served him well from that standpoint. I think he would say that it was a very sober and realistic assessment of the race and what it would mean to him.

RICK BERKE: Would you joke about the one pessimist in the group that really thought it wouldn't work out and he shouldn't do it?

DAVID PLOUFFE: No, not so much. As we were during most of the campaign, we were kind of a unit and there wasn't much dissension there.

RICK BERKE: When you would be in these long conversations with him over time about running, what was the worst-case scenario? That he would go and lose all the primaries and his reputation would be soiled? What was the worst fear that he expressed?

DAVID PLOUFFE: You can't underestimate what a strong front-runner Hillary Clinton was. At that time, you had to assume there was a good chance she wouldn't lose a primary or caucus—she would win it all—so it wasn't so much that. I think it was, could we put this together? Would we be embarrassed because we are trying to do in sixty or ninety days what others have spent months and years doing? We did not have a presidential campaign team in the bullpen and that was his big concern. He's a former organizer. He's a very methodical person. Could we put this together? Could we, whether we win or lose, put forth an effort that he would at least be proud of? He would remark a lot about that.

RICK BERKE: Given his interest in organization and planning, how much did he explore your options for raising money and how closely did he look at what the Hillary Clinton campaign was doing early on? Was he plugged into the polls and everything else about Hillary Clinton?

DAVID PLOUFFE: Probably less so. He relied on us for a lot of that analysis. But, as a group, including him, we assumed she would raise well over one hundred million dollars, she would have a formidable organization everywhere she desired it, they would run a very smart campaign, and she'd be disciplined. We had our eyes open about what we were up against.

RICK BERKE: What would Barack Obama say about Bill Clinton and his role? How much did he see that as an advantage for Hillary Clinton, or did he see that would maybe be a disadvantage?

DAVID PLOUFFE: We didn't talk about that too much in the beginning. We assumed that there would be a lot of benefits that come from that relationship in the primary and that there could be some negative. We assumed he would be out there a lot. He ended up not being out there as much as you might have thought.

RICK BERKE: When you did talk about it, what would he say about Bill Clinton?

DAVID PLOUFFE: We didn't really talk too much about it.

RICK BERKE: The first time he went to New Hampshire, he said something like, "Everyone has their fifteen minutes of fame, but this is going on longer than fifteen minutes." He seemed really stunned by all of the attention. How much did that play into his decision, or had he decided by then?

DAVID PLOUFFE: He went there in December, before he decided to run. That was still part of his book tour.[25] That was our first trip to New Hampshire. The book tour and the campaigning he did in 2006 for candidates were instructive. There was just a palpable sense that people wanted something new and different. Some of that was directed at him, and some of it was just he's a vessel. But it was striking and very instructive and it helped further the discussion about him doing this. It was clear to us that we might be able to build a grassroots organization. None of us would suggest we knew it would happen on the scale it did, but that was strategically in our discussions. We had to do that because Hillary Clinton had the best political operation maybe in the history of the Democratic Party, perhaps rivaled by the Kennedy family—in every state, in every county, in every precinct—and the only way to compete against that was to build a grassroots organization. So our hope was that we'd begin to sow the beginnings of what could be a grassroots organization through that fall because the turnout was great, the

---

25. At Obama's book signing in Portsmouth, New Hampshire, on December 10, 2006, 750 available tickets were taken within hours of being made available to the public.

intensity was great, and a lot of people were saying, "Please run—if you run, I'll help you." You didn't know how strongly that would materialize, but it was the hint of something.

RICK BERKE: So two years ago, he was in Hawaii on vacation, you are on pins and needles worrying that he is going to come back and not run for president. Did you talk to him during that trip and try to encourage him to keep thinking about it—you can do it, yes, we can? [*laughter*]

DAVID PLOUFFE: I was not in the encouragement business. I remember he said, "I've been here every year for a long time and lived here for a long time and it's the first time that it's hard for me to move around." He didn't like that. That was one of the things he was wrestling with—giving up that sense of privacy. So, no, we were not encouraging him.

RICK BERKE: When were you absolutely clear that Barack Obama decided to run for president?

DAVID PLOUFFE: When he said, "I'm running." [*laughter*]

RICK BERKE: When he said it publicly?

DAVID PLOUFFE: We have seen a lot of people get up to the line and then they don't run. So until they say, "I'm in, let's file the papers, let's hire people, let's go," they are not running for president. At some point in the second week of January, we finally pressed the go button. Until he said, "I'm definitely running, let's start the engines," we assumed that there was a possibility that he might not run.

RICK BERKE: When you talk about the vaunted Hillary Clinton campaign, what did you all see as her biggest vulnerability early on, going in, before he made the final decision?

DAVID PLOUFFE: The war. In January, she struggled with some questions in Iowa about the war.[26] It was also clearly a change election and they were adopting a message of experience. Then, pretty soon, it was clear that as sure a footing as they had in many parts of the campaign—rapid response,

---

26. During the last weekend in January 2007, on a campaign stop in Iowa, Hillary Clinton, responding to a question about her vote to authorize the war in Iraq, said, "If we had known then what we know now, there never would have been a vote. And I never would have voted to give the president that authority." She did not say that the vote was a mistake.

getting political endorsements, raising money—they struggled with Iowa for a very long time. Since our whole strategy was predicated on winning Iowa, we sensed very early that we might be able to get something done in Iowa. And her numbers, of all the states through mid-February, were the weakest in Iowa. Still, they like to say that they were never leading in Iowa and "poor them" in Iowa. They were very strong in Iowa. They were the front-runner for a very long time. They were ahead for much of the year. But it was clear that she had a lower ceiling there than she did in a lot of places.

RICK BERKE: Given Hillary Clinton's experience, given that her husband was president of the United States and her über campaign manager, was he scared to run against her at all? Was he intimidated by her?

DAVID PLOUFFE: I don't think he was scared by her. I think that he was impressed by her performance. In the first joint appearance we had—in Nevada at an SEIU forum on health care[27]—Obama would say himself that he did not perform as well as he would have liked and that she was very strong. By the way, we tried to limit the joint appearances but we weren't successful. We all got together and said we are not going to do all these things all year long and it fell apart. What's interesting is that his strongest debate performance in the primaries, with the exception of the Philadelphia debate in April, were one on one with her. But there's no doubt that she was a strong debater, and that concerned us. She kept hitting her marks. It really wasn't until I guess the debate at the end of September that she stumbled for the first time. Remarkable, actually—a string of excellent performances by Senator Clinton—although, what was interesting in the debates is we were always viewed more strongly with voters than we were by the press. That was something that was very instructive to us.

RICK BERKE: Two years ago, at this point, who would Obama have said was going to be the Republican nominee?

DAVID PLOUFFE: John McCain. All of us saw what they went through in the middle of 2007 and a remarkable comeback. We talked a little bit about that but we didn't spend much time talking about the general election. To the extent we did, it was, McCain is right out of central casting and he is going to be very hard to beat, if we were to win.

RICK BERKE: Was there a Republican candidate he would rather have seen get the nomination?

---

27. On March 24, 2007, seven Democratic candidates participated in an SEIU forum in Las Vegas, Nevada, to discuss health care.

DAVID PLOUFFE: At that point, we didn't spend much time evaluating the rest of the field. You had to assume that it would be a tough primary and McCain would likely emerge. He had a lot of strengths in the general election that would make him quite formidable.

RICK BERKE: But you all must have been sitting early on, in December of 2006, saying we would be in our best position if it's *X*.

DAVID PLOUFFE: We were forty points behind Hillary Clinton, we didn't have anything, so we didn't spend a lot of time ruminating about the Romney/Obama matchup. We had to figure out how to get offices open in Iowa if he ran.

RICK BERKE: Final question, deep in Obama's heart, when he announced his exploratory committee, how confident was he that he would get the nomination?

DAVID PLOUFFE: We were confident that if everything went right, we would be in the hunt at the end. I think seven or eight out of ten times you run that race, maybe Hillary Clinton wins. She was that strong, but we were very confident. Because we hadn't been planning this for years, he wasn't pathological about this, and that was very important organizationally. It made us very healthy. We didn't have that burden hanging over us, so we could go try things out. We had to be very agile because we were starting from scratch. We were confident that we could put together a very respectable effort. We thought we could probably get it down to us and her, and then some things would have to go right for us to win in the later parts of the calendar. We were very confident about our ability to do pretty well in those first four states. After that, she had such a pronounced advantage that we had to have some things go right.

• CHRIS DODD •

SHERYL COHEN: Senator Dodd gave some consideration to running in 2004 but decided not to do that. It may sound hokey, but in 2008, knowing how talented this field was and what an uphill climb it would be, he fundamentally felt that with the seriousness of the problems that the country faced, and as someone who had really been a problem solver in Washington for many years—a bit more workhorse than showhorse with a lot of accomplishments—that he had something to offer. He fundamentally felt that he wasn't going to sit on the sidelines at what he considered to be the election of his lifetime. That said, he made the decision to run relatively late. It was not until about May of 2006 that he thought he would do this. We scrambled and spent the next six months trying to meet a number of benchmarks by the end of the year that we felt were necessary to even consider taking the next step. Those included the obvious things—money, staff, message and organization.

There is one story I like to share with people, in terms of trying to attract the best staff to the campaign. David Plouffe and David Axelrod did Senator Dodd's Senate campaign in 2004, and we wanted to try to get the best for the potential presidential race. So I had a lunch with David Plouffe in the summer of 2006 where I tried to tell him why, as talented and charismatic and exciting as Barack Obama was, he probably wasn't going to go anywhere and he should come work with Chris Dodd. [*laughter*] I didn't get him. And I hate to say the pundits are right, but the early analysis of the oxygen suck of money, staff and media attention was correct, and all things proved to be very difficult.

In early 2006, our initial premises were twofold. One was that someone in this race was going to emerge as the alternative to Hillary Clinton. With all her advantages and popularity within the party, there was clearly doubt and evidence to suggest that there was an appetite for an alternative in this race as well. So the strategy became, how did you move yourself slowly up the line to become, at the end of the day, that alternative to Senator Clinton? The second operating theory proved to be a little bit less true, but we thought it would be relevant at the time, which was that experience was going to matter deeply in this race—that given the challenges the country faced and the fact that we had seen many years of mismanagement in government and lack of competency and execution on so many critical factors, that candidates who were in the race with some broad and deep experience, who had a demonstrated ability to solve things, to get things done, at some point could catch some relevancy. We actually did focus a lot on Governor Richardson and Senator Biden early on. Our initial goal was to be seen as the fourth in this race—that was job number one. We thought we would do that in the first quarter by having raised more money, by having built a stronger organization, by having a tighter narrative, all the basic things. We hoped that if we did that, and we did it in a significant way, the press would then pay a little more attention to Senator Dodd. The only way we were ever going to have a shot at this was if we started getting a bit more attention. You do campaigns through paid media, free media and retail. Without having the fundraising success, paid media was tough, and you had to work really hard to get the free media. Our hope was if we could be seen as a serious fourth at the end of the first quarter, we would be able to get more attention from the press. Then, perhaps, over time, the second part of our premise would kick in, which would be, in a field of four—Senator Clinton, Senator Dodd,

Chris Dodd's campaign manager, Sheryl Cohen, says their original goal was to be fourth in the race in order to get more attention.

Senator Obama and Senator Edwards—that if experience mattered and had resonance, we would have some positioning in that over time.

RICK BERKE: Was there an element at all of, I know how this works, I'm probably not going to get the nomination but I've been around a long time, I'm smarter than these other guys, I do a better job than these other guys, I want to show the world what I can do, sort of the end of my career? Was there a sense of just getting out there and getting his views out and knowing that he didn't have a great chance?

SHERYL COHEN: No, not at all. I think that he knew he didn't have a strong chance. In a campaign, you've got to have the right mechanics and you have to have the right candidate. We've all seen examples of races that had one but not the other and, ultimately, were not successful. Senator Dodd, like Senator Obama, has two young children and really had no interest in doing that just for that reason. In many ways, he was really motivated by where the country was and where we were going—what kind of world we were leaving these young children. So, short shot but going to take it.

RICK BERKE: He would say, in private meetings, I think I can do this?

SHERYL COHEN: Absolutely, understanding full well that it was a narrow path. We had a path we thought we could do to do that. At the very end, when this was over, Senator Dodd's comment was, "You can't make a difference if you don't try, and I'm glad I tried." To me, that sums up why he ran his race.

• JOHN EDWARDS •

JONATHAN PRINCE: Iowa was really the ball game for us. At the end of the day, we didn't think 240,000 people were going to show up to the caucuses. So, on some cosmic level, we were gratified to come in second, although first would have been more along the lines of our original game plan.

RICK BERKE: Can you go to the decision to run?

JONATHAN PRINCE: Sure. He's seen as someone who was always thinking about this, for years. Many people have heard John Edwards say, "This is personal to me." It really was a personal thing for him. The core of his public service and his public service ambitions are directly connected to what made him a trial lawyer. Watching his dad work in that mill and seeing him taking college equivalency courses on a TV because he was getting passed over by

Jonathan Prince, John Edwards's campaign manager, talks about the importance of being perceived as a "first-tier" candidate.

someone who had just been hired with a college degree kindled a little bit of populist outrage in him. That's been a guiding principle of his and a real core value of his forever. He thought that he really had a message to deliver in this race around the issues of economic populism and economic justice. That's one of the reasons why much of our campaign—and there were strategic reasons for it as well—tried to be very policy driven, very ideas driven. We tried to shape the debate over issues over the course of the campaign. But it really was a very personal thing to him and, in so many ways, it was a continuation of the 2004 campaign and a continuation of his career.

RICK BERKE: What did he think of the rise of Barack Obama?

JONATHAN PRINCE: You had these two candidates who so clearly represented change. Although the Clinton campaign made a decision, that many of us celebrated over the course of the campaign, to not focus on change and how she represented change, I think they could have made a good play for change and they abdicated that possibility. But these two candidates were demonstrable representations of the possibility of change. We saw that we really had to surround ourselves with the hard, cold facts of change and get out there and push a very progressive agenda—really demonstrate it to the country and, in particular, to folks in Iowa. Generally speaking, as [Boston-based political operative] Skinner Donahue used to say, "Issues are tissues, you use them and then you throw them away." [*laughter*] But in the Iowa caucuses, it's a little different. There were caucus goers that knew our policies better than I did, and I oversaw them. [*laughter*] So getting out there and having a very detailed, progressive agenda with lots of meat on the bones of it, in Iowa, can make a difference, and that was one of the ways we saw that we could demonstrate the kind of change that we represented.

RICK BERKE: Deciding to run early on, what was his confidence level that he could knock off Hillary and Obama?

JONATHAN PRINCE: He's a very analytical, logical guy. He thought we could win. We had to win Iowa to win. If we didn't win Iowa, we weren't going to win.

RICK BERKE: Did he expect to win in the way he carried himself and talked about the campaign privately?

JONATHAN PRINCE: He thought there was a very good chance we could win Iowa. The fact that we came in second and 240,000 people showed up proves that there was a good chance we could win Iowa. We did not win Iowa, but he thought we could.

RICK BERKE: Do you think he would have run if his wife hadn't been so enthusiastic about his running for president?

JONATHAN PRINCE: Marriages are complex things.

RICK BERKE: Your sense?

JONATHAN PRINCE: I think Elizabeth [Edwards] certainly wanted him to run badly the first time. They have two young kids also, but they had the luxury of being able to take their kids on the road, and they did this home schooling, so they got around some of those issues. The kids were a little younger, so it was a little bit easier to do. It's hard to say. It is a very personal decision. When Elizabeth's cancer returned, if she had not wanted him to continue with the race, he would not have continued the race. That I'm quite certain about. That was on the table. It was clearly discussed. He assumed he wasn't going to continue and she was absolutely pushing—driving behind that 100 percent. That was beyond a joint decision.

RICK BERKE: Before the primaries, before Iowa, was he more worried about Hillary or Obama?

JONATHAN PRINCE: We always had this obsession with making sure that the press always treated us like we were a first-tier candidate. We knew we had a plan that began in Iowa and we would have the money to execute that plan. So in some respects, we didn't spend a lot of time worrying about either one. We thought we needed to win Iowa and then ultimately we would be in a race, if we won Iowa, with one of them. We had historic problems in New Hampshire. Winning Iowa meant we probably would have done significantly better than we did in New Hampshire. Winning Iowa meant we probably would not have been counted out by the time he got to his native state of South Carolina—he might have won that. So that was the scenario. But we had a plan. We had a budget of forty million dollars, which was enough to execute that plan. So we needed to win Iowa.

RICK BERKE: So you don't have a sense of whether he was more worried about Hillary or Obama?

JONATHAN PRINCE: In December of 2006, Hillary Clinton was the dominant candidate. No one felt differently about that. But we certainly always saw the possibility for either of them to be the nominee.

RICK BERKE: As Obama emerged as a stronger and stronger candidate and was doing well—someone who has barely been in the Senate where

Edwards had been plotting and planning this for a long time—what did he think of that? Did he feel he was cheated out of it?

JONATHAN PRINCE: He and I had long conversations about the experience thing, and he didn't have that much more experience than Barack Obama. He served one term in the Senate. He and I both shared a view that people make much of this experience issue but it's not really what the job is about anymore. The job is about judgment. Knowledge is important, but you get that knowledge by running. The best presidents are not the people who have served in Washington the longest. I don't think John Edwards ever thought that. It would never even have occurred to him, given his life experience and what he thought made him qualified to be president, that Barack Obama was somehow disqualified because of experience. In fact, I don't think he thinks that is really all that important to being president anyway.

RICK BERKE: So, he was saying, hey, neither of us are that experienced?

JONATHAN PRINCE: No. It's not the experience that people talk about when they talk about experience in the context of presidential politics. It's not actually what the job requires.

• HILLARY CLINTON •

Representatives of Hillary Clinton's campaign were not in attendance on the first day of the conference, so the discussion continued the next day.

BILL PURCELL: We have a bonus session here this morning, and this is finishing out our session from yesterday's lunch. Rick Berke is going to take Howard Wolfson through the exercise that we did yesterday.

RICK BERKE: Howard, if you could take us into the room with you, Hillary, Mark Penn,[28] Bill and whoever else was there two years ago at this point, after the midterms in 2006. Tell us what your thinking was about the chances of Hillary winning the nomination.

HOWARD WOLFSON: We thought the chances were good.

RICK BERKE: Who were you most worried about, or were you?

---

28. Mark Penn was chief pollster and strategist on Hillary Clinton's presidential campaign.

Hillary Clinton's senior campaign advisers, Howard Wolfson and Guy Cecil, say their early objective was to project inevitability.

HOWARD WOLFSON: It depends on exactly what time frame. There was still some doubt then that Senator Obama would run. We were following his interest with interest. We were also concerned about Senator Edwards. Those were the two that we were most focused on.

RICK BERKE: Was there one you were more worried about of the two, two years ago?

HOWARD WOLFSON: In the immediate aftermath of the midterms, I don't think we knew exactly how strong Senator Obama was going to be. There was uncertainty as to whether or not he would run and uncertainty about, if he ran, what kind of candidate he would turn out to be, but there was a tremendous amount of potential that even back then was obvious. In Senator Edwards, we knew somebody who had run well and was very strong in Iowa. So we really focused on both.

RICK BERKE: When did you, in your own mind, think Obama was definitely going to do this, and how much of a nuisance did you see him as?

HOWARD WOLFSON: I don't think I would describe him as a nuisance. I think there was a difference of opinion, based primarily on conjecture, as to whether or not he was going to run. For myself, I got the sense that he was—I don't remember exactly when—prior to his actually announcing. Maybe when he went to New Hampshire and had such a great reception there. He just seemed that he was doing the kinds of things that a candidate would do in order to run and he was getting the kind of reception that you would get if a lot of people wanted you to.

RICK BERKE: At that point, who would you have said would be the Republican nominee?

HOWARD WOLFSON: John McCain.

RICK BERKE: Were you thinking he'd be the best one to have to face or were you hoping it would be someone else, like Romney or Huckabee?

HOWARD WOLFSON: Probably hoping for somebody else. We had a fair amount of confidence that she would be the nominee, but we did spend a lot more time thinking about who our Democratic primary opponents were going to be than we did who the Republican nominee was because there wasn't much we could do to influence that process.

RICK BERKE: What was your main objective in the pre-primary period—to show strength?

HOWARD WOLFSON: To project inevitability.

RICK BERKE: What was your intention at that point in terms of when you would actually announce?

HOWARD WOLFSON: That was a floating conversation. In an ideal world, given how difficult it is to actually run for president, how exhausting it is, I don't think anybody really wants to announce any earlier than they have to. We were constantly assessing when that was going to be.

RICK BERKE: The earlier announcements from the others must have sped up your timetable.

HOWARD WOLFSON: The reality, at least in this cycle and maybe in future cycles, is you have to announce early because the process starts early, and if you are not announcing in an early time frame, you are going to lose out.

RICK BERKE: When Bill Clinton ran for re-election, I don't think he ever announced, right?

HOWARD WOLFSON: If you are the incumbent, you can avoid actually making the announcement, yes.

RICK BERKE: So, was there anyone pushing—

HOWARD WOLFSON: No. That was not a luxury that we had.

The Republican Primaries

2

BILL PURCELL: Welcome to our first afternoon session, which will take us through the Republican primaries. Let me now introduce our two moderators to you. Mark Halperin was named editor-at-large and senior political analyst for *Time* in April of 2007. Despite numerous impressive achievements in the world of journalism, his most important association for us is his connection to the Institute of Politics Student Advisory Committee, where he served as a student and came back as a visiting fellow in the spring of 2007. Joining him as moderator is Lois Romano, national political reporter for the *Washington Post*. Lois, too, has a great and very important connection with the Institute of Politics. She spent the spring of 2008 here with us as one of our resident fellows.

MARK HALPERIN: Our task is to cover the Republican nominating process in a little bit more detail and go all the way up through the convention, which covers a lot of ground and a lot of events.

• THE ISSUE OF CELEBRITY •

LOIS ROMANO: The one question we wanted to start with is the issue of celebrity. We started out this campaign on both sides of the aisle with some of the best-known names, politicians, people—not only in our country, but in the world. We had a war hero in John McCain, we had a former first lady, we had an actor, we had a senator who walked on water, and all of those people came to the race with a lot of celebrity. Are we at a point in our process where there is no room for a dark horse anymore? Do you have to establish or achieve some level of celebrity that might not have anything to do with politics, or it may, to even get in the game, to raise money, to become a player? If you look at this race on the Democratic side, the last

Time *magazine's Mark Halperin and* Washington Post's *Lois Romano moderate a discussion on the Republican primaries.*

two people standing were celebrities, and if you look on the Republican side, John McCain. And the person that was nipping at his heels at the end was Mike Huckabee, who turned himself into a celebrity. I would like to pose this first question to Ed Rollins, who has worked for an actor, an oil man, Mike Huckabee and Jack Kemp: do you have to be a celebrity to get in the game anymore? Do we have to look at Sarah Palin as the front-runner for 2012 because she's such a celebrity? And did you aim to turn Mike Huckabee into a celebrity?

ED ROLLINS: First of all, I think you become a celebrity by the Iowa-New Hampshire process. Iowa was nothing until Jimmy Carter went there, slept on the couches in 1976. Ronald Reagan skipped Iowa in 1980, which is what gave Bush an opportunity to win the straw poll there that I won't say launched his career, but certainly made him have a couple weeks of celebrity. The key thing here is that there's a lot to the process and the fact that you're a celebrity may not be relevant. What's always relevant is, are you a good candidate and can you put a good campaign together? I've seen many of the front-runners come along in the game and go down pretty quickly. The difference in this cycle, in fairness to John McCain and Rick and the people who brought him back from the dead, we had never had such a front-loaded process before.

Our race ended up being like a NASCAR race. Barack Obama was not a celebrity when he won Iowa. He was a candidate who surprised a lot of people. He had had one great speech that most of the country had never heard of four years ago.[1] Mike Huckabee, who has great communication skills, was able to be on television 350 times between the first of December and the middle of January and he was very effective at communicating. Fred Thompson, who was a celebrity, and Rudy Giuliani, who was a celebrity, both faltered early on in their inability to connect with the ordinary voters out there in those hinterlands. I think that the Iowas and the New Hampshires still are launching pads. But if you don't have the campaign or you don't have the resources to go on, it doesn't matter. I went down to Little Rock and I said to Chip, "What's your campaign plan?" This was in December. He said, "We're going to win Iowa, then we're going to win New Hampshire, then we're going to win South Carolina, then we're going to win some southern states on Super Tuesday, then we're going to win Florida and everybody else is going to drop out." And I said, "What's the alternative?" "There's no alternative," he said. "Mike just has to execute my game plan."

LOIS ROMANO: Let me follow up with Sydney. You said that you were hoping lightning would strike. In retrospect, could it have struck? Keeping the same question in mind that Mr. Hunter did not have high name recognition, was it possible to get where you wanted to go?

SYDNEY HAY: I think yes. In this era of new media, the Obamagirl became a celebrity instantly, overnight.[2] Now, granted she was talking about a celebrity, but I do think it is possible. It's important that the candidate have those kind of qualities that could have star power. I do think that Duncan Hunter had those star qualities in that he had a great sense of humor and was very likable. Anybody who had an opportunity to meet him one on one or talk to him would come away from the meeting realizing that he was a great person on a personal level and he was also very knowledgeable and skilled on national defense and the issues that matter. Maybe today, because of all the new media and the YouTube channels and the possibility to go viral on the Internet for some reason that no one can even calculate what it might be, it's even more possible than ever before that someone who doesn't start the campaign as a celebrity can become one. Sarah Palin is certainly now a celebrity.

---

1. On July 27, 2004, U.S. Senate candidate Barack Obama gave the keynote address at the Democratic National Convention.
2. In June 2007, an Internet video posted on YouTube featured model Amber Lee Ettinger, who called herself Obamagirl, lip-syncing a song called "I Got a Crush on Obama."

LOIS ROMANO: No question about it. Beth, at a certain point did you feel like you were up against some very big names? They were all skilled, but Rudy was the face of 9/11 and John McCain had run before.

BETH MYERS: Yes. One of our premises in the very beginning was that we wanted to make sure that we became, and remained, a first-tier candidate. That was very challenging for us right out of the box. It, in fact, dictated our strategy in the first quarter of attempting to raise more money than anybody else, which we were successful at doing, because we were running up against two juggernauts.

RICK DAVIS: I think Sydney really said it best. In the early eighties, it was common, conventional wisdom that you had to run and lose in order to run and win. So we always thought okay, you get a candidate like Jack Kemp—you run him once, you lose. You get a list and you get your name ID up. It was hard. That was pre–cable TV. I know that's hard for some people to even think there was a life in politics without cable TV. But it was hard to establish what you're describing as celebrity status. The best you could hope for was a good list and some friends in some of the key states. The example that's been used is Sarah Palin. She had 75 percent name ID in a week. That was the quickest I've ever seen that happen. We certainly didn't anticipate that. We anticipated some excitement, but we didn't think you could get 75 percent name ID in a week and 85 percent in a month. That's just phenomenal. So yes, I think that right now, with all the communications tools and the amount of intensity with which people seem to follow politics, certainly in this race more than any other that we've seen, it actually evens out to celebrity status. When Ronald Reagan ran in 1976, he was sort of a celebrity but, more importantly, I think he was more defined as a conservative than a moderate. He wasn't seen as a celebrity so much, although people were attracted to him outside of his ideology. It was hard to match that. Nowadays, you get hot, you get a good Internet ride, you can build a list overnight, you can improve your name ID in a week, and it flattens everything out. Even though it helped McCain to have a lot of name ID early in the race, that didn't appear to be the case in July of 2007. We certainly hadn't done much with it by then.

LOIS ROMANO: Do you have to have the narrative to go with it? That's where you all were struggling a little bit.

RICK DAVIS: You've got to create the narrative you think you can run best on. I think the Obama campaign is the best campaign I've ever seen at creating a narrative at the beginning of a campaign and having the discipline to hammer away at that narrative all along the way. Aided and abetted by a relatively compliant press corps, they did a terrific job. I'm not sure we would have had the same ability, even if we'd had the discipline to do it, which we didn't. So this whole idea of celebrity is a great debate topic but, at the end of the day, success gets you celebrity status in politics, and it moves numbers. It moves the polling data. It moves the money. All of a sudden, you can raise in a day what you used to have to raise in a month. I think there's a flattening out of all that. Now, if you're a person who doesn't have much name ID and you're not a whole lot of pizzazz on the trail and you have no Internet list, barriers to entry are up. You've really got to know what you're doing to get into a presidential campaign nowadays. Used to be you hit the road, you make some friends, you start building a base in some early primary state. But now, the barriers are much higher to compete and to win. You can always get in and make an impact but, to win, the barriers are pretty high.

LOIS ROMANO: Have you all come to terms with the YouTube phenomenon, in the sense that it is a place where you can develop celebrity? Lew, was it something that you all realized that you could use? Did you use it? Would you use it again?

LEW MOORE: Yes. We calculated very early that we'd have no chance at all to be perceived as a first-tier candidate by anybody unless we raised quite a bit of money right away, and if we got a bigger base of support. So we started from day one. We hired a videographer. He was one of the first people we hired in our campaign. We were making YouTubes every two or three days. Suddenly, we started noticing that 300,000 or 400,000 people were watching them. After the confrontation that Congressman Paul had with Mayor Giuliani at the South Carolina debate,[3] we were getting 400,000 or 500,000 people watching our YouTubes. So it was critical to our getting off the ground as a campaign.

LOIS ROMANO: Brent, you had celebrity going in. Did that help you make decisions?

BRENT SEABORN: It did, and I don't think it's anywhere near as beneficial as people think it might be.

LOIS ROMANO: It's a double-edged sword.

---

3. On May 15, 2007, at the Fox News Republican presidential debate in Columbia, South Carolina, Ron Paul suggested that the United States' interventionist policy invited the 9/11 terrorist attacks. Giuliani asked Paul to retract his statement and Paul refused.

BRENT SEABORN: It is a double-edged sword. You've got a lot of people who know you and like you but that doesn't necessarily translate into them becoming actual supporters—either activists or contributors. That was something that we had to face early on. We had lots of people who really liked the mayor who we weren't easily translating into donors or into activists as we had wanted to, or as we hoped we could have, going into it.

STEVE GRUBBS: The thing that I thought really changed in this presidential cycle more than any other cycle was how quickly YouTube could make you famous or infamous. In Iowa, activists deciding who they're going to support never stops. Republicans are currently starting to assess [Louisiana Governor] Bobby Jindal and Mike Huckabee and Mitt Romney again and decide what direction they're going to start lining up over the next six months for an election that's a few years away. The first YouTube I received was of Mitt Romney in his debate against Ted Kennedy, banging on Reagan—saying he was never really a Reagan supporter and how he was so passionately pro-choice because they had somebody in their family who'd had a back-alley abortion. This was spread around to activists across the state and so, very quickly, you realized that no matter how Mitt Romney reformed himself, he was going to have some challenges. Back then, the YouTube that we were interested in was the one that affected Senator Allen in his campaign and that became a challenge for what we had planned on working on. So it

Bill Lacy listens as Ed Rollins talks about how to run as a celebrity candidate.

can make you famous, it can make you infamous, but there's no doubt that it changed presidential elections in this last cycle.

• TO CRITICIZE GEORGE BUSH, OR NOT TO CRITICIZE •

LOIS ROMANO: This is about George Bush. Barack Obama ended up running an unusually successful campaign against George Bush. If you look back on Bush's numbers during the heat of the campaign, the surge was in March of 2007 and George Bush's approval ratings were 34 percent, with 70 percent of the country or more saying he was on the wrong track. He was still doing well with the base but in June of 2007, there was slippage there. Nationally, in June of 2007, his numbers were 29 percent. In 2008, between February and April, they were 19 to 22 percent. Knowing what you know now about the war and these numbers and the unpopularity of this president, in retrospect, was there more room to develop an anti-Bush campaign—to be the anti-Bush? All of you were a little hesitant to do that. I'd like to get a discussion going on why and if you had talked about it or argued about it.

BRENT SEABORN: We obviously did a lot of research and a lot of us had worked either with or for President Bush at some other time on this campaign, including Rudy, who had an opportunity to work with him on different occasions, not the least of which was 9/11. Mayor Giuliani had a lot of respect for what the president did, and he wasn't going to be critical of him. He also really believes that you make friends in politics and you don't criticize these people because these things come back at you. That held true for Governor Romney and for Senator McCain, but certainly for George Bush. He had a lot of respect for what he was doing and he wasn't going to publicly criticize him. Our research was showing that President Bush early on had very high approval ratings amongst Republican primary voters and caucus goers. So you maybe could get some good national press from this, or you could maybe become more popular overall, but it didn't necessarily help you with the primary electorate. That being said, there were places you could probably contrast without being overly negative. But you also have a lot of other people you're trying to bring onto a campaign, including donors and organizers, most of whom were tremendously loyal to the president. So I don't think there was a lot of room for it. I think some of the candidates could have done it, but I don't think our campaign was in a position where it would have worked very well for us. The McCain campaign certainly could have. They had a history with George W. Bush that was probably more cold than hot—sometimes better than others. They probably had an opportunity to do it. Some of the other second- or third-tier candidates easily could have. I don't think Governor Romney could have done it as easily. I think that would have been hard for him.

BETH MYERS: I think it would have been a challenge for all the reasons that you stated, among our donors and, particularly, among the Iowa caucus voters and the early primary state voters. From our polling, they were still fairly supportive of the president, until the very end. I'm trying to think of a specific place where Governor Romney separated with the president. I can't think of any off the top of my head. You could do it issue by issue but as far as taking him on head-on, no, that wasn't something we ever considered.

SARAH SIMMONS: There are two things that are important to consider when you think about this. One is contrasting on issues. That's one area where we actually did try to take a swing at drawing a contrast between Senator McCain's position on certain issues and the president's position on certain issues. I spent a lot of time talking about immigration, which is an area that was challenging for us to maneuver through the primary process with. And the position on the surge was something that, in November of 2006, John McCain called for, way ahead of the president. He was very critical of the administration and how they were handling the war in Iraq. The other thing is we are dealing with human beings who are candidates. Any of these candidates probably would have been reluctant to go out there and just take a swing at the sitting leader of their party and of the administration. That's the secondary part—trying to do it in a way that's respectful so you don't lose primary voters.

MARK HALPERIN: Isn't it a little bit of a false choice to say you either had to take him on personally or you had to be completely in line? Weren't there issues that all of your candidates had where you disagreed with the president, where it might have gotten you some good, free national press, not worthless in the nomination process, and where your candidate could have spoken out—as Senator McCain did on the surge and Governor Huckabee did on a few issues, including personnel issues? Isn't there a way to have shown that independence that might have been helpful and not have been personal?

SARAH SIMMONS: Yes. One of the survey questions that we asked throughout the course of all of our research was, "Is John McCain an independent voice for change, or is he going to keep the kind of policies of the Bush administration?" That was a measure that at the end of the campaign, we were in decent shape on. But the President Bush issue was overcome by events sometime between September 5 and the Fannie Mae and Freddie Mac failing[4] and the eventual decline of the economy that dominated the news coverage all the way through the middle of October.

---

4. On September 7, 2008, the United States Treasury announced a rescue of two government-sponsored enterprises, Fannie Mae and Freddie Mac—giant American mortgage banks.

BRENT SEABORN: I don't think anybody outside of people who have either worked in Republican grassroots politics or as an operative understand how strong the base responds when you criticize someone they like, whether it's George W. Bush or Sarah Palin. The more the press hates Sarah Palin, the more strongly the hardest-core part of the base is going to be attracted to her. Because the press is beating up on her, they become very defensive. Particularly in our party, it makes it really hard. And it's particularly true with the president. The worse things get for him in the national media, the more the base rallies around him to protect him. There is this feeling that the establishment or the press is out to get him and we need to defend him. It's a really interesting dynamic to have to work in.

ED ROLLINS: It was not so much the issues, particularly among Republican voters. Some didn't like the war, but most basically thought the president was right on the war. Immigration was obviously an issue that there was great debate in our party over. When people looked at Bush, it was the failure of leadership. It's a little hard to go out and critique his leadership when you're a member of his party. He has done a lot for this party over the course of his eight years. What we all tried to do is to say we would be a different kind of leader but we weren't going to pull our troops out of Iraq. We didn't understand the economy would be quite the dilemma it was in the end. So it wasn't like, here are the twenty things we're not going to do that Bush did. What we all tried to advocate is we're going to be a different kind of leader. We're going to lead the country more effectively. That was everybody's challenge.

MARK HALPERIN: Beth, just take two issues which Governor Romney could have based on his record and his positions where he could have been more critical of the administration. He could have been critical of the administration from the right. Most people here probably believe the Bush administration was too weak on holding the line on spending. And on competence—running as a manager and saying Katrina was a failure of management and there were failures of management in the Iraq war. Weren't there ways for you to show independence and more of the message of change that you ran on, at least some of the time, by talking about the failures of the Bush administration?

BETH MYERS: Katrina was probably fairly safe ground on which to critique the administration. Everyone to some degree or another suggested that perhaps it could have been executed in a better way. But when you talk about attacking the president on competence, no, I don't think that that would have been anything. We wouldn't have approached it that way. On spending, I think you can talk about it in a way that's not in direct confrontation with the president. We did, and that was the most productive way to approach it in a primary situation. When you go into a general election, the dynamic changes dramatically. But in a primary battle, no, I don't think that would have been a winning strategy.

LEW MOORE: I ran the only campaign in the Republican primary that was very critical of most of Mr. Bush's policies. What we found both anecdotally and in polling data is the critique of Bush's domestic policy went over fairly well with a lot of Republicans but the critique of the foreign policy was very limiting for what we could do in terms of penetrating a Republican base. Dr. Paul had a very principled position. He had never deviated from his position. He voted against the war. We had people coming up to us constantly and saying, we really like your candidate but it's a nonstarter for us because he's antiwar. There were some areas where some of the other campaigns maybe could have been more critical of the president if they had chosen but I don't think foreign policy was one of them, which is very problematic in the general election.

MIKE HUDOME: From a McCain perspective, advertising-wise, we actually mentioned [Secretary of Defense] Donald Rumsfeld in one of our most effective ads, so we did take on the president. In New Hampshire, one of our most successful ads was a sixty-second ad that we called "Angry," where McCain says, "I went to Washington, I made some people angry. I made the Pentagon angry when I criticized Rumsfeld." He closes the spot by saying, "I didn't go to Washington to win Mr. Congeniality. I went there to serve my country." More than implicitly, I think the McCain campaign did a little bit of what you're suggesting—taking on the president, in a very classy manner, I might add. [*laughter*]

BILL LACY: The way the McCain campaign did it in the general election was outstanding. That would have been risky for the primary campaign, for all the reasons that everybody said here. If you think you have a real shot at any point of wanting to take on the president that is to align yourself against 80 percent of Republicans. You have to keep that in mind.

LOIS ROMANO: What about in the general election—could Mr. McCain have distanced himself a little further? The scenario that you all are portraying, given where the country is, is that a Republican could not have won under any circumstances.

SARAH SIMMONS: I can give two anecdotes where I think our actions spoke more loudly than a direct hit. Going back to the humanity part of the campaign, John McCain was never going to go out and say,

"George Bush stinks." That just wasn't going to happen. But look at our actions—how our campaign responded in particular situations. First, there was potentially a category four or category five hurricane bearing down on the Gulf coast during the start of our convention. We canceled a full day of our convention. We had ads prepared to respond to it that were very critical of the response that had happened after Katrina. We were prepared to show—and I think we did show—in an action-oriented way, a different response to a similar situation. Second, part of our response coming back to Washington during the economic crisis[5] was because we didn't want to be perceived as the candidate who is flying over a disaster area.[6] We wanted to be perceived as a leader who was going to be in the mix and have a hands-on approach to leadership—someone who was actually trying to affect process. It was very central in terms of how we tried to portray our actions.

CHRISTIAN FERRY: At the start of the primary season, there was a big differentiator between John McCain and George Bush on the Iraq war. John McCain had been a passionate advocate for the surge long before George Bush had taken up that strategy. What happened during the primaries is George Bush came to the same position that John McCain had had. That changed the dynamics of the primary and it greatly changed the dynamics of the general election. Here we had this great issue which has been a differentiator and, all of the sudden, we were on the same side as President Bush. I think it had a big impact on us in the general election.

ED ROLLINS: You made the point that no Republican could have won. The likelihood of any Republican winning in this environment was extraordinary. If this had been the third term and Vice President Cheney was the nominee—which he probably would have been if he hadn't taken himself out at the beginning—he would have been lucky to get 39 percent of the vote. John McCain ran as good a campaign as you could possibly run in this environment. He did as well as anybody could. He made this a very competitive race until the economy fell through. I think any of us who have done this for a long time have the ultimate respect for what these guys did. They had to live through chaos. They had to come back. They had an extraordinary campaign against them. And, until the very end, it was a very close race.

---

5. On September 24, 2008, John McCain suspended his presidential campaign to join negotiations in Congress over the government's bailout plan.
6. On August 31, 2005, following Hurricane Katrina, President Bush flew over New Orleans and Mississippi, surveying the damage from the plane as opposed to visiting the city.

• MCCAIN: THE PRESUMED FRONT-RUNNER •

MARK HALPERIN: At the start of this—in late 2006, early 2007—Senator McCain was considered the favorite and, by some, a prohibitive favorite. Chip, we'll start with you. In the beginning of the race in the spring of 2007, how did you view John McCain, front-runner, in terms of his vulnerabilities? To the extent you thought this guy is beatable, where did you see him as vulnerable?

CHIP SALTSMAN: We were not, at that point, a big enough deal to even think in that margin. We knew that he didn't know who we were yet. But we knew that John McCain was "Battleship McCain." We knew there was going to be somebody to come out of Iowa, as always, as the other candidate. At that point, there were a couple of fundamental things, as the field broke off into the boxes that they typically do. Early on in the campaign, the conservative box was going to be checked by either Bill Frist or George Allen. When neither of those two guys made the race, the Romney campaign made a fundamental decision to shift and to try to go into the conservative box because they saw it wide open. I thought that was a pretty smart decision at the time. As I was looking at it, still not involved in the campaign yet, I saw Romney, who was this successful business guy and had been a governor, and I said, "That's the kind of guy that a guy like me from Nashville, Tennessee, could support." But he, all of the sudden, found all the other boxes had been filled, so he pivoted into the conservative box, but that wasn't a natural place for him. As we were going forward, we thought to ourselves, John McCain is there. He's already got a bye. He's going to be there. This is before the implosion. He's got a bye in the first round. There's going to be a few pre-round games to get into the bracket. We think it could come down to us and Romney in Iowa. If he's coming to our turf to play, we've got a chance.

MARK HALPERIN: Brent, early on if you talked to the McCain people, before the mayor's decision to get in, they were very skeptical that he was going to run. Mayor Giuliani was good friends with John McCain. He shared a lot of his views. What vulnerabilities did your campaign see in the front-runner that made Giuliani and his team say, "This guy can be beat."?

BRENT SEABORN: One part of it was that Giuliani really saw this as him running against his friend. He never said, "Boy, John McCain would be a terrible president and I need to get in there to try to stop him." He really looked at it as, "I hope they choose one of the two of us." I don't think he went into it saying, "I've got to beat John McCain." He certainly was aware—we were all aware—that there was at least a part of the party that didn't like John McCain and that there was some room to grow there. John McCain wasn't as popular as he could have been or as other candidates could be.

MARK HALPERIN: Did you see it as just a general unpopularity? Or did you peg it to certain things he'd done or certain issues where you thought you could be the beneficiary or he wouldn't be able to overcome them?

BRENT SEABORN: We knew that there was going to be an alternative to John McCain. We went in naturally believing we could be the alternative. When the first quarter fundraising numbers came out, that really changed the game and made Governor Romney a top-tier candidate. There was no question that seeing how much money they had raised entirely changed the game. Then we had a number of candidates that flirted with getting in, including Newt Gingrich, who ultimately didn't. We went in as the alternative to John McCain—we thought that the party was going to go in and choose one of these two candidates. For the first half of the year, we were looked at as the alternative. Giuliani had his own base of support but he was also the beneficiary of picking up some of the people who were not happy with John McCain as the potential nominee and were at least interested in Rudy Giuliani being the nominee. All this changes as people get defined. Everything changed a lot. But early on, it was just knowing that there was going to be room for an alternative.

MARK HALPERIN: Steve, did Governor Thompson see any weaknesses in McCain that he thought he would be a good alternative to?

STEVE GRUBBS: Our company does a poll every August on Republican presidential candidates for the caucuses. In 2005, our first poll for this last cycle, Condoleezza Rice was the strong front-runner, followed by Giuliani and McCain. In the fave/unfave question, what we noticed was that McCain's fave/unfave was about one to one—just as many Republicans disliked him as liked him. We saw a big opportunity there. We knew Giuliani was very popular but people didn't know that he was pro-choice, and we knew that was a big problem. We felt like Mitt Romney had serious issues. We said, from the very beginning, that there would be two passes out of Iowa, maybe three, and that it would be one of the three front-runners and then some conservative alternative. We were hoping it would be us, but it turned out to be Huckabee.

MARK HALPERIN: Beth, where did you see vulnerabilities in John McCain in the spring of 2007?

BETH MYERS: Instead of a specific vulnerability of the McCain candidacy, we looked at turf that we could occupy. I take a little bit of issue with the way Chip described us as shifting into the conservative box. I don't think that's where we saw our candidacy. We saw the McCain campaign and the

Giuliani campaign sharing an awful lot of turf. Together, that was the largest group but they were splitting it. There was center right, which is where our candidacy was placed. There was a lot of room for growth. There was room a little bit to the right and there was room a little bit, perhaps less, to the left, with both McCain and Giuliani there. We tried to grow on the economic issues at center right. Instead of attacking McCain in the first half of 2007, we tried to focus on that and getting our campaign out very aggressively.

RICK DAVIS: The issues with John McCain's candidacy were more ideological. It was where he sat in the ideological stream of the party, rather than on any particular issue.

BETH MYERS: Right.

MARK HALPERIN: Because of judges? Because of immigration?

BETH MYERS: Campaign finance reform.

RICK DAVIS: Yes.

BETH MYERS: There were a lot of things like that.

RICK DAVIS: What makes up John McCain's ideological position by the spring of 2007 is a composite of all those things. McInturff did something in May of 2007 which gets to what you are alluding to—a chart of where everybody sat within the ideological space of the Republican party. That became our design for the basis of our strategy on how to win the election. We pushed Rudy back into a more left position so that it opened up our left flank a little bit. All those votes would have been ours if he hadn't been in the race. To the right flank is Romney. Then Romney, on his right, had a slew of other people who weren't our competition. We never ran against Huckabee until he was the only guy standing in the race because we knew he was going to cause problems on Romney's right. We didn't want to hurt somebody on his right who was going to squeeze him. For us, it was just a game of being able to cross-pressure each person on the other end of their ideological base. When people chose not to play in certain states, it opened up those features for us. When Rudy didn't go to South Carolina, boom, all of a sudden our left flank is wide open. That's like 10 percent more vote than we would have gotten in South Carolina. When Mitt decided not to go to South Carolina, that opened up our right flank. It didn't help Huckabee as much as it helped us. When you drew a circle around the Huckabee and Giuliani campaigns, movement along our left and right flanks is what really defined us as a candidate.

BETH MYERS: From our point of view, when Rudy stopped advertising in New Hampshire, that was one of the worst days in our campaign. Our polling showed that, up until that point, there was about 40 percent of the vote that Rudy and McCain were splitting fairly evenly. The two of them were tracking almost 100 percent and we were above that—at five or six points more than that. When Rudy stopped advertising, he went down and McCain went right up. That was a dynamic that was very problematic for us.

BRENT SEABORN: We were seeing the same thing. Frankly, no small part of that was that we were at that point of really having to conserve finances. By the end of the campaign, we were struggling financially. But we also saw the same thing you saw. When we made that decision, we were still looking at it in the context of Governor Romney probably winning Iowa and going into New Hampshire. For us, it was a little bit of a consolation that if we got out of New Hampshire, we would at least ensure a fight in New Hampshire. We presumed all along that Romney would win Iowa. We thought if he won two in a row, the race would essentially be over. At that point, we decided we'd rather have John McCain win in New Hampshire than have Mitt Romney go one, two and essentially be done.

BETH MYERS: At that point, we were struggling with two fights on two flanks then. We had a real horse race in Iowa. Then what we thought was a safe fallback position became a real problem for us when you pulled out.

BRENT SEABORN: If we had all the money in the world, we may have stayed up. But, ultimately, we were having to make some very difficult decisions. We saw one of the benefits of pulling down there would be really mixing up the first part of the field.

• MCCAIN'S IMPLOSION . . . AND COMEBACK •

MARK HALPERIN: Rick, although there are seven of you here, there are no seats for John Weaver and Terry Nelson, who were helping early on in the campaign. We're not going to revisit that entire story of how they left the campaign.[7] [*laughter*] But as you were building the battleship in the first part of the year, you had some different people, some of the same people, and you were raising a fair amount of money. You were also spending a lot of money. Immigration and Iraq hurt you a lot, as did some mistakes that were made out on the trail. But looking back, given that what you constructed collapsed

---

7. Terry Nelson was McCain's campaign manager, and John Weaver was a longtime political strategist for McCain. They resigned from the presidential campaign on July 10, 2007.

McCain senior advisers Rick Davis and Trevor Potter discuss the ups and downs of the McCain campaign.

and you had to reconstruct, what were the mistakes you made in organizing and planning the campaign in late 2006 and early 2007?

RICK DAVIS: Money played a significant role in all that. It was interesting because since the 2000 campaign, John had one of the best lists in the Republican party—both Internet fundraising and a donor list. He had maintained that successfully for ten years. Every cycle he'd go out and campaign and offer his list to members of Congress and we'd match up those names and build a good list. What was interesting about that list is the core of it were people who were significantly offended by his position on the surge. When you looked at it, going into 2006, we'd gotten virtually completely through the election cycle, and when we evaluated our own resources—our own assets—we looked at this ability to raise money and said, "Wow, these people have hung with us for ten years. These are the core of John McCain's base of fundraising. We can move forward into a primary election with this great asset, and we believe it's worth *X*." There's a lot of debate about how you write a budget for a campaign and there's a lot of guesswork, but you base it on what you think your assets can produce on the front end and how you'll grow on the back end. We were very ambitious in what we thought we could do. There is absolutely no doubt that one of the greatest problems we had is, at the same time we launched the campaign, John was in the spotlight launching this attack on the Bush administration on the surge. And he was the biggest proponent of the war in Iraq at a time when the popularity for the war in Iraq, which actually sustained itself relatively well up until September of the election cycle in 2006, collapsed. Suffice it to say, many of the people on our donor list were not rock-rib Republicans. They were McCain Republicans. They didn't like his position on the surge. So our fundraising model collapsed right when we went into the mail and decided to start fundraising. The long story short is that ultimately, John McCain's ability to raise money was off of the backs of the more conservative Republican base of donors than it ever was from the past. That whole thing basically churned through the election cycle and came out completely different on the other end.

MARK HALPERIN: Events obviously hurt you—what was going on with Iraq and then Congress taking up immigration. There were some particulars but, speaking as a campaign manager talking in general about running a presidential campaign, were there things that you did wrong that in looking back you'd say, "We ended up winning the nomination but we would rather have won it in a more linear fashion."? Were there things that you could have done differently, in terms of setting up the campaign, that were mistakes, in retrospect, during that period?

RICK DAVIS: Yes, sure.

MARK HALPERIN: What would some of them be?

RICK DAVIS: One of the things that you've got to be leery of is the old model that you build the battleship and that's strong enough to sail through troubled waters—that you can defend yourself. The model we had was South Carolina. Bush had a battleship in South Carolina in 2000. When he lost New Hampshire, he came under assault, both from outside and inside. Bush's model was he had enough of a ship to keep itself right in the intensive campaign through the South Carolina primary, and he won, ultimately undermining our ability to win a nomination. That was probably the last time that will happen in an election cycle where that model is a guarantee for success on our side. There's a new ship in town.

MARK HALPERIN: A billion-dollar ship.

RICK DAVIS: Yes, right. We were chasing a model that was irrelevant. We invited [*New York Times* columnist] David Brooks over for a lunch with some of our policy guys to kick around ideas and things that were going on in the campaign. He said, "Do you mind if I talk about the campaign for a minute, not just policy items?" "Sure, no problem." He said, "A lot of people were very excited about seeing the John McCain 2000 campaign in this cycle, and instead they saw the George Bush 2000 campaign." He was exactly right. You can call it criticism or not—it was the model that we chose. His observation encapsulated exactly what had happened in our campaign in the first six months of 2007.

MARK HALPERIN: We get to the summer and Senator McCain's campaign, according to the pundits, is over and he's the only one who's not acknowledging it.

RICK DAVIS: That's what Charlie Cook told me. [*laughter*]

MARK HALPERIN: Very little of that was caused by the other campaigns. It was caused by events and by some mistakes the McCain campaign made. Did you think McCain's campaign was over? And, as he started to revitalize, did anyone here think, "We'd better stop this guy because he was the front-runner, he's got a lot of strength, we can't let him come back."? In effect, no one did. He fell by himself, but then he came back, and no one tried to stop him from coming back. What was the debate within your campaigns during the period when he was down and apparently out, and then as he started to come back?

ED ROLLINS: I thought he was done. No one laid a glove on John McCain. He took some tough positions on issues, but I don't think that's what hurt him. I think it was running out of money and their internal battles that they all had to live through. To a certain extent, what it showed to a lot of people on the outside was this was a Washington establishment campaign. They were killing each other. At the end of the day, the question was, would John himself be able to function effectively through a long, drawn-out campaign?

MARK HALPERIN: So, you thought he was dead. Did you then, as he came back, think, "He's back and we have to stop him."?

ED ROLLINS: I thought he was dead. I thought he had a singular shot. As we discussed it, his going to New Hampshire was all or nothing. John's a gambler. Rick's a gambler. It was an all-or-nothing strategy. I don't think if he'd have lost New Hampshire there was anyplace else he could have gone after that. He didn't have South Carolina until he won there. We had a NAS-CAR race. We knocked Romney out, Thompson knocked us out in South Carolina, and McCain went right up the middle.

MARK HALPERIN: Beth, did you all think he was done, and why didn't you try to stop him from growing back as he recovered?

BETH MYERS: No one did lay a glove on him as they had their implosion. We did talk about that. There was one person on our campaign who said, "Wait, he's not dead yet, let's stomp on him some more." And we said, "No, no, no, no, we're not going to do that."

MARK HALPERIN: Why not? Because the guy's down and he's out, so why bother?

BETH MYERS: We thought he was down enough. And Mitt just said, "No, no, we're not going to spend money or time or effort." We've got Rudy, in the meantime, because of the dynamic. As McCain went down, Rudy was getting bigger and bigger, and we were beginning to be concerned about Huckabee and Thompson, and a little bit about Brownback, on the right. We felt we had many other fish to fry than stomping on the guy who was the great American hero, who's being ill served by staffers or whatever. So there just was absolutely no percentage in it, although, later on, I will say that this person on our campaign came into my office more than one time and said, "I told you so." [*laughter*]

MARK HALPERIN: Was the governor's reluctance based on personally feeling bad, like no reason to kick a guy when he's down, or just rationally he said, "Look, we don't want to waste resources because our analysis is that he's not a threat to us anymore."?

BETH MYERS: I think a combination of both, but I wouldn't speculate on his motives. But I think that was the general feeling.

MARK HALPERIN: As he started to come back, before this person said, "I told you so," did they raise it before it was too late? You could have probably done things in the early fall that might have been effective.

BETH MYERS: We didn't lay a glove on him.

MARK HALPERIN: Was the debate revisited as he started to show strength?

BETH MYERS: Yes, it was. It wasn't revisited until later in the fall, in New Hampshire, when we started to see the problem we would have if something happened to Rudy in New Hampshire.

MARK HALPERIN: You say you revisited it but you still didn't do very much. There wasn't negative advertising or efforts to stoke his problems.

BETH MYERS: We did a little bit of negative mail in New Hampshire, absolutely.

RICK DAVIS: Don't sell yourself short. [*laughter*]

BETH MYERS: We definitely did revisit it. But I give huge credit to the McCain campaign and to everyone sitting at this table who had the perseverance because you talk about a narrow path, it was a very narrow path back from June of 2007, which they followed beautifully.

BILL MCINTURFF: I want to speak to this and you said you liked to hear stories. I was offered a job on Bob Dole's presidential campaign and I had a little lower-level offer from the Bush campaign. I went to a famous Republican consultant who was also being approached by both. I said, "I've been offered both, you've been offered both, what are you going to do? What should I do?" He said, well, let me ask you some questions. When you think of Bob Dole people, who do you think of? I said, "Sheila and Joanne Coe."[8] He said, "Who else?" And that's it. Then he said, "Other than the state chairman of Kansas, who cares about Bob Dole? Name me a state chairman who cares about Bob Dole." And there was nobody. Then he said, "George Bush. Who are George Bush people?" And the list is endless. He said, "Name me a state chairman other than from Texas who cares about George Bush." The list was endless. What he said was, "Look, Bush has got the weird hand thing and the voice. I can fix all that. I can't fix whatever it is about Bob Dole that he's been a U.S. senator, majority leader, and a vice-presidential candidate and we can't think of anybody who cares about Bob Dole." What he said about being president is, "If you're going to be president, sooner or later you've got to do two things. You've got to drag a dead campaign forward by your own personality, and you have to have people everywhere who would kill for you because they are fiercely loyal." That's the model that I've used to look at who could be the nominee and who could be president. What we all need to recognize here is a lot of us didn't make it through the entire primary for John McCain but not a single fundraising person, not a single county chairman and not a single state chairman quit. Those people, at a time when they're being told this guy is dead, dead, dead, dead, dead, stayed with this guy. Second, in terms of perseverance—I got all the phone calls saying, "You've known McCain

---

8. Sheila Burke was Senator Dole's chief of staff, and Joanne Coe was a longtime adviser to Senator Dole.

for years, will he drop out?" And I said, "What part of the bio haven't you read?" [*laughter*] I said, "It's not the five and a half years of torture. Let me tell you how he won his congressional seat. He moved to a state where he never lived. He moved to a core Republican seat. He ran against the three most popular Republicans. And guess what he did? He spent six hours a day for eighteen straight months going door to door." I said, "Have you ever gone door to door for six hours, much less eighteen straight months?" I said, "This campaign will be over when John dies or when somebody else has the number of votes required to be the nominee. If he has no money, he will campaign door to door in New Hampshire. He will never quit. He will not stop." What it says about why he's the nominee is the story of two things: one, those people all over the country who stayed with him—joining the campaign to raise money at a time when nobody even wanted to be on the campaign; two, a candidate who has more than once proven he can drag a dead campaign forward. It's a credit to many of the people at the table but John McCain is the nominee and could have been president because of John McCain. We all need to recognize that. Lastly, two things. It is because my friend Rudy got out of New Hampshire and because the Romney people didn't do negatives in South Carolina.

ED ROLLINS: That's the only place they didn't do negatives.

BILL MCINTURFF: If Rudy hadn't gotten out of New Hampshire, McCain couldn't have won New Hampshire. And if Romney had done negatives in South Carolina, Huckabee would have won and screwed up Florida.

MARK HALPERIN: Bill, your candidate got in, in part, because he saw his friend Senator McCain had faded. How much discussion was there to say, "There's now this big room because John McCain sure as heck isn't going to be the nominee"?

BILL LACY: We got in at a time when we thought McCain was definitely dead. The most unfortunate part of the election outcome this year is that Rick and his team aren't going to get credit for bringing back a candidate—and the candidate himself for bringing himself back, reinventing himself. It was unbelievable. We were so far behind the curve. We had so much to catch up on that one of the first decisions that I made when I got to the campaign was to suspend opposition research on John McCain. John McCain was gone—he wasn't coming back. We didn't even have time to do research on the guys that we thought we had as main opponents. So there was virtually no discussion until eventually you started seeing all the candidates—all the presumptive nominees—start to fall apart, and McCain is still standing. He comes back and it's a miracle.

BRENT SEABORN: Our campaign had fairly vigorous debates about what to do, knowing that John McCain was basically occupying the territory that Rudy needed to win. There were some people who said, "Senator McCain is dead and he's never coming back." I was one of the few voices who said, "This is probably his best opportunity—he now gets to go camp out in New Hampshire. He has no expectations and he can campaign exactly the way he likes to campaign." I said, "I don't think he's dead." Ultimately, there was further debate about whether we start picking at the corpse and try to finish him. That debate got as far as Rudy just saying, "No, it's not going to happen." Under no circumstances did he want our campaign to be any part of finishing John McCain. This incredible friendship or loyalty that Rudy has or feels toward Senator McCain precluded that, although there were people within the campaign that were drawing up plans—this is how we're going to finish him, this is how we're going to pick the corpse.

MARK HALPERIN: Did your not picking the corpse raw extend to not try to pick up donors?

BRENT SEABORN: It did.

BETH MYERS: We picked at that corpse. We tried to and we were not very successful.

BRENT SEABORN: I know some of our finance people had gone out. And even some of the donors had said, "If he gets out, we'll come your way, but we're loyal." They did have a very loyal base. Lots of them said, "Hey, you're our next choice, we'll come your way but we're not going to do anything until, or unless, he gets out."

MARK HALPERIN: Beth, let me follow up on what you said. Did Romney make calls to big people?

BETH MYERS: No.

MARK HALPERIN: What did you hear back from people?

BETH MYERS: Our finance chair was very aggressive in calling up the McCain donors.

MARK HALPERIN: What did he say he heard back from them?

BETH MYERS: He was surprised there was not much budging. In fact, I can't think of much budging at all. Our direct mail probably did better then because some of those people defected, but the hard-core folks stayed right with McCain.

BILL MCINTURFF: I have one more story. In 1999, Rick asked me to talk to our key donors. He said, "Your job is to lay out the plausible strategy for how to beat George Bush." I said, "That's an oxymoron, there is no plausible strategy to beat George Bush." He said, "Well, yeah, but you've got to do it and you've got to make it sound really good." I said, "Rick, you're the campaign manager, I'm the pollster. I can't make stuff up, you make stuff up." He says, "No, no, you have to do it." So I stand up and I do this whole speech and I'm trying to be as plausible as I can and still be even close to credible. And these men and women are okay, okay, and they're buying it. I said, "Oh my God, they're buying it." Then we do the questions and answer. This one very big player raises his hand and says, "Now, Bill, have we done any polling about who's going to be John's VP?" I said, "No, we're not worrying about the whole VP slot yet. We're not using your money for the VP slot." I walked out and said, "Oh my God, Rick, I was terrified to talk to that group and they're worrying about who the hell's going to be McCain's VP. These people are beyond Kool-Aid stage. Rick, this is scary." [*laughter*]

CHRISTIAN FERRY: I think one of the things that came out of that time period is right before the campaign collapsed, a direct mail piece was sent out. It was this kind of corny direct mail piece that began, "I'm all alone in a hotel room and it's late at night, Cindy's gone to bed and I'm writing you this letter because I have some time to reflect on my own." Our donors, our base and our supporters responded to that direct mail piece by giving their hearts. It was the most successful piece we had done, until the general election campaign, in his entire career. The difficulty John McCain was going through really rallied our people behind him.

TREVOR POTTER: I had a sort of "on the road to Iowa" comment. Bill said that John McCain had carried the campaign through. But when you talk about lessons learned from the whole process, it is hard to think of any other presidential campaign that could have had the implosion that we had and survive and triumph. So I think it's worth noting what that June to December period was like, because when Rick came in to manage—and I'll suck up now, a brilliant manager—the problem was he had nothing to manage. The offices were empty. The desks were empty. The implosion had been a two-stage implosion where the previous management had had to cut most of the staff and had given everyone pink slips. Then Rick walked in and half the staff looked at him and left. What was left was a small core and not what you would consider a presidential campaign. You had John McCain on the road, carrying his own bags and campaigning, which ultimately was the product. But you still had to deal with the fact that you had this sea anchor down there dragging McCain down—the bad news from the campaign, the financial situation. The point I wanted to make is that it was not only John McCain able to pull himself through, but it was the ability to use volunteers—an enormous number of people, who either appeared or Rick was able to call and say, "We really need you now." People who came in and worked, left their jobs or were retired, or people who came in and worked for nothing and bartended at night, were able to carry the campaign through those months. In that sense, it was an extraordinary presidential effort. People called it the pirate ship because it had this very nontraditional flavor throughout the entire fall with no polling, no television, no mail until the very end, when we could finally do something in Iowa and New Hampshire. All the traditional things that you think you need to make a presidential campaign real weren't there. There was a skeletal crew and McCain on the road. I do think that is one of the more unusual features of this season because it continued through Iowa and New Hampshire. In New Hampshire, it was essentially all volunteers. We had a volunteer coordinator who was signing up what ended up to be hundreds of volunteers from around the country who, at their own expense, drove or flew to New Hampshire and shared bunkrooms and did phone banks. You'd go into our phone banks and they were completely chaotic. People were on cell phones because that's all they

Brent Seaborn, Steve Grubbs, and Lew Moore listen to their primary opponents.

had, but they were really enthusiastic. You'd go into the Romney campaign phone banks and they were very well organized and very serious, but it was a different flavor. It almost became more of a crusade for the McCain people—maybe the last campaign you'll see where old-fashioned volunteers ended up surmounting money, out of necessity.

• THE DEMISE OF MITT ROMNEY •

LOIS ROMANO: In canvassing my friends and asking what are good questions to ask, one thing that came up quite a bit was, What happened to Romney? Why did he never really get traction? It looked like he was doing very well in Iowa. He had unsurpassed organization and he had money, but he never got there. He won Michigan and Wyoming. How many primaries did he win?

BETH MYERS: I think he won eleven.

LOIS ROMANO: So what happened? Why did he never really catch fire? The other candidates didn't seem to take to him, either. Can you talk a little bit about what you saw as the dynamic going on there?

BETH MYERS: You'd have to ask the other candidates whether or not they took to him. I think it's a battle. I will say that after the campaign ended, we worked very hard and had a great relationship. Governor Romney and Senator McCain were at a dinner last night that was, by all accounts, a very friendly thing. So I don't really buy into that. I also don't really buy into the premise that Mitt didn't catch on. If you look at Iowa, we were second. New Hampshire, we were second. Michigan, we were first. Nevada, we were first. South Carolina, we were third. Florida, we were second. We placed very strongly in all of those early battles. The problem with our party is that it's mostly winner take all.[9] I'm not complaining. We knew the rules of the game. But I can give you an explanation in each state why we lost. In Iowa, there was this incredible phenomenon of Mike Huckabee on the right, which started at the straw poll, and they very brilliantly exploited it. We fought back as hard as we could, but their insurgent campaign absolutely overtook ours. In New Hampshire, we've talked about the dynamics of how the New Hampshire electorate got a little bit more less right wing, more center right. When Rudy left, that changed the geometry of the race dramatically. Then we got onto good territory for us—Nevada and Michigan. We decided not

---

9. In most states, the Republican primary system is a winner take all system in which the candidate who receives the most votes in the state receives all of the state's delegates.

to compete in South Carolina because we were starting to run out of money and we recognized that we needed to win Florida to go into Super Tuesday. We wanted to husband our resources there. That's what happened. It wasn't a gestalt but rather a piece by piece.

LOIS ROMANO: I spent some time in Iowa and I did a couple of stories on the evangelicals. One of the things that came up quite a bit in my interviews was the abortion situation—that he had stated at one point that he was pro-choice. Did anything in your numbers reflect that voters were a little bit uneasy with that flip-flop? Not necessarily on that issue, but just that he is a chameleon. Did anything in your numbers indicate that people didn't trust him or weren't sure where he was on issues?

BETH MYERS: Let me just correct the record. Mitt has never described himself as being pro-choice because, personally, he is pro-life. That being said, when he ran for governor, he said he would continue to support the state's law. He never did say he was pro-choice. Others may have referred to him that way. And that's a bit of a nuance there that people may take issue with. But as a person, he's not pro-choice and never has been. That being said, yes, there was a problem there for us. Here in Massachusetts, he was faced with an unusual situation in that we landed very unexpectedly in the middle of culture wars—with gay marriage and the very first stem-cell battle. When the legislature changed the definition of when life began, when Harvard wanted to begin their stem-cell research, Mitt, as governor, was put in a situation that we hadn't really strategized for. We found ourselves pushed into a situation where we were talking about cultural issues far more than we wanted to talk about them. We wanted this race to be about the economy and the economic turnaround.

MARK HALPERIN: Ed, did you want to say something about how much everyone loved Governor Romney?

ED ROLLINS: In fairness to the other candidates, you had a lot of resources and you basically attacked every other campaign, including Paul's campaign. The reality is that every debate that went on, some idea that someone had said somewhere along the line became a Romney line in the next debate. That's what created the resentment as it went on and on and on. At the end of the day, my guy is not a hater, but he would not have supported Romney if Romney was the nominee, and I think other candidates felt the same way. He felt that there were so many flip-flops in the course of the campaign that there really wasn't a core. I think that's what happened.

LOIS ROMANO: Can you comment on what role you think his faith played in the whole process?

BETH MYERS: It became an issue that he felt he needed to address and he addressed it the way he wanted to address it in his speech in Houston.[10] During the course of the campaign, there was only one instance where one of the other candidates mentioned it in a negative way to a reporter, and that candidate apologized to Mitt.[11] I take that candidate's apology at face value.

LOIS ROMANO: What about the base? Some polls showed they were skeptical.

BETH MYERS: It would be naive to say that it wasn't an issue. It seems to be a prejudice that is not a taboo to share.

LOIS ROMANO: But you don't think it was an overriding issue? You think it was just one of many factors?

BETH MYERS: It was a major issue. I don't think it should have been. I think the Obama victory will show that the American people do have open minds. We did break it down considerably during the course of the campaign. The problem for Mitt in the beginning was that we didn't want the first thing they knew about him to be he is a Mormon from Massachusetts, which is why we spent money early on to increase his name ID in a way that was not just the Mormon from Massachusetts, particularly in Iowa, where we found a larger residual of some bias against the Mormon faith than we found in other places.

CHIP SALTSMAN: Since we were candidate X . . . the media constantly referred to him as a Mormon and that didn't help any. Just like Huckabee was always the preacher. We got Reverend Huckabee as much as we got Governor Huckabee in the introductions. The media tend to pick out that one thing that could be a problem and then just hammer it home time and time again. That was a big challenge and I thought the Romney campaign did a pretty good job handling it. But it's hard when every conversation starts out with Governor Mitt Romney, a Mormon—it's whatever is after the comma—so that was a challenge.

---

10. On December 6, 2007, Mitt Romney delivered a speech titled "Faith in America" at the George Bush Presidential Library in College Station, Texas.

11. On December 12, 2007, Mike Huckabee said he apologized to rival Mitt Romney after a Republican presidential debate in Iowa for questioning his Mormon faith in an upcoming article in *The New York Times Magazine*. In the article, Huckabee, an ordained Southern Baptist minister, asks, "Don't Mormons believe that Jesus and the devil are brothers?"

Beth Myers and Sydney Hay look on as Chip Saltsman talks about the success of Mike Huckabee's campaign.

SYDNEY HAY: Friends of mine who were involved in the Romney campaign told me that there was a big controversy in the campaign as to whether to make that speech or not make that speech. Could you tell us how that played out?

BETH MYERS: There was never a controversy on that. It was always going to be whatever Mitt wanted to do on that speech.

SYDNEY HAY: Were there lots of people in the campaign who didn't want him to make it?

BETH MYERS: No.

• THE RISE OF HUCKABEE •

MARK HALPERIN: I want to tie together some things that have already been mentioned as we start talking about the several weeks of primaries and caucuses that led to McCain being the de facto nominee. It's already been suggested that it took a series of events for Senator McCain to win this—

Huckabee's rise in Iowa, Giuliani to pull out of New Hampshire, Romney to pull out of South Carolina to some extent, and Senator Thompson to take up space and then take up less space. Let's start with Huckabee's rise. The Romney campaign and the Thompson campaign grew increasingly frustrated at Huckabee rising in Iowa, not getting a lot of scrutiny from the press, succeeding with very little money. I want to ask Lew and Steve and Sydney since you all were working for candidates who wanted to succeed in Iowa, spent time there and, in at least one case, had more money than Huckabee had to spend. What did you see as Huckabee's source of success there and why didn't you duplicate it, or did you try to?

STEVE GRUBBS: The big difference was the debates. There were more nationally televised debates a year out in this cycle than any cycle I can remember—starting eight or nine months out from the caucuses. From the very first debate on, Mike Huckabee was either the best or the second best in every debate. My candidate was not. As voters had that first glimpse at candidates, instead of early TV, these debates became a defining tool and made a huge difference.

MARK HALPERIN: Lew, what did you all see him doing?

LEW MOORE: I think his narrative captured the imagination of the Christian conservative networks in Iowa. Iowa is a caucus state, not a primary state. There was a huge turnout at that caucus and that's a very committed group when they become committed. He captured their imaginations.

MARK HALPERIN: Sydney, did you all see anything you tried to duplicate or copy?

SYDNEY HAY: First of all, when we were involved in trying to convince Duncan Hunter to run for president, it was because many of us in the grassroots base of the Republican party didn't see how any of the top three were going to be able to really mobilize and excite and ignite the conservative base within our party. It ended up being that Mike Huckabee rose to the top of the other potential wannabes and that's what happened. But the price of admission in Iowa is becoming much higher than it ever was in history.

MARK HALPERIN: But Huckabee was not a well-funded candidate.

SYDNEY HAY: No, not at all. But he was able to really focus on that Iowa straw poll and put a lot of resources there that we weren't able to do.

MARK HALPERIN: Chip, how much did you spend on the straw?

CHIP SALTSMAN: A couple hundred thousand dollars—maybe a hundred and fifty.

SYDNEY HAY: Well, we spent about five thousand. [*laughter*] I'm questioning whether that Iowa straw poll will become a victim of its own success. My first experience in an Iowa straw poll was in 1988, when you won it with around twelve hundred votes. Phil Gramm and Bob Dole tied there in 1996 at a couple thousand votes. Then, all of the sudden, Steve Forbes and Bush came in and really started to put all the resources in there. Maybe that will change, but I think this may be the last time somebody catapulted to success in Iowa based upon that straw poll. Duncan had never even been to Iowa and started to campaign at the end of October 2006, so there wasn't much we could do.

MARK HALPERIN: Bill, you've done this long enough that you don't get frustrated anymore, but you had people on your campaign who were very frustrated at Huckabee's success and took some measures to try to get the press to be more interested in scrutinizing him. What kinds of things did you all discuss in retrospect? Should you have been more aggressive about trying to stop his growth?

BILL LACY: I actually was very frustrated. We kept looking at Governor Huckabee and he was, and still is, an extraordinary communicator. But he could get away with stuff that if Fred Thompson had said it, he'd be on the front page of the *New York Times*. That got very frustrating. There's another piece of Governor Huckabee's rise that hasn't been addressed here—our trouble with the religious right. I spent a huge part of my time trying to work with the more conservative elements of the party. Fred, it turns out, had a lot of support early, before he actually became a candidate. But he's a Federalist. He's a very principled man. Being a Federalist means you don't have national constitutional limitations on everything you want to limit. You do that state by state. That was unacceptable on the issues of gay marriage and abortion to the religious right. That, in large part, opened the door for Governor Huckabee to make those dramatic movements that he made in late summer.

MARK HALPERIN: Beth, your campaign had extraordinarily well-organized opposition research. You were seeing lots of things about Huckabee's record as governor of Arkansas that you thought, if known to Iowa voters, particularly conservative voters, would have been a problem for him. You did some comparative negative advertising but it was pretty soft. It started by saying Governor Huckabee's a great guy. In retrospect, could your campaign have done more? Was there debate within the campaign to say, "These soft negative ads are not enough, we need to do more."? Why didn't you run harder negatives against him in Iowa to try to slow him down?

BETH MYERS: We did have that debate. In fact, we had a few really negative ads in the can. There was a small group of people who wanted to run those really strong negative ads. For the most part, I don't think they would have been effective.

MARK HALPERIN: Because?

BETH MYERS: I think they would have caused a boomerang effect. It is a Republican primary and I think we went about as negative as we could go without really starting to damage our candidate. That's why we did the soft openings.

MARK HALPERIN: This is a pretty critical moment in the campaign.

BETH MYERS: A very critical moment.

MARK HALPERIN: Had you won Iowa, it's been said before, you likely would have won New Hampshire and have been the nominee. You lost Iowa to someone who was not funded and not thought to be someone who could win the Iowa caucuses.

BETH MYERS: I'll push back on that a little bit. I think Governor Huckabee was well positioned to win the Iowa caucus. We were always very nervous about a candidate on the right, in the Iowa caucus.

MARK HALPERIN: But if you could turn the clock back to the beginning of the year, a year out, and you saw the future that Huckabee was going to beat you in Iowa and really change the course of your candidacy, what more could you have done to slow him down?

BETH MYERS: I don't know that we could have done anything to slow him down. We may have put less of an emphasis on Iowa ourselves. If we had known that the turnout was going to be 110,000 people, with a huge percentage of those evangelical Christians, I probably would have said that's going to be a more difficult thing for Mitt Romney to win. But, no, I don't think the solution to that problem would have been to run harder-hitting ads.

MARK HALPERIN: So you are saying that to the extent you could have foreseen that, it would not have been to send your candidate there more or run more negative ads? Not to do anything different except maybe de-em-phasize Iowa?

BETH MYERS: Yes. If we had known that there would have been 110,000 caucus goers, with a majority of those being evangelical Christians, I would have thought that would have been a tough situation for Mitt to win.

MARK HALPERIN: Ryan and Sarah, you all were focused on rebuilding your campaign in New Hampshire. But as you watched Huckabee's rise, did you all start to see this sort of careful bank shot that was going to lead to your nomination? Did you say, "Boy, this is really good for us that Huckabee is rising."? And did you do anything to encourage that?

RYAN PRICE: I focused on grassroots on the campaign. We did see that happening and we were all really hoping for it. I was not involved in the strategy with Rick on what to do to capitalize on that, but it definitely was, from a grassroots perspective. We saw Governor Huckabee's support rising in a lot of the other primary states. We were focusing on the fact that we didn't have staff in Florida. The night of the Iowa caucuses was a very happy night in McCain headquarters.

SARAH SIMMONS: I was vacationing because I was still on hiatus. I do want to say that I think any of us who has lived through a Republican primary knows the reality of being the candidate in the middle. It's very easy to second-guess any of the decisions anybody at this table made throughout the course of it. But to be in that middle position . . . I think Romney was in a very hard spot in Iowa. Every attack you take in one direction alters everybody's perception of you. And there are many different paths they can take if you disqualify one candidate. So, retrospectively, you would have to be careful about how hard you attack. In some ways, we did benefit, although the collapse of our campaign was probably not the design anyone had going into the John McCain presidential plan. But, in some ways, it did give us an advantage because attention was pulled off of John McCain. The press probably got lazy covering a lot of John McCain events, and God knows what things were missed that he said along the campaign trail that we got to skate by on—well, not skate by, that's not a fair representation of our campaign. But, I think that those things did benefit us, because the attention isn't on you and you can have less attention on any mistakes that you would have made.

CHRISTIAN FERRY: For our campaign, after the collapse, we did keep staff in Iowa, we kept our organization going in Iowa, and we continued to look at Iowa as a possibility—as an opportunity should it develop. We weren't running TV and we weren't doing much mail but we continued to run a grassroots campaign. But, by early winter, it became very clear that Mike Huckabee was on the move there. For us, that meant a shift in our focus to New Hampshire—seeing his growth and his movement. Because we had remained tactically flexible about how much time we were going to invest in Iowa, it allowed us to divert much more of our attention and resources to New Hampshire as Huckabee rose up.

• RUDY GIULIANI'S FALL •

MARK HALPERIN: Brent, one of the most criticized and discussed decisions was the mayor's decision to pull out of New Hampshire. In retrospect, do you think it was a mistake? What was driving the decision?

BRENT SEABORN: Looking at it in the prism of where we were at the time, it was a mistake. If we had everything going right, we would have liked to stay. There were a lot of things that happened in New Hampshire that ultimately made us arrive at that decision. Part of it was looking at the idea that Governor Romney was going to win Iowa and then New Hampshire, which ultimately didn't happen. Some of it was financial. We were starting to husband resources knowing that we had to go to Florida, and had to win Florida, in order to make it into the February 5 states. You also had a case where you had Governor Romney and Senator McCain, both with natural constituencies in New Hampshire, and us trying to fight upstream against both. Those things made it difficult enough. We had some reasonably good TV ads—some that we were really happy with—that we started airing. Everybody here knows that buying Boston TV is incredibly expensive. We put a lot of money into TV ads for a few weeks. Unfortunately, when we put the ads up, we were already in a saturated market. We were reasonably late to the game, although that was somewhat by design—we were hoping to get in late and be a new voice. But either we didn't penetrate or we were dragged down by a number of other things. Our ads went up the same time the Giuliani security detail story broke.[12] That threw us off of our game at least for a couple of days. Everybody was trying to get all the facts on that and make sure that everybody completely understood what was going on there. There was also a front-page story in New Hampshire. Those things really hurt our ad buy and, ultimately, we made the decision that we had

---

12. On November 30, 2007, *Politico* released information from previously undisclosed government records that showed that, as New York City mayor, Rudy Giuliani billed obscure city agencies for tens of thousands of dollars in security expenses in the Hamptons, amassed during the time when he was beginning an extramarital relationship with future wife Judith Nathan.

to come down. We were looking at Governor Romney being somewhere in the mid-thirties—that's where he was tracking. Both Senator McCain and Mayor Giuliani were behind him somewhere in the mid-twenties. So we were penetrating. We couldn't justify throwing good money after bad to stay up there. Now, I wish we could have. I wish we had unlimited resources or the resources that we had initially planned on, and we could have stayed and maybe we could have finished second—possibly could have won. We were also in a situation where it was hard for us because, at that point, it was the hottest point of the campaign between Governor Romney and John McCain and we weren't able to take advantage of that. We had a couple of strategies and ideas of trying to interject and referee that. Ultimately, we decided that staying out of it entirely was probably best. There was a lot of long debate about how to deal with that fight. Do we just sit it out? The mayor made the call that we were going to sit it out and hope things break our way.

MARK HALPERIN: But you effectively made a decision that you weren't going to be able to win Florida without having won anything before then, even a moral victory, in any state.

BRENT SEABORN: We did think we could not win any. We thought we could not win in Iowa. We essentially had to write Iowa off early. We didn't play in the straw poll there and we knew that we probably weren't going to win the caucuses there, although we continued to go to Iowa. You need to go there as a platform if you want to get coverage because the press is camped out there. Giving that same speech in Illinois means no one's going to cover it. So, you go to Iowa because you need the coverage and you also hope that something breaks. And, all of the sudden, you become anointed by winning Iowa. And we thought if Rudy Giuliani wins Iowa, it means it's basically over—although that was entirely a pipe dream. We knew that New Hampshire would be incredibly difficult and South Carolina would be tough. We hoped for chaos in the early states. And the last bit of hope we had is that Mike Huckabee would win in South Carolina and shake it up again. When Michigan moved up its primary, that really hurt us. We felt we could weather not winning Iowa, not winning New Hampshire, and not winning South Carolina. But Michigan was a big state. Michigan wasn't a state that we were prepared to play in because it had the same dynamic that New Hampshire had. It was a natural McCain state and it was a natural Romney state. Making our case in Michigan in any other election environment would be reasonably easy, especially if you were able to take the New York economic turnaround story to Michigan. That story would probably be very appealing to Michigan voters. But in the environment that we were in, with the Romney candidacy and the McCain candidacy, we didn't have what we thought was an easy victory in either one of those. So we had Florida as our springboard to February 5.

• THE MICHIGAN PRIMARY •

MARK HALPERIN: McCain wins New Hampshire and then it's on to Michigan, where Senator McCain, perhaps foreshadowing the future, said something about the economy that perhaps didn't get played exactly the way he meant it. He said that those jobs are never coming back.[13] Maybe not the same as his saying "The fundamentals of the economy are sound,"[14] but still not that good. Beth, do you think that played a big role in your winning the Michigan primary, or were you going to win it anyway?

BETH MYERS: We were positioned. We'd been set up in Michigan for a while. We had advertised early in Michigan. There was a tremendous Romney good feeling there. And if you talk about a tough terrain for any other candidate, I think Michigan would be it. But Senator McCain had won in 2000 and he gave a vigorous fight there. He certainly didn't roll over and play dead in Michigan. So it was still a hard-fought win for us.

MARK HALPERIN: Ed and Chip, some people questioned your candidate's decision to spend time in Michigan, rather than going straight to South Carolina. Was that a mistake?

ED ROLLINS: Chip and I have never talked about it but I think we both would agree that we had the momentum. We had to go to New Hampshire. South Carolina clearly was our strategic point. We were encouraged by some people in the state and we had two good days there. We just ran out of time. So it ended up being a waste of time.

MARK HALPERIN: Was it a seat of the pants decision? I know you all didn't have a lot of polling data.

ED ROLLINS: We had no polling data.

MARK HALPERIN: What were the conversations that propelled the candidate to Michigan? Did someone say, "That's the next event."?

---

13. In January 2008, campaigning in Michigan, John McCain said, "I've got to give you some straight talk: Some of the jobs that have left the state of Michigan are not coming back. They are not. And I am sorry to tell you that."
14. On September 15, 2008, John McCain said, "The fundamentals of our economy are strong, but these are very, very difficult times."

CHIP SALTSMAN: There were a couple things. I always tell people if you thought the McCain and Huckabee campaigns were coordinated, look at Michigan, because obviously we were not. One of us should have gone and the other one should have gone to South Carolina. We wanted to say we were competing in all the states because the knock on us was we were a regional candidate—we could only win southern states. We also knew that if one of us beat Romney in Michigan, it was a knockout blow. At the end of the day, it's a war of attrition and we were looking to play knockout politics. We figured if we could get McCain one on one in South Carolina, we would do well. We obviously got him one on one, with a little help, and didn't do well. But that was the thinking. We took money from Florida and put it in Michigan, and we took a little bit of money from South Carolina. It's easy now to say we could have let them go at it in Michigan. We could have gone to South Carolina, not given up the three days that we spent in Michigan and stayed in South Carolina, and put more money on TV. It's easy now to say that would have been better.

MIKE HUDOME: Michigan is a very conservative primary electorate. It's a perfect state for Huckabee. You've got evangelical conservatives out west and you've got a very big NRA membership there—one of the biggest in the country. It was a perfectly logical thing for them to try to fight there.

ED ROLLINS: The interesting thing is we were gaining in New Hampshire. If the thing would have been spread out a little bit. . . . Every day that Huckabee was anywhere he was gaining momentum. Any place he could go with the free media, we did very well. We just didn't have the paid media to compete and we ran out of time.

CHIP SALTSMAN: We never ran an ad in Boston. All of our New Hampshire TV was cable. We did some direct mail here. In Michigan, we didn't have any bit of mail. We had TV. We had some radio. But, it was a three hundred thousand or four hundred thousand dollar buy in Michigan, so it was very targeted to just a few key areas. We couldn't compete with the money the rest of the way.

• THE SOUTH CAROLINA PRIMARY •

MARK HALPERIN: I just want to cover two more primaries. Beth, you said you pulled out of South Carolina because you were running out of money and you wanted to save your money. But it's not a very expensive state. So, why didn't you push harder in South Carolina, where you invested an extraordinary amount of time over many months?

BETH MYERS: The truth of the matter is we hadn't been in South Carolina that much. We did not have that much of an investment going in.

MARK HALPERIN: Well, he made many trips there in 2007.

BETH MYERS: Not as much as you would have thought. We never really pulled the trigger on South Carolina. We had an organization there. We did buy some TV there, but not a lot. And on the same day as South Carolina was Nevada. We wanted to make sure we won Nevada, which we did. We were looking at what was going on in South Carolina.

MARK HALPERIN: To the extent that it was not a good state for him, the three Ms—Massachusetts, millionaire, Mormon—that you mentioned before, were those a bigger problem in South Carolina than in other states?

BETH MYERS: Perhaps, but we had some good support there early on. When Fred Thompson got in the race—when it became clear that it was a Fred/Huckabee/Romney/McCain thing going on there—we looked at winning in Nevada even though it's not as big of a state as South Carolina. We wanted to win going into Florida. So it was simply where do we put our time and our money. We decided to put it into Nevada.

MARK HALPERIN: Does anybody else want to say anything else about South Carolina?

BILL LACY: I just want to make the point that we had gone through this severe cash crunch in the fall and then we found, with Fred's performance in the *Des Moines Register* debate, that our money was starting to come back. So on the evening of the Iowa caucuses, Fred and I talked and he asked me if we should continue and I thought that we should because I thought that he was hot. He'd gotten hot like he did in 1994 and I thought we could get ourselves back into it. We felt there was still a real strong opportunity there for us. But, ultimately, we knew we had to win or finish ahead of Huckabee to have a chance to continue after that.

• THE FLORIDA PRIMARY •

MARK HALPERIN: Rick, although things went on beyond Florida, Florida was really decisive. You got a couple big endorsements. You obviously had momentum coming out of South Carolina. What would you say were the elements of your ability to win Florida that really mattered?

RICK DAVIS: It helped to have the win in South Carolina. Momentum probably mattered as much as it usually did in this election. I think it always matters. But the last piece of our original strategy was to come out of South Carolina with a win and use that to basically dig our way out of Florida. We were, by far and away, far behind two weeks out of Florida. We always assumed that the Rudy thing would collapse after four losses. We couldn't imagine a scenario where you could sustain popularity in a Republican base after loss after loss after loss, and that just came true. That collapse began. We were worried about Huckabee, especially in North Florida, where we had been relatively weak. We had one staffer in the state of Florida for the entire campaign prior to that period. I don't know how many folks you guys had down there, but it was a lot more than one. So we flooded the state with a lot of volunteers and a ton of TV. By now, we had righted the financial ship and we were cash flowing literally every week, each primary. We were able to compete financially on par with all the campaigns at this point. Huckabee had a lot more money at this point than he'd originally had.

ED ROLLINS: Yes, but we had to dump our direct mail program in Florida for South Carolina.

RICK DAVIS: There was a great opening there for us. We got some good endorsements at the loss of Rudy, who had worked it a lot harder and a lot longer than we did. It's an interesting story. After the South Carolina campaign, on a Saturday, John went down to Florida. He loves the Keys. First time in a year, he's got a day off in the Keys. We had this great plan to come out of the Keys and go into Miami and get the endorsement of Senator Mel Martinez that Monday, except Martinez didn't endorse us that Monday. He just sort of disappeared. So we were scrambling around, not really sure what was going to happen with that. That was a really important thing for us because we needed to connect the dots with Florida Republicans, which we hadn't done.

MARK HALPERIN: He had said he was going to show up and endorse and then disappeared?

RICK DAVIS: Yes. It was our impression that he was going to show up at our first event down in Miami with the Cubans. It was really going to be fun. It was still fun—Miami and the Cubans are a blast. [*laughter*] But with no Martinez it just didn't have the feel you really wanted. So we worked really hard that week and, frankly, we didn't think we had much of a shot at Governor Crist's endorsement. We thought Rudy had a commitment from him.

BRENT SEABORN: So did we. [*laughter*]

RICK DAVIS: That started softening up by about Wednesday, and, honestly, I don't think we would have gotten the governor until we got Martinez. Once Martinez locked in and did it, I think that then spurred the governor to say, "Wow, I want to get in on this action." It created a series of events that Friday and Saturday before the primary, on top of a very aggressive ground game and TV game. This was the first state where you had everybody throwing everything they had, whatever was left in the till, into TV and into robo calls. I don't know how many robo calls. I felt sorry for people in Florida. I really did. They must have gotten a thousand robo calls apiece by the end of that primary.

TREVOR POTTER: If you look at the Democratic primary, you might say it was a long march by the time it was over. Our primary was a slalom course. You had Iowa, New Hampshire, Michigan, South Carolina and the capstone of Florida in one month. It was totally different than it was in the 2000 cycle. What you're hearing as everyone talks is you simply can't turn that quickly. You can't win New Hampshire and produce a campaign in Michigan out of nowhere in a couple of days. McCain's entire Florida campaign really started post–South Carolina and it was ten days long.

MARK HALPERIN: It does show that despite all the debate about whether you front-load, it really depends on the situation—who wins what—not on the calendar itself.

RICK DAVIS: One of the things that it portrayed in our cycle, which I'm not sure is applicable to future campaigns, is that a lot of the early TV was a waste. If you were doing anything beyond one month out, other than ground game, building supporters, putting an organization in place and getting some name ID up, it was a waste. Once you were thirty days out, it was a whole new campaign in every one of these states. It was like nothing else matters, which, by the way, was the only way we were able to survive because we basically had a thirty-day campaign in every one of these states.

CHIP SALTSMAN: To underscore that, most all of these campaigns sat atop the national polls for a certain amount of time, somewhere between October and January 1—the time of the first caucus. We were a little bit after that. Everybody got a shot at the top. I can't underscore the resentment that every one of us had on all these campaigns toward Rudy Giuliani if his Florida strategy worked. We were slogging it out in Iowa and New Hampshire, and he was on South Beach. I told him time and time again—"If this works, I'm going to hate you forever." [*laughter*]

BRENT SEABORN: We needed a lot of things to go right. It was a hell of a lot nicer campaigning for all of January in Florida than trudging through the snow.

CHIP SALTSMAN: That's why we all resented you. Because we were slugging it out with the Romney folks in Iowa in a foot of snow and you guys were in South Beach.

RICK DAVIS: We didn't resent them—we were thrilled that they were in South Beach.

CHRISTIAN FERRY: We talked about the early investment of "Battleship McCain." South Carolina and Florida were two states we were able to do well in late in the campaign because of that early investment. We had built an incredibly strong organization in South Carolina that stayed with us after the July collapse. We had built a volunteer leadership team in Florida that when we pulled all of our staff and all of our resources out of that state, when the campaign collapsed, they said, "Don't worry, we'll keep things going, we'll keep working hard, we'll keep the campaign alive until the point where you can come back in and put resources in." It was because of that early investment in organization and ground game that we were able to take advantage of it later in the campaign.

RYAN PRICE: That's absolutely true. We didn't have a paid staffer in Florida until after Iowa. It was a strictly volunteer basis. It was a pretty amazing job. That's the way it was in every early primary state outside of the top big three. We would just shift our staff around from state to state.

BRENT SEABORN: Working in Florida almost all of January, the volunteer McCain organization really was just incredible. Their discipline, their organization and their focus was really something to behold, and it was a real grassroots campaign that was very impressive. We were at some point close, or very close, to Senator Martinez's endorsement as well. He called and let us know that he wasn't going to do that. He said he was going to endorse Senator McCain, which we certainly understood. He was very gracious about letting us know. Governor Crist's endorsement—we found out literally minutes before it was going to happen. We had gone from planning events to announce his endorsement to a promise that he was going to sit it out. That flipped instantly, with virtually no warning.

MIKE HUDOME: I want to congratulate the Giuliani campaign for an irritatingly good spin in Florida by saying that they had all these votes banked because of their absentee ballot campaign, even though they were pretty much out of it by then. The press bought that hook, line and sinker. It was good.

BRENT SEABORN: We had a great organization moving out there and we had, I think, very good mail. I do think we had a good program. The problem was that by the time it was going full swing, we were already starting to fade. Had it been spaced out more, and had we not been losing New Hampshire and South Carolina and other states along the way, we probably could have banked a lot more votes. But how compressed the schedule was limited how many votes we were able to get in there very early on.

TREVOR POTTER: It is a classic example of the problem with early voting, particularly in primaries. The race completely changed from the time many of those people cast votes to when primary day actually occurred.

BRENT SEABORN: We were keenly aware of that—that we were going to have fewer losses the earlier people voted. So we were encouraging and driving out as many votes as we could as early as possible. Unfortunately, it just wasn't enough. But if we had been able to space it out more and there had been fewer losses between there. . . . Frankly, we thought that if Senator McCain hadn't won South Carolina, we probably still would have lost, but it would have been a much more chaotic field coming into Florida. I don't think you can underestimate how important the South Carolina victory was for the McCain people.

• THE SELECTION OF SARAH PALIN •

LOIS ROMANO: We're going to start a discussion on the vice-presidential choice. Rick, what went into the calculation that led you all to Sarah Palin? And maybe you could share who the finalists were at a certain point?

RICK DAVIS: Nobody else wants to talk about this probably. [*laughter*] One thing to point out is a little bit of the conditions that existed generically in the political environment in the country before we got there. We obviously locked up the nomination. After Ohio, we had some time to work. We won the nomination with the same forty people in the headquarters—a very small staff. Broke. We had cash flowed our campaign literally on a day-to-day basis. We were not your typical nominee, and we had designed the victory in Ohio and Texas that day to try and get away from as much of the party symbolism as we could. So we immediately, the next morning, went to the White House, met with Bush, went over to the RNC, met with the RNC and never had John McCain near the White House again until the meltdown,[15] which is the only other time he went anywhere near the White House during the entire campaign. We had a massive undertaking to prepare for the general election as the smallest, brokest nominee in any party's history. The good news is the Democrats were very busy and, frankly, the media turned their attention elsewhere. That was fine with us. We weren't looking to try and win the election in March, April and May. We put together a fundraising operation at the RNC—knowing we were going to be taking the government funds—that would be able to raise enormous amounts of money. We raised two hundred million more than Bush did in 2004 in a six-month period. It's noteworthy that the effort that was put together with the joint committees, both in the states and at the federal level, did a phenomenal job of supplying campaign resources with what we knew was going to be a great fundraising effort by either of those two candidates. The other piece to this that we wanted to do was to make sure we didn't make a mistake that I think many campaigns have made in the past—many of them I've been involved in—where once you've won a nomination, you just assume everybody knows who you are and why you won the nomination. It was very important to us to make sure we got around and reintroduced John McCain to the American public and reinforced the messages of his heroism and his maverick nature—and, frankly, to try to move beyond what we just spent a year doing to win a Republican primary and try and get him back into the status of the original John McCain, which we knew had more saliency in a general election. That was the only area where not having much media coverage hurt us, because we weren't able to get much of a bandwidth while this very exciting Democratic primary was going on. We started the process of looking at potential vice-presidential running mates relatively early. We put a process in place which was a typical McCain process—very low key. We had a lot of advice from a lot of people—you gotta go get some very important Republican to head up a process that's very visible and do it all in the public eye. That's just not who John McCain is. Campaigns are just like their candidates. This was the process he selected, and it was very low key and quiet. Most people didn't care about it anyway because the media was still following a very interesting campaign. We got maybe one or two questions a month for four months on our vice-presidential nomination process. We started with a very large screen of people, twenty or more, and narrowed it down through the process on an irregular basis of meetings and discussions. Suffice it to say that virtually everyone we looked at had assets and liabilities. Every campaign goes through exactly the same process. There was no obvious choice—oh, I could have had a V-8 kind of thing. It didn't exist. In the process of doing

15. On September 25, 2008, President Bush held a summit on the economic crisis with Senator McCain, Senator Obama and top congressional leaders at the White House.

that, we spent a lot of time looking at what kind of environment we were running in. It's probably a good time for Bill to chime in and set a little bit of tone of what that environment looked like to us.

BILL MCINTURFF: Well, it was grim. [*laughter*] Here's the brief summary. We've heard people in this room admire the president and we've talked a lot about a lot of people in this room and their deep commitment with the Bush family and their admiration for the president and the job he did. But, from a neutral polling history, we've had polling since the 1930s and we can say that this president is the least popular president, as measured by the number of months under forty, in polling history. We had an unpopular president, we had an incredibly weak economy, we had wrong track in the mid-seventies and we had an enormous war fatigue—this country was tired and wanted resolution in Iraq. And, as we like to say, we were winning. Then we imploded the financial markets and wrong track hit ninety, and you cannot sustain the same party campaign with 90 percent wrong track. When I was asked to meet with John in late August, when he was making this decision, I said, "Looking at the Michigan consumer sentiment index, there is no precedent in American political history, post–World War II, for the Republican nominee to win." Wrong track is too high. Two-thirds of wrong track voters will vote for the Democratic nominee. That's about 48 percent of the vote—that alone could elect somebody. The other thing we're really missing here is what happened with party ID. We went through 2004 where party ID was equal on an exit poll, and I'd been spending months saying we're going to be minus six or eight. That party ID gap at minus six or eight will be the largest it's been since 1980—1992 was minus five. So you're going to have to run six to eight points ahead of party ID, which means you need 15 percent of Democrats and you need 56 percent of Independents, when we got crushed by eighteen points from Independents in 2006. The other thing we showed was how incredibly parallel the 1992 numbers were on all these barometers to 2004. They were eerily parallel, except these were worse. The point is that by any conventional political standards, sooner or later that environment is going to crush the campaign. We had to be in a situation where very extraordinary things happened. We had to disqualify the Democratic nominee—we had to make sure the fall campaign was, in fact, focused on the Democratic nominee. The last thing I will say is by late August, we had run Celebrity.[16] We were getting closer to tied in the polls. In late August, consumer confidence was drifting back up. Party ID was beginning to close. Then, tracking the image of the party through the NBC/*Wall Street Journal*

---

16. On July 30, 2008, McCain released a television ad titled "Celeb" that referred to Obama as "the biggest celebrity in the world" and compared him to Britney Spears and Paris Hilton.

poll, in terms of positive/negative, the image of the party had gone from minus sixteen to minus seven. We were minus three after the convention. John McCain was beginning to transform this from being a George Bush party to a John McCain party. I was saying in late August that we were seeing signs of life and breathing room that had not existed for months. That was a function of what Rick was describing we were doing in the campaign. By the way, what happened is we went from minus sixteen in party image in April to minus seven in August, then minus three after our convention, and then we have the financial collapse. Late September, NBC track, we're minus thirteen, minus sixteen the last track in November. In the poll released today, it's minus twenty-five.

RICK DAVIS: Now that we have a picture of where the election was, you can imagine then what kind of decisions we had to make and what kind of recommendations we had to give to Senator McCain about the last major act of the campaign before the debates, which were the only other things that were going to create any kind of significant movement in the polls. We were very straight with him and said that under any normal circumstance, under any sort of routine conditions, if we continue to run a campaign just like we're running it now and we don't do anything that significantly mixes it up, you're going to lose. It's an unfortunate thing and a tough conversation to have, but it was very practical. There wasn't a single dissenting opinion as to where we stood or what we needed to do, which was significantly alter the landscape and try and get it in a place where we thought we could get a shot at this thing. The other thing that Bill didn't mention is that we were sporting a pretty significant gender gap in those days. The structure of the vote that we needed to get included significantly increasing our share of women. We were doing pretty well with men—we had a pretty strong testosterone campaign going. In fact, in early August, we were probably overperforming on our model with men. But, we were significantly underperforming with women, probably the biggest gender gap we've had since 1984. That had something to do with the way we looked at the race. We had a lot of good conventional choices we could make prior to the convention and a lot of good unconventional choices. Nobody came without a downside. We looked at a half-dozen semifinalists and everybody basically brought something significant to the table but had a unique problem. One of the things that posed a very big problem for us was the timing of the conventions. We didn't like the fact that we were in September, Labor Day weekend, first night of football, all those other things combined—it was like a gift, our final kiss, from the Republican party. [*laughter*] It was also butt up against the Democratic convention. So there was literally one day to recharge before the weekend before our convention, which was that Friday. What do you do? Do you roll out a vice-presidential nominee the week before a Democratic convention and let them steal back the momentum? That's a lousy choice to make. But you would prefer to have a different ability to roll out a plan. Do you roll it out the day of your convention? Then you're giving up a whole weekend's worth of good news to them. We knew of Obama's plan to have this magnificent coronation ceremony at their convention, which was great. It was exactly what we thought we could get away with on the celebrity sort of spin that we created off of his European trip.[17] That was a relatively successful initiative that really brought us all the way down to the convention, which was one of our original concepts behind the ad strategy to begin with. So, we really had one day. The trick for us was to be able to do it in some degree of secrecy, in order for it not to spill out and then get tangled up in the Democratic convention—because you're not going to compete with Barack Obama on a Thursday night with a hundred thousand people in a stadium. Any practical person will tell you that that's crazy. There was tons of media speculation that we were going to try and step on his event. Any normal person will look at it and go, "That's a silly thing to try to do." So we had a very difficult task to try and get a clean announcement of a nominee. Regardless of who it was, the same timetable would have occurred. It was one of the bright spots of the campaign that we were able to effectively put our nominee out on a day and on the terms that we wanted to. It had a great effect. One thing that people tend to forget is that we had scheduled previously, in order to build some momentum coming into our convention, three major rallies on Friday, Saturday and Sunday. We had never done a major rally. We had always done these sort of town-hallish kinds of things—a thousand people, two thousand people, five thousand max. That was just part of our strategy—to be a little bit more connected. But we decided that we wanted to throw some momentum into the convention, so we planned these in advance. Everybody knew we had these three big rallies. The decision we kept to ourselves was in which one would come the nominee. We had the ability to do any one of the three. We kept our options alive.

LOIS ROMANO: When was the decision made?

RICK DAVIS: The decision was made about two weeks out that really trying to stop the momentum with a major announcement that next morning would be the most effective thing. The only downside to it was that a lot of reporters were going to be getting on an airplane that morning and traveling to our convention so they'd be out of circulation. But the bandwidth is

---

17. On July 24, 2008, Barack Obama gave a speech titled "A World That Stands as One" at the Victory Column in Berlin's Tiergarten Park. The rally drew about 200,000 people.

so wide at this point, if a thousand are in the air, you've got five thousand sitting at your event. So it really didn't matter to us.

LOIS ROMANO: The decision to make the announcement that day was made two weeks ahead of time, or the decision for it to be Governor Palin was made?

RICK DAVIS: We made the decision that Friday was the best day, regardless of who it was going to be. That really started the clock ticking for a final decision by the senator. In order to be able to keep it secret, it meant that we couldn't get too far ahead of that decision process because the minute you make a decision, it gets leaked. So we wanted a late decision. It was designed into the deal in order to try and preserve some level of impact for that next morning. I think it worked great. You barely heard the word Obama on Friday. I thought it was a good plan. I was really stunned that it worked as well as it did. Gave us great momentum into the convention. We were always looking for that, especially in the latest convention in history. We wanted to come out of the convention ahead. When we cooked up this plan sixty days earlier, we were actually starting to meet our goals on making it a competitive race. Even as late as early August, nobody would have bet that we could have had a competitive race on September 5. The convention was a difficult time for us. We got a very good announcement—15,000 people. Governor Palin did a spectacular job having walked out on a national stage for the first time with an immense amount of pressure and scrutiny. The public, for at least one day, got to see a relatively untarnished image of a newcomer to American national theater. Frankly, the confluence of getting to St. Paul with 15,000 reporters all cooped up with a surprise on their hands and no opposition research, I don't know if that was part of what pissed them off, but the press really wasn't very happy. [*laughter*] It was the worst treatment of a political candidate in the history of American politics in the shortest period of time that I've ever seen.

LOIS ROMANO: When did you start narrowing down to Governor Palin? Were there, at any point, several candidates—finalists? Did you have a short list of three people?

RICK DAVIS: There were about a half-dozen finalists in the process.

LOIS ROMANO: At the end, in the last couple of weeks?

RICK DAVIS: It was a winnowing down process that lasted three or four months. I think we did a very good job. Our whole goal was always to keep alive as many options as we could, based upon the ever-changing circumstances that were going on, that would allow us to give the best advice to John without taking decisions off the table that he could have otherwise made. He had all the opportunities all the way down to literally two days before the announcement to make any decision he wanted to make, and to be able to have three options to announce it.

BILL MCINTURFF: When we had that August 24 meeting, in preparation for that meeting, Rick had asked Sarah and me to do a couple of things. He asked Sarah to go back and look at previous conventions, bounces and all that kind of stuff. He asked, where did we think Obama was going to be, what was the margin we could sustain, what would be a margin that would mean that we were going to win or lose? He asked for previous history. When we did that August 24 presentation, he said, "Well, what should we expect?" There were a few things. One, there will be a bounce and we believe that it's going to end up we'll be down six to eight. I think he's capped at around forty-nine. Just give him the doubts or hesitation and we'll drop to the low forties. We can sustain minus six or eight, and that's where we think it's going to be. If we're wrong and this convention pops this guy to fifty-four, we're minus fourteen. Then, I'm sorry, we won't make that back through any kind of convention and we'll lose. He said, "Why do you say that?" I said the last person to actually win the presidency after being behind after the convention was Harry Truman. There was this stunned silence in the room, and Rick said, "Oh, great, more good news from Bill McInturff because I wasn't feeling enough pressure as there is about this pick in the convention." Starting in July, Rick said, "What's the model, Bill, what do we do need to do, what's the model, what's the model, what's the model?" And I said, "Well, what we need to do is by their convention we have to be about tied. They have to go through a convention with no more than eight points ahead and then, historically, we've got to make up those eight points and then at least be ahead. We won't be ahead by much, but we'll be ahead by a couple of points. Then, we have to sustain that through the conventions." I'm a little sensitive how it got misinterpreted when I said that the black hole starts around the debates.[18] All I meant was not that we didn't have plans but that debates become unpredictable in terms of what happens in terms of the model. The point I'm making is that starting in early July through the first debate, even with the Lehman implosion[19] and all this stuff that happened, we were still on that model. That's why I'm saying that we all believe the Lehman collapse and what started happening on September

---

18. In September 2008, McCain pollster Bill McInturff called the period of the presidential and vice-presidential debates "a two-and-a-half-week black hole."

19. On September 15, 2008, the Wall Street investment bank Lehman Brothers filed for bankruptcy protection after the U.S. government refused to bail it out.

15 is sort of determinative. It was the first thing in two and a half months that threw us off the model that said, even despite everything we were facing, we're still on a track to win a campaign.

RICK DAVIS: At one point in time, it was predictable, bad but predictable.

SARAH SIMMONS: Over the course of the summer, and certainly we started off in the spring, we were competing for attention against this very interesting Democratic primary. We started banging away, trying to drive numbers in a very traditional way, doing thematic events and those kinds of things. What we were finding was that this steady drumbeat of message—how campaigns have done it in the past—just wasn't really breaking through. When we released that Celebrity ad, that sort of explosive energy into the race was the first time we saw numbers change in a dramatic way. That was part of the other rationale going into the Palin pick. We knew we needed to do something dramatic, not in a cheesy, teenage girl kind of way, but we knew something that would inject that sort of energy into the race would be to our benefit. I was on the outside of that decision tree in our campaign. But watching it, I know there was a conversation in my office many times—we cannot pick somebody typical, that will not be good for us. So that was another part of the underlying decision-making process that was going on.

The Internet and Presidential Politics

BILL PURCELL: We have Chris Cillizza from WashingtonPost.com with us tonight. He writes "The Fix," an American political weblog that he writes every day.

CHRIS CILLIZZA: They gave me the relatively small task of handling how the Internet affected politics in the 2008 campaign. It's obviously a massive undertaking to try and figure anything like this out. Joe Trippi, who managed Howard Dean's presidential campaign in 2004, is here, so I'm going to talk a little bit about 2004 because I think that was really the year, at least from my perspective, that the Internet became a "thing" in politics. You always

Chris Cillizza moderates a discussion on the role of technology in the 2008 election.

hear these big rumors that the Internet is going to change things. Most people who do politics or cover politics for a living are used to having heard that for quite some time. In 2004, the Internet actually did, at some level, change things. I do think that Howard Dean's campaign, although it wound up coming up short, is incredibly important and helps us understand what happened. You saw massive amounts of money raised, fifty million dollars or more, and organization being done on the Internet. For the first time a lot of smart people, like David Axelrod, paid attention to the way in which politics was moving on the Internet. The lesson learned in 2004 for Howard Dean was that the Internet was something that could be used—not just something where you type in your name and see what comes up—for something meaningful in a political sense, for money and organization. In 2008, the story was that we had to reorient ourselves to the Internet. When I say us, I mean political campaigns, media types, anyone with any interest in this. Because in 2004—and this is a terrible metaphor but I do think it's true—the Internet was a spoke on a wider campaign wheel. In 2008, the Internet was the hub of that wheel. It was from there that everything grew. We knew money could be raised and, in 2006, we saw a lot of House and Senate candidates raising money from the Internet. Then, you saw the criticism, from some people on the left, that the Internet is not just an ATM. In 2008, it became more than just money—it became message. It's not by accident that Barack Obama and Hillary Clinton both announced their campaigns via YouTube. Mitt Romney used YouTube relentlessly to sort of push a message. An ad that was never really an ad—the Apple takeoff of throwing the hammer through Hillary Clinton speaking—became a huge thing.[1] It drove messaging. Barack Obama used it to drive message and to involve the grassroots in a way that it had never been involved before. The other part of it is organization. In 2004, there was a skepticism among the political community. After Iowa, people thought, Howard Dean is going to bring all of these people who have been going to these Meetups to these house parties—they are all going to come into Iowa, he is going to overwhelm Iowa. They are not going to know what hit them. Well, it wound up coming up short, as we well know. Coming into 2008, organization was the piece that I think many people were skeptical of. We have heard this before, online can translate to offline—that these people who involve themselves online can involve themselves offline. We didn't think it would happen, but it did happen. Barack Obama's campaign gets the credit, and rightly so, for its organization and for the way in which it turned voters out. But in John McCain's campaign and in a lot of the campaigns in the primary, you saw record turnout everywhere. This was not something

---

1. In March 2007, an online attack ad by an anonymous filmmaker that took the iconic 1984 Apple Computer commercial and replaced the menacing "Big Brother" image with that of Senator Clinton was circulated on YouTube.

that was isolated to the Democratic side. The level of interest and the level of excitement was there, and I think the Internet really helped to drive that. It became an organizing tool in a way that many of us were skeptical about. That's the broad overview.

We have so many great people here—journalists and political folks—that you probably want to hear from them. I want to start with David Plouffe. We'll start with you, the man of the moment, the man featured in so many YouTube clips from his dark office that I don't think they ever let him out of. [*laughter*] Can you talk about how you guys envisioned the role the Internet would play? I know that's an incredibly broad category, but it played such a central role. Did you know that Obama had the fundraising and organizational capacity that he wound up having? If not, once you saw it, how did you move to try and take advantage of it?

DAVID PLOUFFE: I don't think that David [Axelrod] or I would say that we saw the scale from the beginning. We thought there was the potential there. Hillary Clinton was such a strong front-runner—such an organizational behemoth—that the only way to think about beating her in Iowa or anywhere else was to build at the grassroots level. That was Obama's intention about how he wanted to run, so those two were married. We thought we could raise money online. We ended up raising over five hundred million dollars online, much more than we thought. We had a lot of people—six thousand, seven thousand or eight thousand people—who became bundlers online. They would track their money that they raised and they'd raise ten thousand dollars or fifteen thousand dollars or twenty thousand dollars, so it was a great tool. We thought message delivery was going to be important. There were so many people, particularly younger voters—and I don't mean college kids, I mean people under forty—and even a lot of senior citizens, who searched for their own content, whether it was to fact-check a claim a candidate made, or they wanted to view videos. So we thought it was very important to have as much information out there as possible. It became clear to us, over time, that the most effective way to do that was from Obama directly to folks. David [Axelrod] will attest to this. Every time we tested an ad or a video presentation, we would have all these clever devices—narrator spots, real people and, time and time again, voters said, "I just want to hear from Obama." Some of that was reassurance; some of it was that he was clearly a compelling messenger. We thought from a message standpoint, you can target messages online. We did an enormous amount of advertising. One thing that I don't think has gotten a lot of attention is that we did a lot of advertising. It was very rudimentary. In every caucus and every primary and in the general election, we would buy advertising—Google ads. If someone searched "Iowa caucus location" or "Minnesota caucus location" or "Virginia primary location," our sponsored site would come up. In Hawaii, over

35 percent of the people who went to the caucuses used our caucus lookup tool. In Iowa, we had over twenty thousand people, in the last few days, go to that caucus lookup tool, so we knew who those people were. Some of them were undecided, so it was an opportunity to talk to them. Given that we had to expand the electorate, it was remarkable to see, time and time again, that there were a lot of people out there who did not know how to participate. Rather than calling their local governmental election office, they had the ability to go online and then we would offer them rides to the polls and give them information. That's really an old-school online technique. It paid huge dividends for us. The big trick was organization, which was, how do you turn this into something that has organizational value, aside from just collecting names? We allowed people to organize online. If someone in Iowa said, "I've got fifty people I want to e-mail with," we said, "Fine," we had electronic supporter cards. We might verify those a little bit more carefully than we would someone who was attained at a door. Most people in this room probably live their life through technology. Why should their interaction with politics be anything different? Why should they have to go to a phone bank? The truth is most of the people who signed up online ended up phone banking and canvassing, but it was a remarkable tool to allow people to organize. The other thing I would say is, particularly in the primary, we would enter a state and the state would be organized and we had nothing to do with it, in terms of staff. In Colorado, Minnesota, Virginia and Washington state—I could go on and on. We would send five or six staff and in every county, sometimes in every precinct, there were Obama groups already organized. It was a remarkable thing and it gave us a huge head start. So I think we saw the need and the potential to reach a scale that I don't we would have envisioned, but it was the backbone of our campaign in many ways.

CHRIS CILLIZZA: David Axelrod, once you see the potential that exists, once you see you can raise a lot of money—I don't know if you ever thought five hundred million dollars—and you can use it to organize, how do you do that? The truth of the matter is you were also running a very traditional campaign—door knocking, phone calling. How do you integrate it and make sure that it's additive, rather than duplicative?

DAVID AXELROD: Let me just say that when we started the campaign, we started with nothing; the cupboard was bare. We decided we were going to run for president of the United States, we were up against the Clinton organization, we were like the little sisters of the poor, and they were the Green Bay Packers. [*laughter*] We said we've got to raise a significant amount of money in the first quarter in order to be considered viable by all you folks who are unofficially designated the judgers of such things. I'll say parenthetically, David Plouffe was the best campaign manager in the history

Obama strategist David Axelrod talks about how new technology empowered an old style of politics.

of presidential politics, there's no question about it. [*applause*] One of the reasons he was so good is that he was always conservative in his estimates. Our target was twelve million dollars in the first quarter, which was a lot of money. Remember, four years earlier John Edwards raised 7.3 million dollars in the first quarter. That vaulted him into legitimacy in the presidential race. We wanted to raise twelve. We figured Hillary would do twenty or something like that. Plouffe said maybe we can do a million on the Internet, and we ended up doing six or seven in that first quarter. None of us had any notion of this. By the way, being from Illinois, I'm not that comfortable hanging around with a guy named "The Fix." [*laughter*]

CHRIS CILLIZZA: Especially lately. [*laughter*]

DAVID AXELROD: The thing that was so exciting about this campaign was that the new technology empowered an old style of politics. We returned politics to people at the grassroots, and it was a tool that we were able to use to give people the ability to organize door to door. All the bells and whistles that David talked about were extraordinarily important to us but, ultimately, what was most important to us is that there were millions of people across this country who felt a part of this, who were communicating with us, who went door to door. I think this was the vision that Joe Trippi had in 2004. The technology was a little bit more primitive at the time—we've made a lot of advances—but he started us down this road. So, in many ways, this combined the best of the new and the best of the old. All we did on the macro message front was to provide air cover for the efforts that were going on on the ground. We tried to synthesize all of it so that the message was consistent. I think that the great thing that's happened in American politics through this election is that we've once again reinvigorated people at the grassroots to believe that they could make a difference, and the technology helped us do it.

CHRIS CILLIZZA: Rick, you guys are obviously watching this. You win the nomination. Barack Obama and Hillary Clinton continue to battle it out for several months. You are watching every measure of online donors and are seeing these huge numbers. Are there things that you guys did from a logistical perspective in an attempt to combat what you knew was coming?

RICK DAVIS: We were probably the only campaign in history that was underwhelmed by our Internet performance. [*laughter*] We initially had higher expectations than we actually realized. I've always been a big believer in the Web as a technique and as a tool. I told people about three or four years before this election cycle that I thought the Web would be the hub, not the spoke, in this election cycle, which is what would make this election different than before. In early 2006, we put a group of about six or seven companies together to meet once a month at my office. One of them was a Trippi acolyte, Nicco Mele. My view was the great work we had done in 2000 in the McCain campaign—creating a record online donation performance, up to that point in time—had been really turned on in a big way by Joe Trippi. He really did a spectacular job. It's not all great news. You've got to be careful what you crave. It can sometimes take over your campaign and tell you what to do. No manager likes that process. So we really studied it hard. We thought this was going to be the future. Some of the organizational stuff that David did will revolutionize national campaigns in the future. We thought the communication piece with the video was going to be really revolutionary—we bet on video. It wasn't so much the list manufacturing and the development and communication tools for "get out the vote." That stuff was pretty much around, and it could be improved significantly. We really thought the ability to communicate large-scale broadband with voters would minimize the impact of the cable news cycle. We could get five hundred thousand, six hundred thousand, seven hundred thousand people looking at our information rather than a cable broadcast which didn't have the kind of spin on it that we put on it. That would be the most competitive thing that we could accomplish. Our campaign ran into a lot of different issues related to the Internet, and not everybody in politics believes this stuff works as well as it does. I don't think anybody is going to doubt it after this cycle. There is a generation of true believers in the Web as being the hub, not the spoke, and it's only really up to your own imagination as to what you want to do with it from this point on. We did one hundred million dollars in fundraising on the Internet, which we thought was extraordinary. It's interesting—that was probably seventy-five million dollars more than Bush did in 2004, and he was an extraordinary fundraiser. We have the pleasure of paling in comparison to our opponents, who have done an extraordinary job. I am a true believer in the marketplace. When we start platforming TV on the Internet, the Web will change everything as we know it, including advertising.

Let's not fool ourselves. One of the reasons that Barack Obama's campaign has been so successful is because of Barack Obama. Part of the reason John McCain was successful on the Internet is because of John McCain. Not everybody gets the performance levels on the Web that these two individuals, who have a dedicated grassroots following, will have in this regard. So the standard isn't so much what we did this cycle. It's the outer limits. We'll continue to push those outer limits as to what more can be done and how many more people can be involved in the process. One of the real debates that will occur over the course of the next cycle is, how does everybody else play this game? What works for you in your congressional district, your mayoral city, your Senate district, your governor's race? How does all this then impact you? How many e-mails can one person read in the course of one cycle? How many video clips are people going to gravitate to for a mayor's race? There is a saturation level. I don't know what it is, but I think it's part of the debate that will occur on an ongoing basis.

CHRIS CILLIZZA: Rick, let me ask you one more thing. Your candidate publicly professed uncomfortableness with the Internet. He was not as familiar with it. I know you guys didn't talk about it during the campaign, but did that get in the way of what you were trying to do online? Or did it reinforce the idea that Barack Obama is a younger guy who is with it and John McCain is out of touch in some way, shape or form?

RICK DAVIS: We were going for the out-of-touch vote. I mean that was our whole strategy. We figured not everybody can do this BlackBerry stuff, and we want you. So if your fingers don't work, screw it, come with us. If you can't read those little digits, you're our kind of guy. Why bother with technology? Stone Age, that's what we were looking for, and we got it. [*laughter*]

CHRIS CILLIZZA: Thanks, Rick. [*applause*] Rick mentioned one thing that I do want to get into, which is video and the way in which YouTube and other video influenced everything that we did. I want to turn quickly on this to a campaign that was not expected, in many ways, to do what it wound up doing and used the Internet. Chip, talk about your challenge—you had a very little known Arkansas governor in a field of Rudy Giuliani, Mitt Romney and John McCain?

CHIP SALTSMAN: You don't have to keep reminding me. I got it, I was there. [*laughter*]

CHRIS CILLIZZA: You guys used video, with Chuck Norris[2] among others, to boost your guy up because you didn't have the money. Can you talk about how you used the Web?

CHIP SALTSMAN: Nobody would listen to us any other way, so we figured the guy was good on TV, we could put him online and at least he could watch himself and feel better about the campaign. Online, for us, was the only outlet that we could find where people would actually pay attention to us. We would come to Washington to talk with some big-shot reporters and we'd get "The Fix." Dan Balz, the national political reporter for the *Washington Post*, was too busy, so we'd get "The Fix." We figured that we had to do something that was different in a way that we could communicate—we had to go around the typical campaign. We threw out the traditional Washington, D.C., playbook because we couldn't afford it. We wanted to buy it, but we couldn't. So we decided early on to go online. We had a candidate who was a great communicator—he's funny, he is somebody who really connects with people. Our job was to get him in front of as many people as we could. The Chuck Norris ad was one of those things you luck into. I'm not sure that any other presidential campaign puts their candidate up with Chuck Norris. We had to grab their attention, and that's why the opening line in the campaign commercial was, "My plan to secure the border: two words, Chuck Norris." Everyone said, "What is he talking about? This guy is running for president?" But over a day and a half, 1.5 million people watched that ad on YouTube. We put up a sixty thousand dollar cable buy with that commercial in Iowa, and nobody in Iowa that I talked to ever saw it. We didn't have many staff people, so we had to use our online volunteers as an extension of the campaign. It was interesting listening to David say that when they got to these precincts, they were already organized. That was

---

2. On November 18, 2007, Mike Huckabee began airing a sixty-second ad with actor Chuck Norris, titled "Chuck Norris Approved," as the first ad of his presidential campaign.

what was happening to us as well. You have got to build an online, living, breathing community outside your own campaign structure and let it grow. It becomes a force multiplier for your own campaign. We had it in "Huck's Army," and we had it in a couple of other places. We had zero control over what they were doing, but when we showed up, they had already built an infrastructure, they had already put a precinct plan into place, and they were ready to go. For us, that was the only way we could survive in states outside of Iowa.

CHRIS CILLIZZA: The messaging part, for most of the people in this room, is the most interesting and maybe the most innovative part. You want people to have free rein to say what they want to say but the traditional campaign is always, "We have the message, we dictate the message." I want to ask Alex Castellanos, because he was one of the media folks on Mitt Romney's campaign—how do you live in a world where you know that a YouTube clip is going to distract for three or four days? Or that something one of your supporters says that happened to be caught on a handheld camera by someone who is not a reporter is up on YouTube, and you are going to have to answer it? How do you try and drive a message in an environment that's so crowded message-wise?

ALEX CASTELLANOS: Money. [*laughter*] What we've learned from the Obama campaign is that it takes about a half-billion dollars and Mitt Romney's challenge was that we didn't spend enough. If we had only liberated him before the stock market crashed, he would have done much better. Message discipline? It starts and ends with the candidate. You have to have a candidate who knows that the more fragmented the market, the more important it is that the candidate be a cohesive whole. We saw that in the Obama campaign in the general election this year. But in the primaries, everybody was trying to figure out how to be not Bush. In the Romney campaign, the challenge for Governor Romney was to have confidence in his best and truest self—the transformational figure that he originally was, the guy who transformed business, transformed the Olympics, transformed government in Massachusetts. What's next? It's not a hard call to make—you change Washington. That was not a message he was very comfortable with, but it turned out to be that was the train that was leaving the station and he just didn't get on it. Again, I think it's message discipline that comes from the candidate.

CHRIS CILLIZZA: Because there are so many reporters here, I want to involve some of them, and I'll start with Dan Balz. Dan, when it comes to message, it used to be that if campaigns wanted to get out a message, they would sit down with Dan Balz or John King or a major media outlet. I ran into any number of times where I would be pretty sure that a campaign had given something to Matt Drudge[3] or Huffington Post[4]—that they were moving around the traditional ways in which they would manage their message. How do we play in that world, knowing that sometimes it is easier for them to give it to someone who isn't going to have the filters that we might have?

DAN BALZ: This is something that has evolved cycle by cycle. There was probably a greater leap between 2004 and 2008 than there had been in previous cycles in the way information moved around and the role of different aspects of what we now call "the media"—not just the mainstream media but the media in its entirety. In 1988, there was a sense then that the mainstream media had a gatekeeper role about certain kinds of information. That's no longer the case. There is no longer one entry point for information. What we have all learned is that campaigns always look for a way to leverage the smallest piece of information into the largest impact. In this cycle, the smart campaigns knew that the way to do that was to move information as quickly as they could, and the way to do that was through the Internet. The smart campaigns understood what the different entry points were. That part of the game in this cycle—in a way that I don't think we've seen in previous cycles—was to plant a piece of information, if they could, through a blog or wherever, and once it was out, then to leverage it by sending it out elsewhere as if they hadn't originally planted it. That was the way of moving information. The other thing that was different about this cycle is the degree to which nothing lasted very long. In a sense, the new always pushed out the old—no matter whether the new was more or less important. Small could push out big simply because it was new. I think smart campaigns understood how to take advantage of that or how to protect themselves against it. It was one reason why certain things never stuck on certain candidates—and why we were constantly trying to catch up with what was happening in campaigns. I think this was a watershed in terms of the way information moves, the role of the media, and the intersection between campaigns and the Internet.

CHRIS CILLIZZA: People always say to me, "Wow, you write a lot, how do you do it?" Ben, you came into this from more of a bloggier background than some of us. Can you talk about the speed of it? How you fit what you did, in a smart way, into what was already out there?

BEN SMITH: I come from a traditional journalism background, as most people at *Politico* do, and I kind of eased into it. I was working for a weekly newspaper, the *New York Observer*, and was having all this stuff that didn't fit

---

3. Matt Drudge is the creator and editor of The Drudge Report, a conservative news aggregation website.
4. The Huffington Post, founded by Arianna Huffington and Kenneth Lerer, is a liberal news website and weblog.

the weekly story, so I started putting it online. There was this hunger among the audience, who was hitting "refresh" frantically, all the time. For them, the number one question was who was going to win. There was a big drop-off after they found that out. There was a huge appetite for the new, which distorts what is important—what's new can replace what's important. Something small, that you can take in a lot of little bites, gets blown up. The Obama campaign really mastered that. I think most newspapers have figured this out now. You are leveling with your audience about what you know all the time, and you are giving them what you know as you report it, piece by piece, which is how they want it. You are treating them with a level of respect—there is no reason for you to hold things back from them. In return, they feed you enormous amounts of information that they are seeing around them all the time.

CHRIS CILLIZZA: We would be remiss in this conversation not to include the role of television, the ultimate sort of speed entity. John King, the online world is obviously this huge burgeoning thing, but TV is still a dominant force. The Obama campaign was genius in many ways. One of the ways it was genius is that they outspent the McCain campaign three to one in swing states on TV toward the end, which is to their credit because they had the money to do so. That said, how do you fit into a world in which everyone is going to the blogs, which competes with what you guys are doing—trying to be the newest, the latest, the fastest?

JOHN KING: I'm an old wire guy so I'll start from the perspective that the business has changed enormously. I used to live in a world where if I got home at night and saw "[*Washington Post*'s] Dan Balz reports" or "[*New York Times*'] Adam Nagourney reports," you knew that was serious business and you would start making phone calls. One of the dangers of our business is there is sometimes no longer a distinction. I will get an e-mail from a very senior person saying, "I need you to chase this," and it's some guy in his underwear in Missouri just writing what he thinks. It's not journalism—that guy in his underwear in Missouri has every right, we live in a free country and free speech is a wonderful thing—but the lines have been blurred. The lines have been blurred between journalism, as I know it and was taught it, and what we see out there. That's not a bad thing. It's good for democracy. But, internally, as a media enterprise, we have to think longer and harder about how we make our own distinctions. We at CNN, I'm incredibly proud to say, saw the appetite that people had early on, and we had to hustle to improve our online product. For all the ratings successes that CNN television had, CNN.com was actually a bigger driver in our growth. And I believe it was a driver in bringing people to watch us on television because they enjoyed the product they were getting online. As a guy who, in eleven years in television, has missed writing longer form pieces, I wrote more in the past year for the Web than in the previous ten years that I had been at CNN because I enjoyed it. It was a great campaign and there was a lot out there that I couldn't say on television or I couldn't fit in a two-minute piece, so I started writing more. There was a lot of reaction. You get e-mail and people post their comments to the pieces. It was refreshing, in a way, that I could still actually put subject and verb together in the same sentence. [*laughter*] The one lesson we all have to realize is that you can't change what's happening out there. I'm not making fun of the guy in his underpants or places like the Huffington Post, which has an agenda but still contributed to the journalism of this campaign. Remember Mayhill Fowler? I'm sure David Axelrod and David Plouffe love that moment when the Huffington Post ran that article—the "bitter cling to gods and guns" story came from a woman at a fundraiser who worked for a liberal website.[5] She recently said at a panel that she sat on that story for seventy-two hours. One thing we need to remember is the difference between them—with no disrespect to them—and us is if you or I were at that fundraiser, that would have been online—

CHRIS CILLIZZA: In seventy-two seconds.

JOHN KING: Right. But she said she knew it would hurt Barack Obama and she wanted him to win, so she actually had a debate with herself and then a debate with her editors about what to do with it. We are never going to change that, and we don't want to change it. We can't change it, even if we did want to change it. We can't stop the evolution of the technology. So you have to study it and learn from it—watch what your competitors do well, steal and copy it, and try to get better. But, we need to keep our standards. The one thing that scares me about the business is you hear, "Well, it's out there, so we can report it." No. But there is a lot of pressure because it's out there that we can say it, or we can talk around it, or we can get close to it. When it comes to the personal stuff, we live in a much more dangerous world, and that's frightening.

CHRIS CILLIZZA: Sam, anything to add from the broader perspective of having to figure out, in a world that is demanding information constantly, how you adapt what you do from a programming perspective, as opposed to a reporting perspective?

---

5. On April 11, 2008, Mayhill Fowler posted an entry on Huffington Post, quoting Barack Obama at a San Francisco fundraiser saying, "You go into some of these small towns in Pennsylvania, and like a lot of small towns in the Midwest, the jobs have been gone now for twenty-five years, and nothing's replaced them. And they fell through the Clinton administration, and the Bush administration, and each successive administration has said that somehow these communities are gonna regenerate, and they have not. And it's not surprising then they get bitter, they cling to guns or religion or antipathy to people who aren't like them or anti-immigrant sentiment or anti-trade sentiment as a way to explain their frustrations."

SAM FEIST: Both in terms of programming on TV and what we've done online, 2008 was the campaign that reminded everybody why we need the mainstream media. In some ways, people were starting to think of the mainstream media as a dinosaur because you've got all of these blogs that provide so much more interesting, fresh and up-to-date information. 2008 was the campaign that we learned that Barack Obama, from what we thought were responsible websites, had attended a madrassa in Indonesia and that Sarah Palin's baby son wasn't actually hers but was her daughter's. That was from the Daily Kos, which we thought was a responsible website. It was the year that we learned that Barack Obama refused to put his hand over his heart when he said the Pledge of Allegiance and that Sarah Palin had banned most of the books from the Wasilla library. All of those were completely wrong, but they were reported on what we thought were responsible websites. It was ultimately up to the mainstream media to disprove those stories, to go and actually do reporting in many cases, to find out that those stories were wrong. Now, a lot of people still believe those stories—they got them in their e-mail boxes, they saw them on these websites that they thought that they could trust. It turned out that they couldn't trust them. So that was something that is refreshing for those of us who work in the mainstream media. There actually is a role for the adjudicator of the truth, or at least some of the truth, because there is a lot of stuff that's out there that's wrong. As far as programming, we had to be careful. We were constantly seeing this material out there—something would be on Drudge or Huffington Post or Daily Kos—and there would be a lot of pressure to put it on television. I would get calls from producers in the same way John King would get calls in the middle of the night to say, "Can we report this?" The first thing you have to do is put the brakes on and say, "No, wait, let's check it out, we don't know this to be the truth," and then work from there. Sometimes that means that we were slower than others but, in the end, hopefully you're right.

CHRIS CILLIZZA: That is the world in which we live. David Axelrod, was part of the Barack Obama thought, in terms of media, to find friendlier outlets that would put the message out there exactly as you wanted it?

DAVID AXELROD: We're still looking. [*laughter*]

CHRIS CILLIZZA: How did you approach that? How do you deal with that?

DAVID AXELROD: I think you have to participate in the world in which you live, and I think maybe we were a little slow in the uptake on that. I don't think that was our first instinct, but we had to participate in the environment as it existed. I would hope, and I believe, that we didn't inject toxins into the environment. I don't think that we did that, but I think we were competitive in that environment. Let me just say a couple of things about this, though. First of all, I am an old newspaper man. But, I do think, on the one hand, that there's something incredibly vital about the Internet and the ferment of the Internet involving people. It's not a genie you can put back in the bottle, and it's not one you should. But, when I was writing, there was a news cycle. There are no news cycles anymore. There is no filter. It's very hard to be contemplative about the information. It's very hard to verify. Maybe because of competitive pressures—maybe in some cases just sheer laziness—there is this utter trash that gets dumped on the marketplace and gets treated as if it's news. That's part of the circus of American politics today, and it's something that you have to cope with. In many ways, I saw in this campaign some of the things that bothered me about reporting when I was doing it—and I committed some of these same sins. There is an instinct to take what happened before as a template for what's going to happen in the future. In other words, we've never elected a black candidate, we are not going to elect a black candidate now, or Hispanics don't vote for African Americans, or Jews won't vote for a guy named Barack Obama. When we started this campaign, my friend Mark Penn, who was with the Clinton campaign, said one of the things he highlighted on the first day that we announced was that we were losing among African Americans by two to one and the Clinton brand is strong among African American voters. That was reported, and I got the question a lot—how can you win? I kept saying, "Look, give this time," and I explained where I thought the evolutions of these kinds of things would be. We ended up getting two thirds of the Hispanic vote, 78 percent of the Jewish vote and probably 98 percent of the African American vote. We did as well or better with working-class whites as John Kerry and Al Gore did. We defied every single elite hypothesis that was out there. I think it would behoove everybody who looks at these campaigns—and there are some really good reporters in this room who I really respect and who do this—to be able to look forward and not back, and to not assume that what happened before is what's going to happen again. We live in a dynamic society. We are evolving all the time. I used to get the question about the Bradley effect[6]—will white people lie to the pollsters about whether they are going to vote for a black man? Well, that was 1982—it was twenty-six years ago. I've been involved in a lot of campaigns for African American candidates running for offices that have never been held by African Americans before. I've seen the

---

6. The Bradley effect is a theory that proposes that some voters tell pollsters that they are undecided or likely to vote for a black candidate but then, on election day, vote for the white opponent. The theory is named after Tom Bradley, an African American candidate who lost the 1982 California governor's race despite being ahead in voter polls going into the election.

evolution of this country. We are well past where we were in 1982—and there is even some question of whether there was really a Bradley effect in 1982. Yet that was a big subtext of this election. So my admonition to all of the practitioners in the room who are in the media is next time—for those of you who are still doing this next time—look forward and not backward. Try and understand the dynamic of the world as you find it and not the one that existed four or eight or twelve years earlier.

CHRIS CILLIZZA: I want to do one last quick thing because I feel like if you get referenced thirty-five times, you get to say something. Joe Trippi, manager of Howard Dean's 2004 presidential campaign, was in many ways the progenitor of everything that came in 2008. Joe, can you tell us where the Internet and politics is heading in 2012?

JOE TRIPPI: No one can tell you that. We didn't have YouTube in 2004, and Facebook was sitting on some college campuses but hadn't really gotten off the ground yet. If you had sat all of us down the day after the 2004 election and said, "What's it going to look like four years from now?" there's no way I ever would have sat there and said where the Obama campaign would have taken it. So, just like we didn't have YouTube, we don't know what 2012 or 2016 is going to look like. The one thing I can tell you is I guarantee you there will be a campaign eight years from now that will make this one look ridiculous, just like the Obama campaign made the Dean thing look ridiculous, because the technology and people's ability to use those tools are growing every day. The number of people on broadband, for instance, is constantly moving, growing and changing. Millions more Americans are involved now because of the Obama campaign and the McCain campaign than were involved in 2004. The last thing I would say is that we are still scratching the surface. I am here celebrating with everybody that thirteen million Americans signed up with Barack Obama and sixty-seven million Americans voted for him. I believe there are going to be thirty million people who will be involved in something. The other thing is to get ready for this presidency because it's going to be completely different. Even compared to the practitioners, and the brilliance of what they did, they are now the Wright Brothers because no one has ever done this one before. John F. Kennedy said, "Don't ask what your country can do for you; ask what you can do for your country." If these tools had been in existence at the moment he said that, millions of Americans would have joined right at that moment to help the president pass his agenda. I'm in awe, waiting to see how this is all going to play out. It's going to be a pretty amazing presidency, and I think more people will be participating. Hats off to them for pulling it off.

The Democratic Primaries

4

BILL PURCELL: For our session now with the Democratic managers and strategists, we have two moderators. Marc Ambinder is an associate editor at *The Atlantic,* has an award-winning daily blog, contributes to the magazine and is a contributing editor to the *National Journal.* He is also a 2001 graduate of Harvard. Our second moderator is Susan Page, Washington bureau chief for *USA Today.* She has served on the selection committee of our Kennedy Library Foundation and our Institute of Politics committee to select the recipients of the New Frontier Awards.

USA Today's *Susan Page and* The Atlantic's *Marc Ambinder moderate a discussion on the Democratic primaries.*

• THE CANDIDATES: RACE, ETHNICITY AND GENDER •

SUSAN PAGE: One reason the Democratic primary campaign was so interesting was because we had this breakthrough field—a credible black candidate, a credible woman and a credible Hispanic candidate.

JONATHAN PRINCE: And a white guy.

SUSAN PAGE: And a white guy—always an underrepresented demographic. [*laughter*] We would like to start there, talking just briefly about the impact that these qualities had on the race from the start. Start with the Obama folks—what degree did you think, as this race was beginning, race would play with Obama's candidacy, as an advantage or a disadvantage?

JOEL BENENSON: Even before I joined the Obama campaign, I spoke to *Newsweek* for a story on the possibility of a woman or an African American getting elected president, and I thought that an African American Democrat would have the opportunity to expand the map. This was in late November, early December of 2006. I said I thought states like North Carolina and Virginia would be put in play in a way that they might not be by other Democrats, so I thought it was plausible for both of them. I thought there was a potential to broaden the map, in part, as a result of Senator Obama being an African American. But a lot of the conversation about race that ensued during the course of the campaign, I thought, was obsessive to a flaw. I always believed that if there were voters out there who were not going to vote for an African American candidate, they weren't likely to vote for a Democrat under any circumstances. The party brand over the last couple of years had been painted in a way that a lot of those folks had decided to not vote Democratic. It was also one of those things we couldn't control. I think David, who was involved in the campaign a couple of months before I was, would say you've got to, in a campaign, deal with what you control, and it was a factor that was a reality. Senator Obama himself, during the campaign, would say, "I'm not going to win this election because I'm an African American, and I'm not going to lose it because I'm an African American."

MARC AMBINDER: But weren't there a good number of voters who wanted to vote for Barack Obama who may have had some cultural resistances because he was African American? You seem to use an either/or thing. Did you completely write off those voters as well, or was there a program in place to make them more comfortable with Obama or to persuade them?

JOEL BENENSON: You use words like "make them more comfortable" with Senator Obama. Strategically, we knew that we had somebody who was the youngest candidate in the field and the least-known candidate in the field. Despite the excitement around his early candidacy, one of the things that we knew was that people didn't know him that well. Even African American voters didn't know him that well. There was this assumption, in the beginning in particular, on the part of the media and the elites to think, "Why isn't he doing better with African American voters?" They didn't know who he was. And a lot of other Democrats didn't know who he was. He had a certain degree of celebrity, but we had a lot of time, given the early start of the campaign, to fill in who he was with people. We weren't focused on people who were culturally resistant to him. We felt that there were always thresholds that we were going to have to clear with voters that didn't relate to race. They were related to readiness, steadiness and being a figure that they saw as presidential.

DAVID PLOUFFE: It would frustrate us sometimes. I think this was completely overblown. I was pretty clear about that during the campaign. In the primary, the gates we had to get through were Iowa and New Hampshire— there are not many African American voters in either one of those states. And in the general election, it just was not an issue. We spent a lot of time on what Joel termed "up-for-grabs" voters—the undecided voters. Anybody we felt was a true "up-for-grabs" voter had clearly decided that race was not going to be an impediment to their selection. We got 94, 95, 96 percent of the vote—record turnout—amongst African Americans in some states. I don't think that would have happened for any African American candidate. He sparked a degree of excitement, particularly with younger African American voters. So I do think there was a positive electoral consequence to it in states like Indiana, North Carolina, Virginia, even in Florida. But there was an obsession in the fall with, are a lot of white voters going to bail on him? People who are saying they are going to vote for him aren't going to vote for him, the so-called erroneous Bradley effect. It didn't come up in any of our research. And we talked to voters a lot every day. In the primary, our sense was that in order to defeat Senator Clinton, who was such a strong candidate, later in the calendar, we had to get 75–80 percent of the African American vote. Our sense was that if we succeeded early, that dam may break open, and it did. So we weren't that worried that in South Carolina in December, we were still trailing amongst African Americans because we figured the race would be a lot different a month from then if we succeeded. And if we didn't, then it was a moot point.

SUSAN PAGE: Was your strategy basically—since it wasn't something you could change—to ignore it, except in cases where you had no choice to address it, like after the Jeremiah Wright[1] stuff came out?

DAVID PLOUFFE: Yes. Honestly, it wasn't something we spent a lot of time talking about—it was what it was. When he first got into the race, we didn't spend much time talking about it because he had been successful in Illinois. If that ended up being a barrier we couldn't overcome, there was not much we could have done about it, so it just wasn't a huge factor for us. We tried to register younger African American voters and get them to turn out. That was important in some of the primary states, and it clearly was important in the general election. But we spent a lot of time talking to voters—at their doors, in focus groups—and this wasn't something that they were bringing up a heck of a lot.

SUSAN PAGE: You said it expanded the map in places like North Carolina. Didn't it also contract the map in places like West Virginia or Arkansas?

JOEL BENENSON: West Virginia and Arkansas were states that Democrats only won sporadically. A starting point for us was, how do we expand from the [2004] John Kerry map? He had gotten 254 electoral votes. In fact, the three states that we probably looked at earliest, that we had to win to win the election if we held the Kerry map, were going to be Iowa, Colorado and New Mexico. Those were the first three—we won the election if we got those. None of those have high African American populations. We knew Virginia would be the beginning of a much bigger total number for us, and that was probably the fourth state on the list.

SUSAN PAGE: To what degree do you think Hillary's gender created special issues for you?

HOWARD WOLFSON: We were aware that not only had no woman ever won a primary or caucus but no woman had ever won a delegate in a contested primary or caucus. So in the one sense, many people saw her as inevitable. We tried to project her that way. On the other hand, we were aware that a woman had some barriers to overcome in terms of people being

---

1. Rev. Jeremiah Wright was the Obamas' pastor for twenty years at the Trinity United Church of Christ in Chicago. During the campaign, it was revealed that he had a long history of making inflammatory remarks, including saying that blacks should not sing "God Bless America" but "God Damn America." Obama said he was not at church when those comments were made, and he denounced them. He severed ties with Reverend Wright later in the campaign.

comfortable with her as a commander-in-chief. No woman had been successful in crossing that threshold in the history of this country, so we were aware of that challenge.

SUSAN PAGE: Did the fact that she refused to apologize for her vote on Iraq, which became a big issue among some Democrats, relate to the desire to show that she was tough enough to be commander-in-chief—that she didn't have the option of apologizing when a male candidate might have?

HOWARD WOLFSON: Actually, it related to the desire for her to be consistent with what she thought, which was that she didn't make a mistake.

SUSAN PAGE: In what ways did your strategy reflect a need to demonstrate that she could be commander-in-chief?

HOWARD WOLFSON: Ensuring that she had—and she does and did—a facility with foreign policy and defense issues and making sure that people knew that she had served on the Armed Forces Committee. Showing that she was conversant and had a facility with those issues was important.

SUSAN PAGE: Governor Richardson, the first credible Hispanic candidate, to what degree do you think his ethnicity played a role?

MARK PUTNAM: It played very little role. For us, Iowa was the game, and there are very few Hispanic voters in Iowa. So that was not a part of our game plan. If we got to Nevada, it was going to be helpful there. But he would joke about how he had a very un-Latino name, Richardson. It was something he would poke fun at himself about. It really was not a part of our game plan. We were organizing with Latinos and it was a source of fundraising, but it was not a major focus of our strategy.

SUSAN PAGE: Was it a disadvantage in any way?

MARK PUTNAM: No, we never saw it that way.

SUSAN PAGE: *USA Today* did an analysis of voter typology in March, and we found that John Edwards was doing very well among white men who did not agree with him on issues but had the demographic qualities of being white and male. I wonder if you think that he benefited from voters who might have had some qualms about voting for a woman or an African American.

JONATHAN PRINCE: I don't think so. First of all, as the process began, Iowa was the game for all of us. I don't think any of us encountered any evidence that this made a difference to Iowa caucus goers. For us, one thing that was definitely an issue was that our two dominant opponents represented change in a very progressive, obvious way—as soon as you looked at them. For us, that was really a change there, and we were glad that they spent less time focusing on change as a message for a while. Our challenge was to make sure that we got out there and were able to cast John as a real candidate of change, given the obvious change and powerful progressive change that both of these candidates represented just by who they were and the history-making nature of their candidacies. That's why we spent so much time focusing on trying to drive a progressive agenda and surrounding him with that. I don't think any of us encountered any evidence in Iowa, or any of those early states, that it really made a bit of difference to caucus goers or primary voters.

HOWARD WOLFSON: The only thing I would say to that, in slight disagreement, is that we were not unaware that Iowa had never elected a female statewide in its history. I am not quite sure why that is, but it does make it unusual in the fifty United States.

JOE TRIPPI: For one thing, in Iowa, Joanne Zimmerman was lieutenant governor. There had been women elected to office in Iowa. But push that to the side. Iowa is a unique place. There aren't a lot of minorities there, and there was no sign—whether you were white, male, Richardson, Obama, Clinton—that ethnicity or gender was a problem. When Obama came in first in Iowa, what it did do though was, regardless of what was going on in the rest of the country—where people had some doubts, where African Americans may have doubted whether the country was ready for Barack Obama—when he came in first in Iowa, it released all that. There were a lot of people out there who went, "Damn, this can happen," and that actually alleviated a lot of the question.

• RUNNING AGAINST HILLARY'S INEVITABILITY •

MARC AMBINDER: I want to start and ask each campaign, who is not Senator Clinton's campaign, to describe Clinton's specific, chief vulnerability you saw and you thought could be exploited when you were thinking about a race. This was at the time when everyone assumed Senator Clinton would be the nominee. Then, if you could briefly give your map from candidate inception through Iowa through the nomination. What was your road map? We'll start with Senator Dodd's campaign.

SHERYL COHEN: In looking at Senator Clinton, there weren't a lot of vulnerabilities. It wasn't like you went into it thinking, "Oh, this is going to be easy." But my response to that would probably be that she was so well known and so well defined that to the extent that some of her numbers weren't getting above 50 percent or some of the negatives were there, you felt that there was room within the caucus for an alternative to her—based on some of the polling.

Our strategy, going forward, was, in the first quarter, to try to be seen as the fourth in this race. We thought we could do that through fundraising, through the strength of our operation, through the narrative we were trying to create around Senator Dodd and his message, and through the broad base of experience that he had. We fell short in terms of the money. We were surprised at how well Governor Richardson did—that kind of knocked us off of where we thought we would be. But if that had happened, the theory would have been that in the second quarter, when the debates began, if we could have moved into a credible fourth position in the eyes of the national media, we could have gained a little bit of traction. That, in turn, would help increase our fundraising numbers and then do all the things that we needed money to be able to do. There was some potential in the second quarter, if this field began to winnow a bit, to be able to do that. Then, from there, it was potentially wide open, in terms of other mistakes people might make or other opportunities. That was our quarter-by-quarter goal for trying to move up in the track.

MARK PUTNAM: In regards to Senator Clinton, the Clintons were not a part of the factors in Governor Richardson's decision-making.

MARC AMBINDER: Really?

MARK PUTNAM: Honestly. He was grateful for the years of service that he had been able to do for President Clinton, and he had great respect for Senator Clinton. Some in the campaign might have thought that, in a general election, she might be polarizing, but she clearly was going to be a force in the primaries. We were focused on our own campaign with a candidate that we thought was uniquely qualified, and our goal was to get past one of the top three. There was a clear division of the first tier and the second tier. Our goal was to do well in fundraising every quarter. We wanted to take advantage of the governor's personality. The job interview ads,[2] which were the first humorous ads ever run by a presidential candidate, tried to take advantage of that unique intersection of a candidate's personality, his status in the race and his breadth of experience. Our goal was to be first on the

---

2. Governor Richardson ran campaign ads in Iowa that featured him in a mock job interview in order to discuss his qualifications for president.

air, among the Democratic candidates, to get some momentum, to drive the fundraising and to get past one of the top three.

MARC AMBINDER: There really wasn't any consideration given to the behemoth that was Senator Clinton's campaign—the fact that many people viewed it as inevitable? What was the way to beat her?

MARK PUTNAM: All of us in the campaign saw ourselves as an underdog. You've got two extremely formidable fundraisers, and you have another candidate in Senator Edwards that was very popular in Iowa, so we were not uni-focused on Senator Clinton or Senator Obama. We saw that our opening, in our early polling, appeared to be Obama voters—voters who were attracted to a change candidate but also were a little concerned about his level of experience. So that was actually more of our focus than Senator Clinton's campaign.

LUIS NAVARRO: We had two phases of the campaign. Once we came back on the screen in April of 2007, we had three objectives. Senator Edwards was on an unsuccessful national ticket, and Senator Clinton was running as an inevitability candidate. Those sorts of candidacies had not historically worked well in the Democratic primary and electorate—or at least had had a checkered past. So we didn't buy into the notion that inevitability or having been on a national ticket would necessarily work to their benefit come January of 2008. What did that mean for us? There were three things. One, in trying to dominate the national security/foreign policy arena, our first opportunity at that, we thought, was our plan for Iraq. No matter where anyone was, in terms of Senator Obama's opposition to the war or Senator Clinton's unwillingness to apologize for it, the question was how to get out. We felt we had the best marketable plan for arguing that point. Second, when the other two campaigns had both come out early to say that they would vote for the troop funding in May of 2007 and then did not do so,[3] Senator Biden had already committed himself to that—both from a consistent policy standpoint and because of his legislation, which he thought was another way of talking about concrete solutions to the most pressing challenge. Third, we did think that, as a function of the residual support that we had in Iowa coming out of our 1988 presidential campaign, we might be able to sneak into a distant third place as a result of a three-way fight among the better-funded and better-known candidates, and that that would be our projection. We would live off the land, culminating in a fight in South Carolina, where we thought we

---

3. On May 16, 2007, Senator Obama and Senator Clinton voted to end funding for U.S. combat operations in Iraq by April 1, 2008. They were both previously reluctant to limit funding.

would win beyond expectations, perhaps coming in second, and that would allow us to move on to February 5.

MARC AMBINDER: David, as the primary period progressed, before the Iowa caucuses, who were the Clinton supporters who switched? Was there an issue profile of Clinton supporters who switched to Obama?

DAVID PLOUFFE: In most states, with the exception of Iowa—although our initial survey had Senator Clinton ten or twelve points ahead of us in Iowa—she was in the mid-forties to 50 percent. I don't think any of us quite understand exactly what happened in New Hampshire. Like in Iowa, Edwards fell down to the high teens and then climbed back to 30 percent—almost all of those people that he got back to 30 percent with had been with him at some point. In New Hampshire, Senator Clinton is in the mid-forties in the very beginning and then falls down. So those people still liked her—they had been for her at some point, so they are easier to get back. In almost every state that concerned us, as her numbers dropped, most of those people still had high favorable ratings of her and they had been for her at some point, so we watched that very carefully. We had open eyes and great appreciation for their strength in the race and knew that we had a very narrow path. It was a change election clearly. She was running as the inevitable insider. Particularly in Iowa, and in New Hampshire to some extent, that did not resonate terribly well. It gave us an opening. Secondly, we thought we might be able to sneak by her in Iowa. For us, our strategy was we had to finish ahead of her in Iowa. In the very beginning, that might have meant coming in second to Edwards, but it increasingly became clearer that we would have to win. We thought we had to win the New Hampshire primary to be the Democratic nominee because her strength later in the calendar was so pronounced. We felt we had to have a terrific January. That was one of the surprises—looking back on it. We lost two of the first four states and we were still able to be the nominee. That happened for a couple of reasons. One, in the very beginning, we assumed we would only have the organizational and financial ability to transact the first four states. We would have to run the table there and try and catch lightning in a bottle.

MARC AMBINDER: How much was that budget, by the way?

DAVID PLOUFFE: Maybe fifty or sixty million. It became clearer, after the first two quarters, we were going to have the ability to put together, and maybe even exceed, what they were going to do financially and organizationally in these later states. All that did was put more pressure on us because actually it became less of a pipe dream. We began to see it because in the beginning the odds were very low. We began to think, wow, we are going to be able to transact February 5 and the states after if we can just get out of the gate. If we don't get out of the gate, all that money and organization is moot. We had to win Iowa. We thought we had to win New Hampshire. South Carolina ended up providing us a unique momentum that we didn't expect. We had a very narrow path, and had we not won Iowa, it would have been game, set and match. Our ability then to be ready for what came next was a big surprise because in the beginning—January, February, March, even in the second quarter—we were just focused on those first four states. Then, the world opened up to us because we began to see all these people organizing. We sent staff into Minnesota and Colorado. Our initial surveys in all of those states had us losing to her in every February 5 state and every state that came after. In some cases, like in Minnesota, we were only down four or five points. The reason we were behind is the people who said they were going to caucus tended to be the core Democratic caucus goers. So we had to expand the electorate. We put aside five or six million dollars for February 5—that's all we did—but that was a big deal. It enabled us, in the fall, to put staff in all of those states. We'd send five or six, seven or eight staff in, and they would literally have thousands—sometimes tens of thousands—of full-time volunteer help. That was a big advantage.

JOEL BENENSON: Let me add one thing on the profile part of the question. The one group that we always saw a big overlap on, between people who were favorable to Clinton and those who were favorable to Obama, were white, college-educated women, particularly in New Hampshire. As the numbers swung in New Hampshire—as they did from February right up until the end—it was always white, college-educated women who we saw moving back and forth. They liked both candidates. Keep in mind we were looking at favorable ratings for all three of these candidates in New Hampshire in the mid to upper seventies. They liked all of them—less intensity around Senator Edwards, but a lot of mutual intensity around Senator Clinton and Obama. So that was the group that we always saw as a movable.

MARC AMBINDER: Senator Edwards?

JONATHAN PRINCE: In terms of the overall strategic approach, our approach was Iowa, Iowa, Iowa. It was much like David described their earlier approach, without having the benefit of the massive financial readjustment that allowed them to expand. We were always in that four state, get out of the gate thing. Our budget was a little less—a little more than forty million dollars for that. We always thought, as evidenced by our performance in Iowa ultimately, that we had a credible case to make that we could win the caucuses. If we had won the caucuses, our expectation was that we would have to do better than we did in New Hampshire but not necessarily win. The Clintons were always very strong there, and New Hampshire has always been tough for him. Putting aside the matter of Nevada, because it was such an unclear context—it was on a Saturday and the union politics were so wrapped in it. We expected then to go to South Carolina and be in a face-off with whoever was the ultimate winner of New Hampshire and whoever followed us—whether it was Obama or Clinton. South Carolina was a state that John had won in 2004—a state he was born in. If we were coming off the benefit of having won Iowa, his performance, I think, would have been very good there, and we could have won. Then we'd be off to the races. That was the tactical notion.

JOE TRIPPI: Our thing was to win Iowa and raise forty million dollars. Go after forty million dollars and do it. Hillary's vulnerability was the inevitable part. The toughest thing to do is try to go wire to wire. In 2000, Gore was able to do it against Bill Bradley, but it wasn't as competitive and as talented as this field was. We thought "inevitable" was going to be a big problem. When you looked at the modeling, if African Americans ever started moving away from Clinton and moving to Barack, that was going to be a huge problem later on in the other states.

JONATHAN PRINCE: The inevitable would then be both candidates.

JOE TRIPPI: Right. Then what you have, hopefully, if Obama takes second, she takes third, African Americans start moving off of her a bit, and, as we get to South Carolina, it really could be a three-way race and we could do well there. Could we make it happen in Iowa? If so, we had a shot. It might have been a lot less of a shot than a lot of other people, but we would have a real shot at it. We took our best shot at Iowa and it didn't happen. We really did try to, during that entire period, help frame Clinton as status quo. Whether fair or not, they had moved more to experience and the inevitable thing—it's hard to be the change candidate when the world is saying you're inevitable. We did everything we could to keep shoving her in that direction. In some of the debates, John did an effective job at doing that. But it ended up benefiting the Obama campaign. We were trying to paint status quo on Clinton, win Iowa, pop the inevitable button, see African Americans shift away from her and, hopefully, create a three-way race.

JONATHAN PRINCE: I'll give you one other little piece of color that is interesting. We, very consciously, allowed ourselves to drop into third place in Iowa—eyes wide open. We felt like we had to do that because of the way that our spending was over the summer. We knew we had a lead. We knew they were going to outspend us significantly. We needed to husband our resources so we could get back in there very strong in October for the finish. We felt confident that those people who were with us would come back to us when we started to look credible again. We were right about that. We didn't expect to turn out 240,000 caucus goers, but with a turnout of 140,000 or 150,000 or 160,000, we probably would have won—that's what our modeling was based on. We did make a very conscious decision, in terms of resources and media expectations, that if we stayed dominant in Iowa all along, it very easily could have been written off as, oh, that was just Edwards in Iowa, now we'll get to the real Obama/Clinton race in New Hampshire. For both those reasons, we made a conscious decision to allow ourselves to fall back in Iowa.

JOE TRIPPI: John and Elizabeth thought this strategy was a little crazy.

MARC AMBINDER: It seemed to me that you guys were much more aggressive during that period against Hillary Clinton and kind of had kid gloves against Barack Obama. Is that true? Why was that true? Did you worry that there was an overlap in terms of supporters?

JOE TRIPPI: You are running against two historic candidacies.

MARC AMBINDER: And you are only putting gloves on one of them?

JOE TRIPPI: Right. The press is only going to watch two people. The press—everybody—was conspiring to narrow this down to two people really quickly. They had already started to do that, and it was Clinton and Obama. So we had to beat both of them, and the best way to do that was to get some of her stuff in Iowa. She was the target, and if we could be the change candidate, push her off as status quo, then we gained. Then we win Iowa. That was our best way to get there. There wasn't a deeper strategy about fifty states. We are just trying to live to win Iowa and, at the time, the best way to do that was to shove against her on the status quo/change thing, realizing that some of those voters might go to Obama. That's also the reason we had to be more aggressive. Who else was going to report anything John Edwards said unless we were aggressive and said something? One of the reasons Richardson, Dodd and Edwards were, at times, so aggressive was, hello, how do you get attention? At one point, John Edwards turned to me on the plane and said, "What do I have to do, set myself on fire?"

JONATHAN PRINCE: No. Howard Dean tried that. [*laughter*]

Luis Navarro and Sheryl Cohen listen as Mark Putnam talks about the Iowa caucuses.

JOE TRIPPI: I said to him it won't work, or we would have tried it already. Trying to get attention with these two giants rolling across the country was a very tough thing to do.

MARC AMBINDER: But you found a way later to get attention.[4]

• THE IOWA CAUCUSES •

SUSAN PAGE: Guy and Howard, there was a memo that was leaked in May of 2007, in which Hillary Clinton's strategists suggested skipping Iowa—not a friendly state for the Clintons, not a good state for women, for whatever reasons. Was that seriously considered?

HOWARD WOLFSON: Our initial poll in Iowa was terrible. We had real doubts about whether Iowa was viable. By the time that memo was leaked, we were pretty far down the road towards having made the decision to compete in Iowa. At the time, and certainly in retrospect, it was difficult to see how the inevitable candidate could walk away from the first primary. Either

---

4. On August 8, 2008, John Edwards acknowledged, in an interview on ABC's *Nightline*, that he had an extramarital relationship with Rielle Hunter.

you are going to be inevitable or you are going to walk away from Iowa, but it's hard to do both. By the time the Mike Henry[5] memo had leaked, we were more than half pregnant on Iowa. Our polling did get better there as time went on, but our initial polling in Iowa was cause for enormous concern.

SUSAN PAGE: Do you think that there was a strategy in leaking the memo, either to raise the possibility of skipping Iowa or to make sure that you could not?

HOWARD WOLFSON: I don't know the answer to that.

SUSAN PAGE: Why do you think Iowa was unfriendly territory for Hillary Clinton?

HOWARD WOLFSON: Iowa did not have an enormous history of being all that friendly to women running statewide. I don't know why that is, but it was a reality. There was a lot of concern in the campaign about our ability to compete in Iowa. Mike Henry, in that memo, laid out, fairly and honestly, what those concerns were and suggested a path to deal with them by not competing there. But by that time, the decision had been made.

JONATHAN PRINCE: I actually have a simpler theory, for what it's worth, which is there were three very popular candidates in Iowa. You guys did very well in Iowa, and in other years you posted a number that could have won. Obama did the best. We were almost tied. There were three candidates who were very strong in Iowa, which hasn't happened in a long time, and they all stayed strong all year long. We were in first for a while, Clinton was in first for a while, Obama won it.

HOWARD WOLFSON: It wasn't just the top lines that gave us some cause for concern.

JONATHAN PRINCE: I understand that.

HOWARD WOLFSON: We had some underlying concerns.

---

5. Mike Henry was the deputy campaign manager for Hillary Clinton's presidential campaign.

JONATHAN PRINCE: So did we. We had the house,[6] haircut[7] and hedge funds.[8] We all had our things that gave us cause for concern.

MARC AMBINDER: What were some of the underlying concerns?

HOWARD WOLFSON: You asked the other campaigns what some of the vulnerabilities of Clinton were, and nobody mentioned the one which we actually seemed to get attacked on—character. Our polling showed that. And the other campaigns were proficient at raising the issue of her motivation and raising some of the unflattering residue from the nineties.

SUSAN PAGE: Senator Obama did win Iowa. You did that by changing who participated in the caucuses there, as you did in later caucus states. Talk about your approach in changing the demography of the Iowa electorate and, especially, the incredible appeal that he showed among young people who, despite the skepticism of many of us, actually turned out for you that night.

DAVID PLOUFFE: It was clear to us from the beginning that if the 2004 electorate showed up, we had very little chance of winning. And as time went on, that became more and more pronounced. In September of 2007, three-quarters of our identified supporters had never attended a caucus before. That meant that we were doing a good job of attracting support, but it also was a source of great concern because there was a lot of skepticism. It had never been done on this scale before. I think the final numbers were two-thirds of our ones and twos[9] had never caucused before. Some of those were reliable primary voters, some were reliable general election voters, and some were new registrants. One of the more remarkable statistics of the entire election is that there were as many people under thirty as over sixty-five who caucused in the state of Iowa. If you had asked anybody that on January 2, they would have said there is no way that could happen. It was helpful

---

6. John Edwards and his family lived in a 28,200-square-foot home on 102 acres in North Carolina—the most valuable home in Orange County, with a building value of $4.3 million and land worth $1.1 million.

7. John Edwards's April 15, 2007, campaign finance report listed two four-hundred-dollar haircuts and nearly five hundred dollars for spa treatments as "consulting" expenses.

8. In the fall of 2005, John Edwards served as an adviser to Fortress Investment Group, a New York–based hedge fund, and, according to his April 2007 campaign finance report, he raised at least $167,700 from individuals associated with the company.

9. In the Iowa caucuses, candidates must meet a threshold 15 percent requirement. Supporters of candidates making up less than 15 percent of the vote in a particular precinct have the option of making their vote count in a second tally for a "viable" candidate—one who got at least 15 percent in the first tally.

to us, from a selfish perspective, but it was also great to see. We organized just about every high school in Iowa—this was where resources and great organizers came in. One of the untold stories of the campaign is the amazing field workers who gravitated to our campaign early. They were remarkably talented. They would go to Algona, Iowa, and Charles City, Iowa, and live there for nine or ten months and become part of the community. They were just terrific. Our precinct captains in Iowa, as happened throughout the whole campaign, were quality people and inspired. Our precinct captains worked around the clock. We had to turn precinct captains away. In some precincts, we had four or five people who wanted to be precinct captains. We got a lot of criticism for not going to a lot of county or state party dinners. Our Iowa staff eventually bought into it, but it caused them great angst. You are only going to be in some of these counties two or three times. Our view was if we are going to a county party dinner—if your one trip there is to speak to 400 people who gave fifty dollars to the county party—we would come in third amongst that universe. So we had to go where we could invite Independents and Republicans and people who hadn't caucused before. That was how we thought about our schedule. It was, "How do we put him in front of as many people as possible to help us expand the electorate?" We measured that very carefully.

If 150,000 or 160,000 people had turned out, we would have come in third. We structured the schedule in pursuit of finding these people. We'd send people out to community events and shopping centers. We just had to find people. So we were working off lists, sure, but part of it was just to have a huge basket that we tried to collect people from. We needed a high African American turnout, the few who there were. We needed high-school kids. We needed college kids. We needed Republicans. We needed Independents. We just had to put them all in a basket and hope enough of them showed up.

ALYSSA MASTROMONACO: I was the director of scheduling for the Kerry campaign, and this was so different than how we approached things four years before. All of our schedulers were field people—these weren't people we brought in from D.C. They were field staff, they were from Iowa, they had worked in Minnesota, they were from the Midwest. They knew what needed to be done. We sent them to Iowa and they lived there. We told the advance teams we found from Iowa and the people we sent in, you are not part of the national advance team anymore, you are part of Iowa, and you work for Paul Tewes,[10] and you work for me. In the beginning, there is always a little bit of disconnect, but by the end, I had advance staff calling me saying, "We really need to do this picture with the Barack Stars," our high-school organizers. Everyone was really part of a team. It wasn't the

---

10. Paul Tewes was the Iowa state director for Barack Obama's presidential campaign.

usual advance in Iowa, which is a historic problem. They were part of the Iowa family. I worked with state staff directly.

They would call me up and send me a crazy schedule for approval that included five hours in a car getting to a tiny town, and they said, "If we can just get ten people to sign up from this town, we are going to meet our local goals." It meant putting a lot of faith in them. It meant trusting them, which I think was really important in the beginning.

SUSAN PAGE: The night of January 3 was the end of the road for some candidates and the beginning of the end of the road for others. Could we go around the table and have each campaign describe briefly what it was like that night? Were you surprised by how well or badly your candidate did? The Clinton people are laughing, so we'll start with them. [*laughter*]

GUY CECIL: It was not fun. I was in New Hampshire at the time but listening in on Iowa calls. It was almost like we were in this weird middle ground where we knew that the Edwards folks were doing well with the regular caucus goers—caucus goers who had participated in 2004. We also knew a lot of the Obama organization's focus was on expanding the universe of potential caucus goers. In some ways, we tried to do both. When you look at those folks who were Hillary voters, they tended to be older. We spent a lot of time reminding people that they didn't have to stand up the entire time. We got rid of the phrase, "Stand up and caucus for Hillary Clinton," so that they knew they could sit down. [*laughter*] But our capacity to expand, to compete in a 240,000-person caucus, was somewhat limited by who was most likely to be with us. When you get e-mails from friends who are traveling to Iowa who are excited about recruiting some additional wheelchairs for the caucus, you recognize there are a lot of challenges. They would do a lot of home visitation with voters who were over the age of sixty, who had not participated in a caucus before, who were excited or motivated, particularly women, by the fact that a woman was on the ballot. In some ways, by trying to do both, maybe we didn't do enough of either in terms of continuing to reach out to the 2004 caucus goers and doing enough to expand capacity with new caucus goers.

SUSAN PAGE: Did you think these young voters could actually be relied on to show up for Obama?

GUY CECIL: Not to the extent that they did. Did we think that there would be an increase? Sure.

HOWARD WOLFSON: We were skeptical.

GUY CECIL: Did we think it was going to be 240,000? No.

DAVID PLOUFFE: We thought around 200,000. We did think the kids on Facebook would show up but not at that level. Actually, I think that the Clinton campaign got a healthy number of that increase.

HOWARD WOLFSON: We had this weird Goldilocks strategy, where it was like, if it was too small, Edwards was going to win, if it was too big, Obama was going to win. So we needed to increase it, but not by that much. In the end, it was a much larger increase than we anticipated—maybe than even they had.

JONATHAN PRINCE: There were macro effects to the increase in turnout that went beyond any of our efforts, which was just the excitement over the race—a lot of that generated by their candidacies, but by ours, too. We had twenty-five thousand or thirty thousand more caucus goers than we had in our own models.

DAVID PLOUFFE: Our campaigns were so large and organized in every corner of the state. The Republican contest was completely different, so Independents participated in our caucus in huge numbers, and we had a lot of Republicans participate. I think that was a big factor. It worked to our benefit. We did voluminous research with these people who hadn't gone to a caucus before to figure out why they hadn't gone before and what the barriers were. For a lot of people, we just had to convince them that they weren't going to have to be there very long and find buddies for them. We spent as much time in the end trying to figure out how to get these people there as we did converting undecideds. It was a big challenge.

SUSAN PAGE: But the standing up issue was not one that you faced?

DAVID PLOUFFE: No.

HOWARD WOLFSON: We even had a special video explaining to people how to caucus. There was a real sense that unless we got people who had never caucused and were indifferent or suspicious of the process, we didn't have much of a shot.

JONATHAN PRINCE: The one group of folks, by the way, who got the massive turnout right was the *Des Moines Register* in their Iowa poll. Howard and I were having dinner together on New Year's Eve and we tried to debunk that poll with every national reporter that walked by our table. We Clinton/ Edwards two-teamed the poll, which then turned out to be exactly right.

HOWARD WOLFSON: For the record, Ann Selzer is the pollster.

JOE TRIPPI: What happened is three campaigns had enough people there that night that would have been enough to win in any other election. Roughly 30 percent was going to be about near eighty thousand people—that would have been 50, 55 percent any other year. So there was a lot of success. And I do think because the Republican side had no energy that the Independents played a role. I'll tell you exactly what happened on our side. We looked at the first reports and said this thing is going to be 240,000 and it's over. Then what happened was we stayed there. We stayed with Obama. You guys won and you won big in the numbers. But we expected as the numbers came in that we would be dropping off because we didn't have that many ones and twos identified. Our organization hadn't identified them. But 30,000 more people showed up and voted for Edwards than we thought, and that actually kept us in second place, which wasn't good enough. It was a really weird feeling of immediately realizing it was over and then seeing bigger numbers in these precincts than we had thought were going to be for us. We were trailing but keeping up with Obama as it went on. We started to think maybe, if we were lucky, we could win. But, it was pretty obvious midway through the count that they had scored a huge victory.

SUSAN PAGE: After all that campaigning, after Iowa, Senator Dodd and Senator Biden immediately dropped out. Tell us what that night was like. Was it a surprise? Was it clear to these candidates that the time to go was now?

SHERYL COHEN: Yes. We were working off about 150,000 turnout. If that had been the case, based on where we thought our ones and twos were, we would have done significantly better than what we did. We would not have been anywhere near where the top three were, but we might have been a fourth. We thought we might even get somewhere closer to 6 percent, believe it or not. The numbers were completely blown out. If you don't get 15 percent, you don't qualify. A lot of people showed up that night for Dodd and, to some extent, for Richardson and Biden. When they lost people in the first round, all of our numbers moved elsewhere. There was support for these candidates there, but it just doesn't show up in the way the Iowa caucuses work. We were definitely taken aback by the size of the turnout. We had a strategy in place if we had come in fourth. We would only continue if we were fourth, and only if we were in a reasonable distance from, who we thought would be, Senator Edwards. For example, if he had ended up closer to 15 percent and we were at 6 percent, we thought that made sense and we'd take one more shot in New Hampshire. We budgeted for that.

SUSAN PAGE: Given what the results actually were, was there discussion that this was not going to work and it was time to go?

SHERYL COHEN: Yes. Even if the results were better, we were potentially not going to continue. It needed to make sense for us. But we planned for it.

VALERIE BIDEN-OWENS: There was no discussion about continuing because you wouldn't be in the debate in New Hampshire. You would be nonexistent. We thought that the earth moved under our feet in Iowa. We went in and we had the third number. Our strategy in Iowa was to do well in the debates. Joe's a great retail politician. We worked to get him out and exposed to as many people as possible. We were the third best in endorsements from legislators. We really thought we were a viable candidate for the endorsement of the *Des Moines Register*. In the afternoon, one of the principals in Iowa said, "You are going to come in third." The news commentators thought that we were coming in third. If you look at it in a vacuum, it looks like, "What in God's name were you thinking?" But what we were thinking is that we were not thinking in the universe of what these guys did with 240,000. We were viable. But we weren't there after the first round because, in some precincts, it was 400 percent turnout. We certainly weren't satisfied because we wanted to win. Clearly we were in this to win because when we entered, we thought we were the most qualified person, especially given the situation in the world where the most important issue in the world, in our country, at the time, to voters, by three to one, was Iraq. Joe was the most authoritative, respected voice on foreign policy and national security. With that as a background, we gave it our best shot. We ran a campaign that was honest to Joe. We responded to the needs of what we thought the country wanted. We didn't win.

SUSAN PAGE: Governor Richardson did a little bit better and waited a week before dropping out. What was his view that night?

MARK PUTNAM: Iraq was a key issue for us. We not only ran the first humorous TV ad of the campaign but we also ran, in my recollection, the only comparative ad of the Iowa campaign, which was on Iraq. It said that Governor Richardson was the only candidate who would pull out all the troops, and it was a belief that he strongly felt. It was something that he got into a lot of debate with Biden about. In the end, we saw the Iraq pull-out vote as our key to respectability. We wanted to come in fourth, at a minimum, just for respectability's sake, so we really focused in the end on pulling all the troops out of Iraq. We spun it as we made the final four, but the writing was on the wall.

SUSAN PAGE: Did he realize that that night?

MARK PUTNAM: Yes, he did. He wanted to go on to New Hampshire and have a chance one more time to make his case against the top three. There was some desire within the campaign to go on in Nevada, just because we did have a lot of folks out there who were counting on us to stay in the race, but it became very obvious that he needed to pull out.

MARC AMBINDER: There were reports that night that Richardson field organizers had been told if Richardson didn't make viability in the caucus to support Obama. Was there any truth to that at all?

MARK PUTNAM: You can't tell Iowa caucus goers who to go vote for.

MARC AMBINDER: Was there any instruction? Was there any sense that that's what they should do?

MARK PUTNAM: No, there was no coordination like that.

MARC AMBINDER: From the Obama perspective, you certainly must have picked up the reports that a lot of us did that that was happening to an unusual degree. Was there any communication?

DAVID PLOUFFE: There's always a lot of intrigue around this, but people aren't going to be told what to do. The truth is, in a lot of these precincts where Richardson wasn't viable or Biden wasn't viable, we were clearly the stronger second choice, in competition with Edwards. That was one of the problems that the Clinton folks had—they were not anyone's second choice. The Clinton number didn't really move because they didn't pick much up on the second round. A lot of the staff and a lot of the supporters, particularly from Richardson, if their guy wasn't going to be viable, moved to us. If 150,000 or 160,000 people showed up, Richardson would have been viable in a lot more precincts. He fell short in some places, and I think we picked up the lion's share of that.

• THE NEW HAMPSHIRE PRIMARY •

MARC AMBINDER: I'm going to ask two obnoxious questions—one of the Obama folks and one of the Edwards folks. How did you mess up New Hampshire?

DAVID PLOUFFE: First of all, if we had entered that day where we thought—every poll showed the thing 34–34—and lost a two-point race,

I think we would have had a hard time coming back from that. Honestly, the way it went down, we kind of shrugged our shoulders and said, "Something strange just happened, we don't quite understand what it is, and let's move on." First of all, Clinton was always very strong in New Hampshire and again, she ended up getting 39 percent. The people she picked up—she moved from 30, 31, 32 to 39 those last twenty-four to forty-eight hours— were people who were still highly favorable to her. A few things. One, if we had won New Hampshire, we would have been a comet streaking across the political sky. Looking back on it, maybe it was good we lost because it gave us a little more texture and people could see how he dealt with a setback. Voters through this process wanted Obama to earn it, and I think there were enough people in New Hampshire who said, "You know what? Maybe not quite yet." The coverage was, if Obama wins Tuesday night, and he is going to win, it's over. Second, because people thought we were going to win, we hemorrhaged Independents to McCain because the McCain/Romney race looked closer. We were very concerned about that and it happened. It happened in big enough numbers to hurt us. Third, I think she had a very good debate. There were dynamics coming out of the debate I don't think we fully appreciated that night. I think her moment on Monday[11] really helped her get back some of the people who she had bled. They had a good organization, and we had a good organization. In New Hampshire, we did everything we wanted to do—knocked on every door, made every phone call. We slapped ourselves around about the campaign those last four or five days. We probably, in retrospect, looked a little too celebratory. Honestly, though, it would have been hard, given the crowds we were getting, to do a lot of town hall meetings. In my view, we probably focused a little bit too much on that internally as a reason. So there were a lot of different things that happened, and it ended up with her winning. We could have done some things differently. There's no doubt about that. We probably should have looked like we were hustling a little bit more. The truth is we did a lot of on-the-record interviews those last four or five days, a lot of shaking of hands, up early. But all the coverage was, "Look at these enormous crowds, he is going to win." That was a terrible dynamic for us, particularly with Independent voters. The McCain/Romney race was seen as a dead heat with Independent voters. It was a McCain and Obama contest. I think a decent percentage of folks, at the very last minute, said McCain needs my help more than Obama, and that was part of the reason we lost.

---

11. On January 7, 2008, at a campaign event in Portsmouth, New Hampshire, when Hillary Clinton was asked by a voter how she keeps up with her arduous campaign, she replied with her voice cracking and tears in her eyes.

MARC AMBINDER: Jonathan and Joe, both of you had said that Iowa was the be all and end all. If he didn't win Iowa, that was basically it. Was one of the reasons why Edwards decided to stay in because there was a sense that culturally conservative Democrats might not move to Barack Obama and that Hillary Clinton's inevitability was punctured, and therefore that would give room to John Edwards?

JONATHAN PRINCE: One of the fascinating things that happened that night when we came in second in Iowa, and the next day, is you got a great glimpse of the disconnect between the parameters that the national media and all of us operatives and the whole chattering class sets on these races, compared to the rest of the world. Our biggest fundraising day ever was the day after Iowa. The e-mails poured in congratulating us because we had beaten Hillary Clinton. The media had been telling everyone for years that no one else could possibly win. We had just beaten one of the two inevitable candidates. So the perception amongst voters, the general public and our supporters was, wow, we just had this massive achievement. Internally, did we know that the road was a lot more difficult? Of course. But we weren't entirely sure what was going to happen in New Hampshire, and there was a good possibility that if Obama won, Hillary would be out. We are going next to the state John was born in—a state he won before. We might as well play it out. We had money. We had resources. He was a very good debater. We were suddenly looking at a situation where Hillary Clinton, after two contests, may not be in the race. It seemed like we still had a couple of hands left. It was way beyond an inside straight that we were trying to draw at that point, but it wasn't like there were no possible outs, as they say in poker.

JOE TRIPPI: That night, John called and said, "Does anybody think there's any way, give me the reasoning for how to keep going, what's the way?" The way was if Obama won New Hampshire, he would be the streaking comet and Clinton would have been in deep trouble. At that point, it's just the way a race happens. The press still has to make it two people, and we would probably have a good shot—in South Carolina or somewhere—as emerging as the other person. This wasn't like Iowa—going after Clinton as status quo. It wasn't trying to figure out how we get a demographic for the long haul. It was, how do we just keep alive? We have a message. We have someone who is doing extremely well at communicating. People are responding to us. But we were fighting two giants. How the hell do you try to stay in there and get by? For us, it probably ended when she won New Hampshire. When you are going through it, you don't realize what the moment may have been, but the final nail was probably Clinton winning New Hampshire.

JONATHAN PRINCE: Then, suddenly, you are actually in the position that the press decided we were going to be in all along.

GUY CECIL: Since we got to talk a lot about why we lost Iowa, I thought I would just add a couple of comments on why we won New Hampshire. I don't think there's any doubt that the debates and her moment on Monday—although we weren't sure at the time how it would play—played a role. I think there were two other factors. First, it was the same dynamic that existed when it was announced that we loaned our campaign five million dollars and the next day was our best fundraising day. It was the flip side of the inevitability argument. Once our folks realized we weren't inevitable and that we actually needed their help—whether it was giving money after the five-million-dollar loan or losing Iowa—there was a dynamic there that changed for us internally as an organization and also changed amongst our supporters. Second, I don't think you would find many people inside the organization through those four or five days that thought we were going to win. But there were a couple of things that we did notice. Number one, we weren't losing ones and twos at any more of a rate than we had been at any normal point in the campaign—5 percent. You always lose folks from the time you ID them three months earlier to the time you call them again a month earlier. So we felt like our numbers, from an organizational perspective, were in fact holding. We knew that there was something wrong and it was either that our numbers were wrong or the poll was wrong, and there wasn't going to be any way to figure that out until the election actually happened. Two, I think Hillary made a decision about how she was going to campaign—taking questions at every stop from the minute she landed on the ground. Despite the fact that, at times, the staff encouraged her to just go in, give the speech, shake hands and get out, she was like, "No, we need to do this differently. I want to answer questions at every stop." We expanded the day, we added more on-the-record interviews—which I know the Obama folks did as well. So I think that it all fed into the story about her saying she found her own voice. All of that played into this role of a different type of Hillary Clinton that I think, one, helped bring women back to the fold for us and, two, changed the dynamic in terms of the way, at least temporarily, that the media looked at her.

JOEL BENENSON: The polls weren't wrong in New Hampshire. We had the race tighter than you did. I think you guys had it at about fifteen. We actually had it at about ten but we saw it tightening on Sunday, which was our last night in the field.

HOWARD WOLFSON: We had it at twelve.

JOEL BENENSON: Twelve? Oh, I thought fifteen. We had it at ten. We saw the last night tightening to eight. We still thought we would win comfortably. We were always cognizant of a certain slice of Independent voters who we thought could bail on the Democratic primary if they thought Obama was winning and get the race they wanted, which was Obama/McCain. We took those out of our Sunday night sample. We then took that group of women—largely white, college-educated women—who we saw overlap in and reweighted them to vote for Hillary Clinton as opposed to Barack Obama. The result came out thirty-eight to thirty-seven for Hillary Clinton, almost exactly what the vote was. I think you won by two points. About the moment on Monday—it wasn't just that people saw that Hillary Clinton needed their help. The media piled on when they saw a woman choke up for a minute, which people do all the time. She got pounded for it. I think these women, who were back and forth on us all the way through New Hampshire, said, "I'm not going to let them run her out of the race for this. Obama's got a comfortable margin. I can give her a little shot in the arm here."

In hindsight—which I continue to get ribbed about by everybody, including the president-elect—I think losing New Hampshire did help us. In fact, the first thing Obama said to me when he saw me afterwards was, "It's better this way, it shouldn't be this easy." We got back to the hotel suite—it was his sister Alma's birthday and we had a cake—he came into the room where we were all gathered, which was our workspace. He came up to me almost immediately. I think he knew I probably felt like crap, and he said, "It's better this way." I think he was right. I think people wanted to see Barack Obama earn this and not glide through in Iowa and New Hampshire. I think it did serve us over the long run.

SUSAN PAGE: To the Clinton folks, was it clear to you, when you heard the first reports of the moment on Monday, that this would be a positive, not a negative? Because the commentary was divided.

HOWARD WOLFSON: No. We were very concerned that it would be a negative. Everybody remembered the Pat Schroeder moment.[12] She was exiting the race at that point, but certainly that was not remembered fondly in American political history. It didn't accrue to her benefit. So there was enormous concern that this was a problem. There wasn't really much we could do about it. We basically said that she was genuinely expressing her emotions, which was the case, and I think it absolutely played to her benefit. I don't know how much of it was the result of the media piling on or how

---

12. On September 28, 1987, Congresswoman Pat Schroeder cried when she announced her withdrawal from the presidential campaign.

much of it was the result of people actually feeling a connection to what she was feeling at that moment and relating to her in that way, but I think it clearly helped us.

GUY CECIL: It seemed like it took eons to actually see the video because, as often happens when you get reports from the field, they vary widely from "she teared up" to "she bawled on camera." Sitting there, we thought this is probably not a good thing.

HOWARD WOLFSON: The first report I got was that she had been weeping.

JONATHAN PRINCE: We heard that she was hysterical.

GUY CECIL: We got just "she was hysterical." That's literally what came across to us.

JONATHAN PRINCE: It was a little much.

• THE SPOUSES: BILL CLINTON •

SUSAN PAGE: Let's go to the role of spouses. Obviously, several spouses played significant roles in this contest. The reason we thought this would be the moment to talk about it is because Bill Clinton's comments after South Carolina caused some controversy. I wonder if you could assess for us the ways in which Bill Clinton was an asset and the ways in which he was a problem for your campaign.

GUY CECIL: Howard, you want to handle the problems? [*laughter*]

HOWARD WOLFSON: Sure. I'll do that easily by just saying he was an unalloyed asset. At the end of the day, it was our view, and you could see it in the way in which we consistently kept deploying him, that he was an asset, that where he went he got votes for us, that he made a strong case for her, that there was a huge segment of the Democratic primary electorate that liked him, related to him and respected him, and we kept using him. Even in the face of an awful lot of criticism about the comments in South Carolina, we kept him out on the road and put him in all kinds of places throughout the country. So it was our view that he was an asset, and I think that was a correct view.

SUSAN PAGE: What about the Obama team—was it your perspective that he was a total asset, or do you think that Bill Clinton caused some problems for Hillary?

DAVID PLOUFFE: Alyssa and I would see his schedules, particularly after February 5—it would annoy the heck out of us because he would be doing six, seven, eight, nine events in areas that we may not get to. I think he was a big help. I think he campaigned very hard. The issue with South Carolina was we were facing February 5, a day that we always feared and thought was lined up for Senator Clinton very well. Our whole strategy was based on trying to develop enough momentum to survive February 5 because we knew we had some good, positive real estate after that. Having lost New Hampshire, it was hard to see how we were going to get that back. We always thought Nevada was going to be hard. I think there was an education moment for the press about delegates that day, but they won Nevada from a raw vote perspective.[13] I think in South Carolina the fact that they contested it so heavily turned it into a meaningful contest. He was down there a lot more than she was. If they had decided we were going to win South Carolina, I don't think we would have had the momentum required to do as well as we did on February 5. So it turned into a meaningful contest—a lot of the polls had it tightening. There was the infamous NBC poll that had us hemorrhaging the white vote and her within striking distance.[14] I know that there were some reporters who thought that we could lose South Carolina. We won it by twenty-eight points. Fairly or not, the coverage said this was a rejection of Clinton tactics. That was our message wheelhouse. Big win, did better with white voters than the press thought, and the coverage was that this was a rejection of Clinton tactics. Then we had Ted Kennedy and Caroline Kennedy come out, and their message echoed that.[15] It was a confluence of circumstances that gave us what we needed, which was momentum. That's not insignificant because it was a big part of how we won the nomination. That aside, I think Bill Clinton was a big asset. I'm actually quite pleased that they did not use him in Iowa like they did in the later contests because if he had been bouncing around those smaller counties, he would have been a big asset. He was a good campaigner. He drew a crowd. He was pretty disciplined, for the most part, except for some rope lines.

---

13. In the Nevada caucuses, Hillary Clinton received 51 percent of the vote compared to Barack Obama's 45 percent, but Clinton received eleven delegates compared to Obama's fourteen delegates.

14. A January 2008 *Wall Street Journal*/NBC poll showed Clinton leading the Democratic race nationally among white voters 53 to 24 percent compared to 40 to 23 percent a month earlier.

15. On January 28, 2008, Senator Ted Kennedy and Caroline Kennedy endorsed Barack Obama for president.

• OBAMA'S ENDORSEMENTS •

MARC AMBINDER: Was the Ted and Caroline Kennedy endorsement the biggest single endorsement that Obama got? The most important?

DAVID PLOUFFE: We never cared too much about endorsements. I think the John Kerry endorsement mattered because it happened right after New Hampshire. Kerry endorses us, Governor Napolitano, Senator McCaskill. That sent a signal because I think most people that night thought it was over. She was okay, Obama had his little moment in Iowa.

MARC AMBINDER: Were they all in the can there, waiting?

DAVID PLOUFFE: We had a plan. I think most of those folks thought they were endorsing the winner of the New Hampshire primary, not the loser, but they stuck with us and so that was important. I think the Caroline Kennedy endorsement and the Ted Kennedy endorsement were very important because we needed everything we could have before February 5 to give us the momentum we needed. And what they said echoed our message. So, yes, if you had to pick one, it was the Kennedys.

GUY CECIL: I remember walking into the war room and every TV for three to four days was Ted Kennedy and Caroline Kennedy. As a single endorsement, if it had happened and it had gone away, but, literally, for days that story was covered, recovered, over and over again, every nuance of it, every conversation that happened between Kennedy and our campaign, why he did it, old tapes of them together. It was a pretty well-covered event leading up to the fifth.

HOWARD WOLFSON: Mark Penn did some analysis internally about how much free media there was around the Ted Kennedy endorsement, and it was, in dollar numbers, some enormous amount of tens of millions of dollars. I think it was generally thought, in our campaign, that the two most important people, outside of your campaign and the Obama family, to contribute to the Obama victory were Ted and Caroline Kennedy.

SUSAN PAGE: David, was there anybody that you thought might endorse you as the winner of the New Hampshire primary who held off when you lost and either didn't endorse you or waited a while?

DAVID PLOUFFE: I'm going to save that for my book. [*laughter*]

SUSAN PAGE: We'll take that as a yes.

DAVID PLOUFFE: I will say this. Almost everybody stuck with us, and we needed that. We were concerned that there was going to be a sense out there that, okay, the world is restored to order, she wins New Hampshire, she is going to be off to the races here. I do think that Kerry and Napolitano and McCaskill were really helpful in that period. It sent the signal that this thing is going to go on for a long time. It was really helpful. It helped us regain our sea legs after New Hampshire.

• THE SPOUSES: MICHELLE OBAMA •

SUSAN PAGE: Let's talk about Michelle Obama, clearly a big asset in South Carolina. But, a few weeks later, on February 18, she made the comment about being proud of America for the first time.[16] How much damage do you think that comment did, and how did you respond to it afterwards?

DAVID PLOUFFE: First of all, she was a huge asset in Iowa. She would actually have Bill Clinton–like schedules. She would go to all these counties, and she would get pretty good turnout and she would convert people. She really was a secret weapon for us in Iowa. She did great work in Iowa, good work in New Hampshire, and good work in South Carolina. She just got Iowa. She liked talking to our precinct captains. She liked talking to the high-school kids. She really connected well in Iowa. So, overall, she was a huge asset. There is no doubt that the "proud of my country" comment took a little luster off for a while. One of the things we were so pleased about was from her speech at the Democratic convention, she gained almost twenty points in favorability and never lost it.

SUSAN PAGE: Before we jump to that, the Clinton people were very candid in talking about how they first heard about the Hillary Clinton moment in New Hampshire and their alarm about it. Can you be similarly candid about how you heard about the "proud of my country" comment and what your initial thoughts about it were?

DAVID PLOUFFE: Our staff who was with her said, "Hey, she just said something that could be picked up." Then we saw it on cable, and it doesn't take much to know you are going to be in the bunker for a little bit on it. Although, honestly, it didn't last that long. It was a couple of days, I think. In the right-wing blogosphere and talk radio, they talked about it incessantly for the whole campaign. But we didn't. For instance, if you look at Ohio

16. On February 18, 2008, Michelle Obama said, "Hope is making a comeback and, let me tell you, for the first time in my adult life, I am proud of my country."

*Joe Trippi, Jonathan Prince, Howard Wolfson and Guy Cecil talk about the race
for delegates.*

and Texas, it wasn't something we were dealing with in those primaries very
much.

SUSAN PAGE: Is that Clinton's view, too—that it was a couple days and
not a big impact?

HOWARD WOLFSON: Yes, actually.

• THE RACE FOR DELEGATES •

MARC AMBINDER: I want to move forward a little bit and get to the
heart of the post-Iowa, New Hampshire, South Carolina, Nevada strategy.
David, you said that if Florida had been treated as a legitimate contest,[17]
three days after South Carolina, and Hillary Clinton had won it, Barack
Obama might not be the nominee. It goes back to a question of strategy
for the Clintons. In 2007, the Rules and Bylaws Committee—which I don't
know if the Clintons necessarily had a majority on it, but they certainly had
a plurality of those who were voting—decided to strip Florida completely of

---

17. In December 2007, after the state legislature decided to move Florida's primary election date to January 29, the Democratic National Committee announced it would not
seat any of Florida's delegates at the national convention and had every candidate sign an
agreement not to campaign in the state.

all of its delegates. And yet, had it been a state that even had half-delegates, it probably would have been really important for Hillary Clinton. Guy, what was the impact of not having Florida count early on to Hillary Clinton's strategy? Was there always a hope that you would win Florida, it would give you momentum into February 5, and that would be the end of the contest?

GUY CECIL: It changed after South Carolina. The effects of South Carolina were deep and long lasting because the campaign made a decision that we were going to contest it and it heightened the importance of it. Rightly or wrongly, one of the narratives that came out of it reaffirmed some of the things that had been written before—wrongly, in my opinion, of course. I was talking to someone about February 5 and the first question I always ask is, "Are you talking about February 5 before South Carolina or February 5 after South Carolina?" I do think the impact was significant for us. We saw it in our polling. There is no doubt that Florida would have been very helpful in stemming that tide, giving us something else to talk about. Winning an election in a big state with delegates allocated to it would have changed the numerical delegate math, which was beginning to develop as a story line for the press, as they were starting to understand the archaic process by which we allocate them. So I think it would have been significant in terms of ending, or at least lowering, the South Carolina discussion to a level that we could deal with. But there is no doubt that we dealt with the repercussions of South Carolina into February 5.

HOWARD WOLFSON: Guy and Harold[18] used to come up and brief me on what they anticipated the delegate allocations were going to be during the process. We had a much more optimistic—I think realistic—scenario about what was going to happen on February 5 prior to South Carolina than we did afterwards. I remember them coming in after South Carolina with a different assessment of what February 5 was going to look like, based on what we were seeing in the polling after South Carolina. So South Carolina had a tremendously important impact on what happened on February 5. Criticism of the campaign has been that there was not a plan B strategy. In some respects, that's unfair. The plan B strategy was that we were going to come out of February 5 with a much bigger lead in delegates than we ended up having. In part, that was because of what happened on January 26.

GUY CECIL: By big, we don't mean hundreds. There was never really that scenario because of the way the delegates are allocated. Whenever you have two candidates that are reasonably well funded, who are competitive, it is very difficult to develop huge delegate leads, and we knew that. It did drop

18. Harold Ickes was a political strategist for Hillary Clinton's presidential campaign.

pretty significantly and started looking like, okay, maybe we win by five, six, ten, maybe we lose by five, six, ten, as that week developed.

MARC AMBINDER: Virtually all of the Obama campaign's delegate leads, though—if you look at the margin of how much they led at the end of the campaign, not on February 5—came on the string of eleven states, many of them caucus states where there was virtually no Clinton presence and a huge Obama presence. The Obama campaign racked up these states and racked up delegates. Looking at the math, it was inevitable that they would do that and, afterwards, it was not impossible but virtually impossible, unless Senator Clinton did much better than demographics would project in later states, for her to win. There has been a lot written about this.

HOWARD WOLFSON: I think that the math looks different on January 25 than it does on January 27. We had anticipated coming out of February 5 realistically, with, I don't know, a hundred-delegate lead, an eighty-delegate lead, a seventy-five delegate lead—with a delegate lead that would have been more or less sufficient to cushion what we anticipated to be a very bad stretch of two and a half or three weeks.

MARC AMBINDER: You did anticipate that?

HOWARD WOLFSON: Oh, yes.

GUY CECIL: We always knew that that three weeks were going to be really bad for us. One, the demographics of those three weeks, in terms of how the election panned out, was not that much different than what it was when we contested some of the states. We knew Louisiana was going to be a difficult election for us. We knew that Maryland was going to be difficult. It wasn't about caucus versus primary alone. It was about the demographics of those individual states that we knew they were going to be problematic for us. One was South Carolina and two was a resource question. I can speak from only October on, when I joined the campaign, but we were doing everything we could just to get through the fifth, which I know people are surprised to hear because, in retrospect, everyone knows what the money situation was. As we were looking at just paying for the fifth, whether it be organizers or TV time, there wasn't much left over for any of those states. So it would have taken a significant amount of money for South Carolina to go differently in order for us to really be competitive during that three-week window. The flaw is the delegate count came out differently after the fifth than we had hoped it would, and so that changed the complete dynamic of the race. We knew that the second half, or maybe the last third, should be better for us and, if we got through the first part—if we could weather that middle ground and then get to Ohio, Texas, et cetera—we would have a chance.

DAVID PLOUFFE: On the delegates, we, for a long time, thought that they would net eighty-five or a hundred delegates on the fifth. It did change after South Carolina. South Carolina has gotten some attention, but in many respects, it was almost as important as Iowa because it did change things. We thought we needed to survive the fifth. We thought we would net a good amount of delegates between the fifth and Wisconsin, and then we would be in a real death struggle after that. We netted fifteen delegates on the fifth, which doesn't sound like a lot. For us, it was a huge deal. The press coverage that night focused a lot on, "Hey, she won the big states." I really thought we were going to be the nominee that night because we knew we had some good real estate coming up. We also knew that, if she stayed in the race, she was going to win a lot of the later states. On the fifth, why did we do so well? The margins—starting to win states over 60 percent. That's the story of the election. Why did we win and why didn't they win? We won more landslides than they did—simple as that. If you win these states fifty-three to forty-six, the delegate allocation is fairly equal. It wasn't just the caucuses. In Virginia, Maryland and Louisiana, we netted a huge number of delegates in big states. We did better on the fifth than we thought we were going to do. Then we had big margins in the rest of those states. We were on a roll. We won Virginia by almost thirty points and in our projections, we had us winning by sixteen. We kept winning by bigger margins than we had projected.

HOWARD WOLFSON: If you look at that period, we knew that we were going to be in unfavorable real estate for us. Combine the fact that it's unfavorable real estate and the fact that we had not made significant investments in a lot of those places because we didn't have the money, and then you add a very difficult media environment in that two-and-a-half-week period, and it all combines to essentially deliver the election to Barack Obama.

SUSAN PAGE: You get to the first part of March, and the assumption on everyone's part is Barack Obama is going to be the nominee. Yet Hillary Clinton comes back and wins Ohio and Texas and, the next month, Pennsylvania. What was the message there? Those were going to be good states for you, and you knew better states for you than the previous set, but was there a message there that there were second thoughts about Obama?

HOWARD WOLFSON: Hillary Clinton was an extraordinarily good candidate. So I don't know if it was so much a referendum on Obama as it was our campaign retooling its message somewhat. One of the things that I think has not gotten enough attention was when John Edwards dropped out of the race, it created some space for us from a messaging perspective. We felt we could make a more populist case to middle-class voters than we had when John Edwards was in the race because that was the space he had occupied. Had we tried to go after that space when Edwards was in the race, it would have been a very difficult struggle to wrest it away from him. So you have John Edwards leaving the race, and you have more favorable terrain for us. You have an infusion of money based on her giving herself the loan. Then, our Internet money comes pouring in, so we have the resources that we need to compete. Our message was much more successful in the latter part of the campaign than it had been earlier.

SUSAN PAGE: There was a time when the arithmetic meant that Hillary Clinton was not going to be the nominee. Was there any thought of "Why stay in?"

HOWARD WOLFSON: Everyone in the echo chamber and the media was asking that question. One of the things I think people came to see about Hillary Clinton is she, constitutionally, is not a quitter. She thought that there was a chance—as long as she was still in the race and Senator Obama had not achieved the requisite number of delegates—that she could be the nominee.

SUSAN PAGE: Was it damaging, Joel, for Senator Obama, looking ahead to the general election, that Hillary Clinton did not get out and that he was losing these big, critical states?

JOEL BENENSON: In hindsight, it was probably less damaging than we thought at the time.

SUSAN PAGE: Talk about what you thought at the time.

JOEL BENENSON: At the time, we thought we were going to have work to do in the general election. David Plouffe was so rigid before Ohio and Texas about keeping us all focused on the fact that this was only about delegates that we didn't actually care that much if we lost these states. We wanted to win them, but it was about how we came out with delegates. We came out of Ohio and Texas in very good shape on delegates that night. They won two big states and it really didn't make a dent in our delegate lead at all. Plouffe was continually keeping us on message about that. He really did force the whole organization to stay focused on that, notwithstanding the echo chamber. On March 4, we probably should have put all our attention in Texas and not worried about Ohio. Had we focused on one state, we'd probably have had a better shot of winning it, and, because of the echo chamber, it might have been a different story coming out of it.

SUSAN PAGE: Why did you not choose to do that smart thing, in retrospect?

DAVID PLOUFFE: We came out of Wisconsin on this amazing roll. Joel polled in Ohio and somebody else polled in Texas. We're down double digits in both states. She was a very strong candidate and was very popular in a lot of these states. We found, particularly in bigger states, that we entered usually with a fairly large deficit. So, we are two weeks out, we just win eleven straight contests, the press is covering us as the likely Democratic nominee, and we are down double digits in both states. As the two weeks go on, we closed the gap. We moved pretty quickly. Some of that was momentum, some was advertising, he's campaigning there, but it was clear all along, demographically, that in Texas, we had a better chance to adjust the electorate— a better chance to get younger voters. Had we spent two-thirds of our effort, time and money on Texas, we might have been able to win. Because we split our time, our scheduling strategy in Texas was all about delegates. We didn't spend much time in the Hispanic communities because those Senate districts offered less delegates. Our view was to just come out of here with our delegate lead maintained. We actually won more delegates in Texas, which was our strategy. But I look back on that with some regret that I was so focused on delegates because if we had been able to outright win the Texas primary, it would have been done. Whenever I think about those three months that the McCain campaign had and we didn't have, it's Texas.

SUSAN PAGE: Is that the biggest mistake you think you made in this campaign?

DAVID PLOUFFE: In the primary, yes, I think so.

JOEL BENENSON: Let me add a point about the big states and about the echo chamber and how it can affect things on a nightly basis. First, I'll talk about Pennsylvania. We had a six-week campaign in Pennsylvania, and we started out down about sixteen or seventeen points. We had six weeks, so we thought we could make it up. We always thought if we got this into single digits, we'd be in good shape. If we could get it down around the mid-single digits, that would be a big win for us. The media set the stakes and set the bar at Senator Clinton needing a double-digit win in Pennsylvania to stay alive, more or less. My guess is she probably would have stayed on anyway. An interesting thing is that all night long on CNN and on MSNBC, the number on the screen was fifty-five to forty-five. You had two hours of dialogue saying she got her double-digit win. By the next morning, it's down to 9.1 or 9.2. Imagine how different the conversation for two hours would have been had all night long it said fifty-four to forty-six. It would have been, "She was denied her double-digit win in Pennsylvania." That had a big impact on the next day. Last point on the big states is that one of the biggest frustrations we had pushing back on was this notion that primary results would be determinative in the general election—both in terms of subgroups and in the kinds of states. We won Pennsylvania by eleven points in the general election—more than Gore, more than Kerry. We won Michigan. We won Florida. We won Ohio. We won states that they didn't win. We never believed that what was happening in the primaries among Democratic primary voters was going to be indicative of what was happening in the general election, so we weren't terribly concerned about that. Our biggest problem, at that point, was a perception in the media that Obama couldn't close the deal because we weren't winning in these states. We thought we were actually doing pretty well in these states most of the time. We would have preferred winning one or two along the way. But at the end of the day, I think campaigning in fifty states helped us, including down through Indiana and North Carolina, where we won by very narrow margins on election day. I don't think anybody in our camp, even though at the time we wanted to be done and move on and start focusing on McCain, would say that having participated fully in those primaries didn't help us in November.

• THE ROLE OF THE PRESS •

SUSAN PAGE: The press has never felt so powerful as around this table because you keep talking about the powerful role of the press. So Marc and I wanted to take a minute to give you a chance to assess press coverage. Everyone except the Obama campaign criticized the press for being in the tank for Obama. Was that the perception that you all had? Howard, I've heard you've been critical of press coverage. [*laughter*] Assess for us the quality of the press coverage in the campaign.

HOWARD WOLFSON: My sense is, from having had private conversations with some of you about this topic, that those of us who have lost don't have much credibility on this subject and that the people who are most biased are, in some respects, us. So I'm going to leave that to others. I'm not going to criticize.

JOE TRIPPI: It is the same every cycle. Sooner or later, the press gives everybody a fair shot for quite a while as they roll around Iowa, New Hampshire and some of those places. They start off fundamentally ranking the first tier, and that's where I think the unfairness comes in. Some in the second tier don't even get a reporter assigned to them. This is just the way it happens every cycle, which means you have to somehow jump to the first tier, which is why the Edwards campaign kept desperately trying to define ourselves as first tier, no matter what the report was.

JONATHAN PRINCE: We had mugs and T-shirts made. [*laughter*]

JOE TRIPPI: The press gets it down to two people pretty quickly. You can see it happening and you're desperately trying to dive between the two of them and get into the mix somehow. If you are with a third-tier candidate, you know what you've got to do. I think Iowa, at least this time around, was a pretty fair shot, except for that division that inevitably happens too early about the separation of the tiers that causes you to have to do something in a debate or something to get attention.

JONATHAN PRINCE: The thing that frustrates you the most—it's not an error of intent—is a shortcutting that happens that doesn't reveal full stories. Joel raised a good example, which is this idea that somehow any candidate's performance in a primary contest has any relationship to that candidate's potential as the nominee in the general election. It's just silly.

HOWARD WOLFSON: In fairness to the media there, that was our message point.

JONATHAN PRINCE: But it wasn't always asserted as your position. It was asserted as fact. There is a desire to make a race about two candidates and to announce what the race is going to shape up as before it shapes up. We always argued we were first tier. As it turns out, we actually beat Hillary Clinton in Iowa. We could have won Iowa, which means, by definition, we actually were a credible first-tier candidate because we could have won the first state. But we couldn't prove that until a year later, affecting our fundraising and our coverage. There tends to be a bit of shortcutting that sometimes happens to make stories have a narrative, which I understand is something you've got to do. I don't have a solution for it.

JOEL BENENSON: At the risk of playing the role of the recovering alcoholic here and, in full disclosure, I am a former journalist and I spent ten years covering politics, I don't think the issue is bias. I love journalists, my wife is a journalist, some of my best friends are journalists. But the point Howard just made goes to the crux of the issue. Journalists are among some of the smartest people I know, and there is a tendency to not be willing to think outside of the conventional wisdom. That's a problem. Secondly, the

Clinton campaign did a masterful job of spinning this, and it boggled my mind that some of the most experienced political reporters in this country thought that somehow because Democratic primary voters were divided among two Democratic candidates in pretty solid Democratic states, they were suddenly going to vote for a Republican. It was bizarre, even the whole Hillary women story that there will be a whole big backlash of Hillary Clinton women not voting for Obama. We have the biggest gender gap since Bill Clinton in 1992. None of that existed, and it just surprises me that folks who I have enormous respect for don't buck against some of the spin and some of the conventional wisdom. I think, going forward, that's a bigger issue than bias. There is always going to be some bias that comes in because it's about the horse race—who raised the most money, who is ahead in this poll.

SUSAN PAGE: Howard, when you were making that spin, did you believe it? Were you surprised that reporters were willing to repeat it?

HOWARD WOLFSON: That's a very good question. If you don't believe it yourself, you can't credibly sell it. So whether or not I believed it or convinced myself of it at some point in the process, I was getting on calls and saying what I thought and what I believed. You get very caught up in this process and become very passionate about it. Unless you are willing to be passionate and believe what you're saying, you are not going to be credible or in any way successful.

GUY CECIL: The number of briefings that we had to do for the media to explain the delegate process was baffling. There were probably two weeks where at least two or three times a day, we did off-the-record briefings—not necessarily on how to win or lose, although obviously that came up, but on how delegates get apportioned. A lot of the confusion about the delegate process and the lack of knowledge about the delegate process—rightfully so, because it is somewhat of a ridiculous process—actually helped us a little bit in that regard and gave us more space to talk to the media in a way that wasn't just about delegates.

SUSAN PAGE: Sheryl, you wanted to make a comment about press coverage?

SHERYL COHEN: Yes, from a little bit of a different perspective. The bias comes into question when you are actually getting coverage, so I mean that's different. [*laughter*] At the risk of making a marketing analogy and turning these guys into products, for candidates who were not in the first tier with the press, this felt a little bit at times like trying to introduce a new cereal against Kelloggs and Post. Kelloggs and Post get the best shelf space in the supermarket because they sell the best. I think that was a huge challenge. Ultimately, you get known by the electorate when you are not known through free media, paid media and grassroots politics. But in terms of free media and press coverage, we really didn't get much. In fairness to the press, I had friends who were reporters who would tell me that they were getting resources cut back, there was only so much staff to go around and there were these two behemoths of a campaign. So that was a huge problem. Secondly, you had advertising revenues that were ten to one. When you are a new cereal trying to introduce against better shelf space and they have better marketing and funds to do that, and the best salespeople want to go and work for Kelloggs and Post, you have challenges. You were reduced to what I call the taste testings in the supermarket, which was retail politics on the ground. So for candidates who didn't have the press coverage or the money or the organization, you still took your shot. I would criticize ourselves. At the end of the day, our product wasn't marketed different enough and better enough to say, "I'm going to change from looking here at this brand and I'm going to go over there." We couldn't come up with a smart enough way to market it to make it different. At some point each of these candidates went, "My God, what do we have to say so differently to get some attention?" There were natural tensions within the campaign because what you didn't want to do is turn yourself into something you didn't recognize at the end of this process. I think it was really to the credit of Senator Biden and Governor Richardson and Senator Dodd that none of them ended up going so far out of the lane and doing something so outrageous or not to the core of who they were as public servants in order to compete. But it was a huge problem, and there were good people who really didn't get known as well as they should have.

VALERIE BIDEN-OWENS: The debates and the grassroots helped with that for us. By all accounts, Joe is a good retail politician. That's why we looked to Iowa a whole lot. I moved to Iowa in August and lived there through January. Where he was, I wasn't. When he went this way, I went that way. That's what we were looking for—a level playing field, the way it used to exist, until these guys were so good to increase the caucus numbers to 240,000 people—which is a good thing for our democracy, but it wasn't good for the Biden organization.

MARK PUTNAM: We did a whole advertising campaign where we made fun of the skepticism among the mainstream media and the decision makers. I don't think Richardson would complain about much of the coverage other than the debates. It would take twenty-five minutes for him to be called upon. There would be a lot of cross-talk between the top three before he would even have a question asked. We were counting the minutes of coverage and sending out press releases about how little chance he had to speak. That was probably the largest complaint that the governor had about the process. Otherwise, he felt he had a fair shake from the print media and the online media.

JOE TRIPPI: It's easy today to forget when a campaign gets so big and it wins, like the Obama campaign, that they were a small campaign with nothing going. It wasn't unlike the Dean campaign in 2004. We were little, we got big, and people tend to remember that and the crash, but they don't remember that we were trying to get attention and said things that actually meant something. The weird thing about this year was Bill Clinton. As stretched as resources were, here we are fighting for our lives in South Carolina, Bill Clinton is running around the state and our entire press plane is reassigned to cover Clinton every time he lands. It was like they were actually sort of megaspouses—Michelle, et cetera—and with the resource problems that the press was having, it was even tougher if you were a second-tier candidate or struggling to stay in the first tier.

MARC AMBINDER: We talked about how the Obama campaign essentially built its campaign as it was taxiing down the runway. The Clinton campaign seemed to land with the fuselage barely attached. Obama overtook the superdelegate[19] lead on May 11, which was one metric that the Clinton campaign used, and then the goal post moves. Then John Edwards endorsed Obama, which, at the time, was a very important endorsement because it signaled, or at least seemed to signal, that the establishment had decided that the race was over. Then Florida and Michigan, by dint of the DNC Rules and Bylaws Committee, get half their delegates back in an interesting compromise.[20] Then Hillary Clinton finally gets out. At what point did she make a decision to stay in until the last votes were counted, regardless of what would happen?

HOWARD WOLFSON: Once we won Ohio and Texas, her heart was pretty set on staying in. If we had lost Pennsylvania, I guess she would have dropped out.

---

19. Superdelegates are delegates to the Democratic National Convention who, instead of being selected based on the party primaries and caucuses, are seated automatically based on their status as a current or former party leader or an elected official.

20. On May 31, 2008, the Democratic National Committee ruled that Florida and Michigan could send all their delegates to the Democratic National Convention and each delegate would get a half-vote. Earlier, Florida and Michigan were told their delegates would not be seated because they moved up their primary dates in violation of DNC rules.

MARC AMBINDER: Did she sincerely believe, up until the day she got out, that she had a chance to be the nominee?

HOWARD WOLFSON: Absolutely.

MARC AMBINDER: What was the thinking there?

HOWARD WOLFSON: The experience of the Clintons in their political lives is that stuff happens and that comebacks are possible, that the media is not always right, that you can be counted out and come back the next day and have a great big victory. Their political life is full of moments like that, going all the way back to when Bill Clinton first ran for office—his first election is unsuccessful, then he wins for attorney general, then he is elected governor, then he loses, then he comes back. Their personal experience was that people are very quick to count you out, that you cannot win unless you are competing, and that politics is a funny business and things happen.

DAVID PLOUFFE: I think if we had been running against John Edwards or Joe Biden at that point, there would have been a little bit different take. There was a belief that the Clintons would find some way to pull a rabbit out of a hat. There was an enormous amount of space given because of that. Some of that was not a great understanding about how all this was going to unfold—that the superdelegates were going to begin to move pretty quickly towards us. There was a belief that, and I think for good reason, the Clintons were the greatest survivors in modern political history and Hillary was campaigning hard. I can't look at the state of Texas on a map without kicking myself, but it went on for three more months. In many respects, that made us a much better general election candidate, but it was frustrating during the time because I do think a wide berth was given, less based on reality, although they were winning contests. At the end of the day, this is a fabric of the campaign. What happened on January 3 is as important as what happened on June 3 because it's about the acquisition of delegates. I thought our delegate position was impenetrable. But there was just a belief that these guys somehow were going to find a way to do this.

HOWARD WOLFSON: In fairness, it's hard to get out when you are winning—when you are out there on the road, on the rope lines, people are coming up to her—"Don't drop out," "We love you," "Keep fighting." She is still getting very large crowds—larger crowds at the end of the primary when she had been given up for dead than John McCain was getting in the general election in some instances. And winning, at least in a couple of states, enormous victories. Her sense that this was possible was also reinforced by what voters were telling her directly and what voters were saying when they went to the polls. It's not like she was in and she kept losing. She was in and was mostly winning—clearly too late.

MARC AMBINDER: The historical record is incomplete when it comes to the negotiations over retiring the debt of her campaign. Did Senator Clinton, at the time, expect that the Obama campaign would use its mechanisms to take care of it, and why?

HOWARD WOLFSON: I was not directly privy to the conversations between the two campaigns, and so I can't answer with specificity. I think it is always the case that there is a hope that the winning candidate will be helpful to the losing candidate, and that has historically been the case, but I can't speak to the specifics of the conversation.

MARC AMBINDER: From the Obama folks, any desire to speak to the specifics of that?

DAVID PLOUFFE: I will not discuss our internal discussions. I would say, for as long as that campaign went on and as strongly as we felt about it,

Joel Benenson, David Plouffe and Alyssa Mastromonaco discuss the vice-presidential selection process.

in the days after she graciously withdrew, most issues were dealt with very easily, and she campaigned very hard for us. I really respect and admire her for that. There was a lot less suspense and tension around these things than people might have thought. We immediately talked about how to get her volunteers involved and hire her staff, and we are continuing to do what we can on the debt.

• SELECTING A VICE PRESIDENT •

MARC AMBINDER: What happened with the vetting for vice president? Did Senator Clinton ask specifically not to be vetted?

HOWARD WOLFSON: That's a question for David.

MARC AMBINDER: Did Senator Clinton ask specifically not to be vetted?

DAVID PLOUFFE: I'm not going to reveal the discussions that the two principals had.

MARC AMBINDER: The way history stands now is a sense that she asked specifically. Nobody wants to go there?

DAVID PLOUFFE: I'm not sure that's how history stands, but I'll let history stand the way it stands.

SUSAN PAGE: Valerie and Luis, I believe that Senator Biden tried to make his case that he would be a good choice as a running mate—that he would bring assets to a ticket. Could you talk a little bit about that period for him? He was out of the presidential contest for some time. What did he do to make his case to the Obama team that he would be a good running mate?

LUIS NAVARRO: The irony of the situation is that, at the very beginning of the process, he made it absolutely clear that he wasn't interested. He was quoted a number of times in the press as saying so. His estimation was that while Senator Obama and Senator Clinton were engaged in the very tough and competitive race for the nomination, and while McCain was wrapping things up very quickly, there was the potential for a circumstance in which Republicans would begin to go after the Democrats on the issue of national security in an attempt to disqualify them as commander-in-chief. As chairman of the Senate Foreign Relations Committee, he worked to ensure that that did not happen—that we were not outflanked. In a series of speeches at Georgetown University and the Center for American Progress, he laid out very clearly, using his credibility both in terms of his relationship with John McCain and also the positions that he had held, to essentially set himself out as the Democratic voice on foreign policy and national security. The intent all along, at that time, was trying to protect the Democratic flank.

SUSAN PAGE: David, tell us what you will about the vice-presidential selection process.

DAVID PLOUFFE: Compared to what our opponent ended up doing in their process, there was a very orderly process. With so much, the primary going long was a benefit, but this is one case where it was a challenge because we were on a compressed time frame. One of the reasons we went to the folks who had done it four years ago[21] was because we didn't have a lot of time. We had to have a whole vetting unit set up immediately, and so Obama went through it in a very orderly way. Alyssa did a masterful job of keeping all of that quiet, through all sorts of cloak and dagger about when and how we were meeting with people. I think Obama spent a lot of time thinking about this. He spent much more time focused on who did he want to be in the White House with, as opposed to who was going to help him. First of all, our orientation was that the vice president historically does not have a huge impact on the election. I think in this case it did, but it was on the other side. It was very unusual that that happened. You didn't want anybody that would hurt you. I was proud of the way he went through it. It was a very personal decision, as it should be. This wasn't a situation where he asked us to gather around the room and we offered our thoughts on who it should be. He certainly bounced things off of us, but it was a very personal decision, and he managed that process in a way that reflected well on him. We were thrilled with our selection. It's been termed a safe selection but, in many respects, it wasn't. From the moment we picked Biden, the press focused on when is he going to make gaffes and how are they going to impact? And he made some comments that became an issue in the election. But if you look at the balance of that, from his first appearance with Obama in Springfield through November 4 on, he filled us out in a way that was very important. Voters said, "That makes sense, we trust Biden, we like his values, we think he's got good foreign policy experience." And he was a great campaigner. Look at Indiana, North Carolina, Virginia, Ohio, Pennsylvania—he would

---

21. Jim Johnson, who chaired the vice-presidential selection committee in 2004 for John Kerry, was selected to lead the process for selecting Barack Obama's running mate. On June 11, 2008, Johnson stepped down from his vetting position after it was reported that he had received loans directly from a company implicated in the U.S. subprime mortgage crisis.

go in there day in and day out and deliver a very strong message. Did he say things from time to time the press would pick up on? Sure, as did Senator Obama, as did Senator McCain, as did Governor Palin. But on the whole, he was remarkably disciplined. We were thrilled with his selection and we think it ended up really helping us. I think vice presidential selections usually don't make the difference, but there is no doubt that Biden could campaign anywhere we wanted him to go. He was great in blue-collar areas and great in rural areas. In many respects, he was a good balance for us because Obama was great out West, with Independent voters and in Northern Virginia. Biden was strong in Ohio and Pennsylvania and Florida. So they were a good complement. If you think about it, in many respects, we had a pseudo running-mate situation in Senator Clinton, who was out there a lot for us and got great coverage. We had a huge benefit from that standpoint. They didn't have Bush out there, so it was really just McCain and Palin. In Florida and Ohio, Hillary did great work for us.

VALERIE BIDEN-OWENS: The way that the Obama campaign handled the vetting process was with a deftness and a clarity—a refined way.

SUSAN PAGE: What do you mean when you say "deftness"?

VALERIE BIDEN-OWENS: Nobody was paraded out. They were disciplined. Nobody auditioned for it. Senator Obama said I'm interested in you. Senator Obama knew Biden. He sat with him on the Senate Foreign Relations Committee. He debated him eleven or twelve or fifteen or however many times. Obama saw what Biden had done as chair of the Senate Foreign Relations Committee by not allowing McCain to take the national security mantle away from the Democrats. My brother had a joke—I don't know who said it originally—one brother ran for vice president, and one went into the Navy, and we haven't heard from either one of them since. But in this campaign, the American public was twice as interested about who the vice president was going to be. Lastly, Senator Obama wanted someone to help him win, which Joe clearly did. But that wasn't it. Senator Obama wanted someone to help him govern after he was there. It was a very fine process.

• THE DEMOCRATIC NATIONAL CONVENTION •

MARC AMBINDER: In general, what were your goals for the period leading up to the convention and for the convention generally? When the convention ended, what threshold did you want Senator Obama to have crossed? How did the convention itself play to that?

DAVID PLOUFFE: First off, from a message standpoint, we still had a lot to fill in about him, even at that late date—who he was, his values, who he was going to fight for. That was a big part of our convention speech and the speeches everyone else made. Michelle's speech obviously was enormously helpful in terms of humanizing him and really filling out his values. Secondly, we thought we needed to lay some wood to McCain. I remember all the commentators, midway through, saying, "It's a disastrous convention, you're not negative enough." These things are four days. The first day we were not going to do a lot of contrast. On Thursday night, he did a lot of contrast, as did the Clintons and Senator Biden. We wanted to lay out, in very clear terms, the differences between these two candidates on the meaningful issues of the day. Thirdly, we wanted to make sure that the party came out fully united. We were well on the path to that. There was a lot of speculation about Clinton and Obama not getting along, about the roll call,[22] about when she was going to speak. The truth is these were very easy, harmonious discussions. We were one unit on this and worked very carefully. One of the amazing things about the convention was Senator Clinton agreed to go to the floor on that Wednesday and move to acclamation. She came down, we were on the nightly news, there was an electricity in the hall. That took us by surprise.

MARC AMBINDER: Having been in a network news control room, the timing was perfect.

DAVID PLOUFFE: That you can control. We thought that would be a good story at 6:30 on Wednesday night. But I think there was a lot of reaction to her doing that. It was, in many ways, closure on the primary. There was an electricity that this is a pretty exciting thing that Barack Obama is our nominee. So we came out of the convention having accomplished really everything. I thought President Clinton and Senator Clinton both gave great speeches. I think Senator Biden gave a great speech. So we hit our marks. There was a lot of discussion about the thing going outside.[23] As a campaign, we were always best when we were on the high wire. We talk about it—going back to doing the announcement in Springfield outside when it

22. On August 27, 2008, Hillary Clinton's name was placed into nomination at the Democratic National Convention and a full roll call was scheduled. Instead, the roll call was cut off after thirty-two states and territories had weighed in when Hillary Clinton moved to make Obama the nominee by acclamation.
23. On July 7, 2008, the Democratic Party announced that Barack Obama would deliver his acceptance speech at the Democratic National Convention at Denver's INVESCO Field, the Denver Broncos' stadium, instead of in the Pepsi Arena, the indoor arena that housed the rest of the convention activities.

was twelve degrees.[24] We were always best when we were on the high wire. I think it helped us regain a little bit of that insurgent feel, and it tested our organization.

MARC AMBINDER: Even the set?[25]

DAVID PLOUFFE: You guys were obsessive about the set.

MARC AMBINDER: Jim Margolis[26] said that when he first saw the set, he was aghast and asked for changes.

DAVID PLOUFFE: We made some minor changes, as we do at events in Ottumwa, Iowa. I remember I did the morning shows Thursday and everyone was asking about the Roman columns. It was a small thing. They were every day talking about small things. There wasn't a single swing voter out there in Ohio or Florida or anywhere else who gave a damn about the set. The fact is it looked great on TV that night, so the people who watched it liked it. People would think the media hoisted us on their shoulders and carried us across the finish line. We had enormous frustrations all throughout the campaign, and that was one moment where we thought the media was giving this way too much attention and was out of sync with the voters.

JOEL BENENSON: Let me add a couple of other things about the convention that we thought about on the way in. One thing we were very conscious of is that we wanted to raise the stakes for voters. We knew that voters thought this was more important than other presidential elections and we believed we benefited the more we could raise the stakes and dramatize for them that this was a critical moment in our country's history—that the choice between change in Senator Obama and Senator McCain, if the stakes were higher, would actually benefit us. The other thing is we were talking throughout the campaign about bringing the country together around a shared common purpose. We did infuse the convention with a lot of real people. They didn't make it into a lot of prime-time TV, but we generated a lot of local news coverage by having people speak at the Democratic National Convention. We had little snippets—sixty-, ninety-second segments—that

24. On February 10, 2007, Barack Obama announced his candidacy for president on the grounds of the Old State Capitol in Springfield, Illinois.
25. On August 27, 2008, Republicans sent a memo to the press criticizing the set of Barack Obama's convention acceptance speech at INVESCO Field, comparing it to a Greek temple and advising the press of proper attire at "The Temple of Obama," or "The Barackopolis."
26. Jim Margolis, a partner at GMMB, was a senior advertising strategist for Barack Obama's presidential campaign.

got us a lot of coverage in states like Ohio, Florida, and Pennsylvania. My favorite was Barney Smith,[27] who got big cheers on Thursday night at the convention. The last piece we did was we had a featured Republican every night. We knew that in 2004, the Bush campaign did a masterful job of bringing in their kind of outside, independent, free-speaking, free-thinking Republicans—Governor Schwarzenegger, Senator McCain and Mayor Giuliani. Those were their featured speakers, and they got mileage out of that. We wanted to do something that related to our message about bringing the country together and breaking down partisanship. So every night we had a Republican, starting with Representative Jim Leach of Iowa on the first night.

SUSAN PAGE: Obviously, a lot of those things worked well for you. Was there anything at the convention that did not work as well as you had hoped?

DAVID PLOUFFE: My orientation was, there are going to be four speeches here that really matter—maybe a fifth if you count President Clinton—so let's really get those right. I think we did a good job of that. But we didn't do a good enough job of thinking through, "Let's have a real person at 10:05." If you look at the coverage we got back in the battleground states off the people we featured, it was terrific. So that mattered a lot. But, the networks—even the cable networks—wouldn't cover these people. We had [Montana] Governor Schweitzer, who gave a great speech, and eventually everyone broke to him because something was happening in the hall, but no one was covering him in the beginning. We probably mishandled the choreography there in terms of thinking, every moment, who actually will get covered? We probably didn't do a good enough job outside of the major speeches of thinking through that. It's a minor thing, but it was a source of frustration because I thought we made a mistake there.

The other thing about the outside convention was that we thought it was consistent with our grassroots campaign, and I think that came through. This was the state of Colorado. If we won those electoral votes, John McCain couldn't be president. Our organization was immeasurably strengthened by that convention and the people who attended it, and if that was all it did, it was worth any criticism we got because John McCain could not win the presidency without winning Colorado. That was a big difference between our two campaigns in the general election—we focused on individual states and they tended, in our view, not to.

---

27. On August 28, 2008, one of the convention speakers at INVESCO Field was Barney Smith, a Midwest factory worker whose job was outsourced to another country. He said, "We need an America that puts Barney Smith before Smith Barney."

MARC AMBINDER: I want to end this in a slightly unusual way. One of the more memorable moments of the Democratic convention was the appearance by Senator Ted Kennedy. Joe, your reaction to that at the time was very interesting, and I'm wondering if you could give your thoughts on that moment and how it mattered to Democrats in particular.

JOE TRIPPI: First of all, I thought his and Caroline's endorsement was a powerful moment that changed the dynamics in a way that made it very difficult for anybody to get near Obama. There are a number of people in this party who have organized out there for years in the grassroots who were motivated by Ted Kennedy back in the seventies and eighties. Those people come of age and here he is, making this dramatic entrance and dramatic speech. It was really one of the most moving moments. It got a lot of coverage and was an amazing moment at the convention.

MARC AMBINDER: Well, we are approaching the end of our time here, but I think we managed to do so many topics and we didn't even touch on Reverend Wright or Rielle Hunter.

David Plouffe, Dan Balz, Jonathan Prince,
Howard Wolfson and Guy Cecil gather during a break.

The General Election   5

BILL PURCELL: This is our last panel and the logical conclusion to all that we've been thinking about and talking about together. Our moderators are the perfect two people for that purpose. Jeanne Cummings has covered politics at every level—state government, local government, federal government, five presidential campaigns—and she currently is the chief lobbying and money correspondent at *Politico*, overseeing team coverage in both these areas. The other moderator is John King, who is CNN's chief national correspondent.

Politico's *Jeanne Cummings and CNN's John King*
moderate a discussion on the general election.

• CHOOSING THE VICE-PRESIDENTIAL NOMINEES •

JOHN KING: We are going to go through the general election. We heard a lot in the Democratic session about the primaries and a lot in the Republican session about the primaries. I think we should start with the two most relevant questions in the general election, which were, do you support the Bush Doctrine[1] and what newspapers do you read?[2] [*laughter*] Some of them are laughing. We are going to actually start with the vice-presidential selections and how you looked at them from a general election standpoint and how they would help you. What we most want to get into is what the other side thought of the calculations the other team was making. Since we did have the Biden selection first, I want to start with the Obama campaign. When you are making this selection, after going through your list—and you can share your list in more detail, if you care to, for the record, now that it's over—why Joe Biden, from a general election standpoint, knowing that you are going up against John McCain, and at that point, unknown?

DAVID PLOUFFE: Even though the election is over, I will still say that the way he made this decision was more about what would happen after the election than before the election. Part of that was our belief that a running mate—certainly you wanted them not to hurt and maybe help a little—at the end of the day wouldn't fundamentally alter the election. So he really spent a lot of time thinking about, if he were to be elected, who did he want to spend those four or eight years with? That's not to serve him well in the aftermath. That's just the way it went down. Partially, because there wasn't anybody there that we thought, from an electoral standpoint, was really going to deliver a state—even [Virginia] Governor Tim Kaine or [Indiana] Senator Evan Bayh. We just didn't subscribe to that. We looked into it a little bit, but it just wasn't going to make that much of a difference. So all things being equal, he got to know Biden pretty well in the Senate and during the campaign. He spent a lot of time talking to him about Iraq and foreign policy issues. He was very comfortable that he would be a good counselor and real added value in the White House. We thought that, despite some of the issues from 1988 that he had, the 2008 campaign had been relatively gaffe free, with a couple of exceptions. We watched him carefully in Iowa, he had a good stump speech, delivered it consistently, and was very good in the

---

1. The Bush Doctrine is a phrase used to describe the foreign policy principles of President George W. Bush. In an interview with ABC News' Charlie Gibson on September 11, 2008, Sarah Palin, when asked, "Do you agree with the Bush Doctrine?" responded, "In what respect, Charlie?"

2. In an interview with CBS News' Katie Couric that aired on September 30, 2008, when asked to specifically name any newspapers and magazines she reads, Sarah Palin responded, "All of them, any of them that have been in front of me over all these years."

debates. The vice-presidential debate is the most important moment because you have to assume they are going to give a good convention speech when they are nominated. The one high-wire moment is the debate, and we really did think he would do well in that debate. So from a political standpoint and an electoral standpoint, that was the major factor. We thought that in that one big moment, he is going to shine. And we thought he rounded out Obama pretty well—lots of Washington experience, a blue-collar person, someone that blue-collar voters responded well to in the beginning and over the course of the campaign. I think he ended up with the best fave/unfave ratio of the four people—well, maybe not, Obama did—but anyway, it grew. He started out pretty well and it got better. There wasn't a lot of eventfulness to it. He went through a process. In the beginning, we didn't have a favorite, meaning there was nobody in the pole position. The process unfolded and I think that he made what, in retrospect, was a very good selection, but it wasn't something that was so clear either. He really wrestled with it and ultimately—I'm sure that Senator McCain did this as well—it's a very personal decision, which I think it should be. While he would consult us on what we thought, this was his vote and this was not something where if two or three of us said, "We think that's a bad idea," he would necessarily listen to us. It's a very personal decision.

JOHN KING: Rick, when I and other reporters were calling into your campaign the day Biden was chosen, there was this sense that Clinton would have been worse. Was that spin, or was that a true belief that if he picked Hillary Clinton, she would have been stronger from an electoral college perspective? Was that just spin to kick their choice a little bit, or was that a genuine feeling?

RICK DAVIS: Probably all of the above. What we were anticipating was somebody who would reinforce the brand that they had already achieved, which was this change agent. What David said is exactly what we assumed would be their strategy, which is they didn't want to fundamentally change the race—they were winning. You don't want to change a race that you are ahead in. We had exactly the opposite problem. We had to fundamentally change the race. Everybody goes into a postprimary general election period thinking that one of the lessons we have to learn about vice-presidential selections is do no harm, because the do no harm ones tend to get elected more often than the more speculative ones. But that is because people who select candidates for vice president who are more of a gamble are doing so usually because they are behind, and people who come out of their conventions behind usually stay that way and lose elections. From our perspective, we were surprised it was such a conventional pick. We thought the danger with Clinton would be that it would redefine their brand as more of the same. It was the same thing we were having trouble with since, by then, you would have thought our running mate was George Bush. We were surprised it was a traditional pick. We were surprised it was somebody from the establishment—another senator, not a governor. But we also thought it was probably a safe pick. There was nothing there, other than a couple of good reels of video, that you could laugh about in the morning. There wasn't much else there. Our hope would be that Biden would give us things to talk about along the campaign trail. He did his best, but it wasn't good enough. We needed a little bit more from him. [*laughter*] We saw it as a tough one to criticize because what would be the point of that? I think that was part of the design. I don't want to guess what they were up to, but it was not a news story and it wasn't going to be for the balance of the election unless something extraordinary happened. And they are probably the best campaign I have ever seen at making sure nothing unusual happens. No mistakes is a good way to run a presidential campaign.

JEANNE CUMMINGS: I'm curious about how much debate there was in your campaign about picking Hillary Clinton as the vice-presidential candidate.

DAVID PLOUFFE: Senator Obama and some of us have spoken about this over time.

JOHN KING: Which is why we are asking again. [*laughter*]

DAVID PLOUFFE: I probably won't add too much to it.

JEANNE CUMMINGS: Can you do a little bit more than that?

DAVID PLOUFFE: I think that he thought about Hillary quite a bit. We had a very competitive primary and it went on a long time, and we definitely had knives drawn there for a few months. That being said, when you share what we went through with these guys across the table, even though we were in a pitched battle, it's something that's unique and you appreciate what they went through and the effort that they put into it. The candidates go through this together—Barack and Senator Clinton debated themselves four or five times and traveled through fifty-four primaries and caucuses. They had a good relationship before he decided to run. It was a little frosty there after that. But he thought that she had, from a qualifications standpoint, few rivals in terms of being the vice president. There were a lot more complications, potentially, in terms of the campaign. But at the end of the day, I think he thought a lot more about her than people think, and therefore she was always somebody that was in the discussion. There is this notion that we never vetted her. I'm not going to get into a lot of the detail, but the truth is we ran against her for sixteen months. We had fifteen people doing research on her. Sure, there was some information we would need to acquire from her if she was really about to be selected, but we had vetted her pretty thoroughly. We had a pretty good sense of what information we still needed and knew a lot of the issues. As you can see by his selection of her to be Secretary of State, he thinks she is an immense talent and can make a real contribution.

JEANNE CUMMINGS: Speaking of the Secretary of State issue, President Clinton had to agree to a variety of limitations in his private business and philanthropy. Would those restrictions had to have been put on him if she had become the vice-presidential candidate? Would that have been a complication? To what degree did his presence weigh into those debates?

DAVID PLOUFFE: If she had been selected, I'm not sure all of the steps would have to have been taken, but a lot of them would have been. By the way, he said if she won the nomination, he would have taken a lot of those steps himself. There is no doubt that if she was to be selected, it would not have been survivable for things like his donor records not to be released, given the spotlight we had shone on that during the primary. It would have been hard not to do that, so I think there would have to have been some accommodations made.

JEANNE CUMMINGS: Do you think they could have been accommodated at that time?

DAVID PLOUFFE: I don't know. I assume so because things have moved pretty quickly now.

JOHN KING: Let's move on to Sarah Palin, and I want to do this in reverse order, just to try to get a little bit more enlightenment than we received in the earlier sessions. I want to start with the Obama campaign. You are leaving Denver, you had a great night, your speech to eighty thousand-plus people, you are the Democratic nominee, you are rolling out of your convention, and before you can pretty much get a plane on the ground, the Alaska governor is John McCain's running mate. When you get that word, what is the first thing you are saying about that choice?

DAVID PLOUFFE: It was the Friday after our convention, and we knew it was coming. I give them an enormous amount of credit for keeping that quiet. We had done some research on Governor Palin—we had researched probably a dozen Republicans—but she certainly wasn't someone at the front of the list, and we were taken by surprise. It was 6:30 in the morning, or whenever it came out, Mountain Time, and we were taken aback. Our first reaction was we had to do a lot of work. Our second thought was, wow, they had been running on experience for the whole campaign, and that was taken away. We had some people in the campaign who had worked against her in Alaska and they said do not underestimate her political skills—she is going to give a great speech this afternoon in Ohio, she is going to debate well, and she is going to give a good convention speech. So, from the get-go, we thought that it was going to provide them challenges because it caused them, in many respects, to abandon the message they had built up over a period of months, but we thought she would probably be a formidable campaigner.

JOHN KING: What did your candidate say when he was told?

DAVID PLOUFFE: I know Senator Biden said, "Who is Governor Palin?" or "Who is Sarah Palin?" [*laughter*] We were all surprised. You spend as much time thinking about your opponent as you do yourself, so we were trying to get in their heads, saying, "What were they thinking here? How is this going to play out?" We were a campaign that liked to be in control of things. At that moment, we were not in control of the compelling dialogue of the campaign, and that was an uncomfortable couple days because it took a little while to figure out how we were going to handle this.

JOEL BENENSON: We did whittle our list down from about ten or twelve to about five. Most of the five had some tactical political advantages—a state that would either bolster the McCain campaign or put us on defense in a state, say Governor Pawlenty in Minnesota or Romney in Michigan. The pick of Palin said, okay, they are not playing a tactical game with this choice—they were really going to try and recapture the change message. She had a lot of appeal on that front. She was young. She was a woman. She was going to get a lot of press attention right away. We did think it was a bit of a long pass in the sense that it is very difficult for the vice-presidential candidate to redefine the top of the ticket. We were making the case very strongly that John McCain was more of the same. It was going to be very hard to rely on your number two to totally transform that. We made a decision at the outset, because we were caught off guard, to not focus on her. We made a decision to focus on McCain—that they'd undercut what we thought was an experience message. Our first response was to talk about the kind of decision he had just made—putting someone who was completely untested a heartbeat away from the presidency.

JEANNE CUMMINGS: Why did you initially even research her?

DAVID PLOUFFE: We researched a lot of people, but we did not give her the same amount of scrutiny towards the end. She wasn't someone we spent as much time looking at as Romney. That week in Denver, we were actually throwing some arrows at Romney because we thought he might get picked. We were excited about that because we thought they would double down on the wrong economic philosophy—how many houses and all that.[3] [*laughter*]

We had done some preliminary research on her, but we were far less prepared, from a research perspective, for her than we were for most of the other people on the list. From the beginning, as much as she energized their base, and that lasted all the way through November 4, she provided us an enormous spark from the get-go. Why did we raise $150 million in September instead of $120 million? It was Sarah Palin. Why did our volunteer hours boost in September? It was Sarah Palin. It helped us both from an organizational and financial standpoint.

JOHN KING: Rick or Trevor, take us in that room because you had to know that picking her would address some needs you had but that these guys would say right away that she undercuts the experience argument and she is untested. Air out here the debate that you had amongst yourselves when you got to the point where it was clear that it was down to one or two people or that it was most likely going to be her, once you got over the comfort threshold.

TREVOR POTTER: Before you go there, could I just follow up on that last comment about Romney? Who did you most fear we were going to pick and who did you hope McCain would pick, in terms of who you thought was going to be vulnerable to you all?

DAVID PLOUFFE: It's such a dynamic process. You don't know how these things are going to play out. A lot of what we thought about Palin in the beginning didn't play out the way we saw it. We probably feared Pawlenty the most because he's from the upper Midwest, which was another electoral strength for us. We thought that perhaps he could eat into that a little bit.

---

3. On August 20, 2008, John McCain said in an interview with *Politico* that he was uncertain how many houses he and his wife Cindy owned. He responded, "I'll have my staff get to you. It's condominiums where—I'll have them get to you."

JOEL BENENSON: Or, if your party could have gotten over the choice issue, Tom Ridge would have doubled in on McCain's national security experience.

RICK DAVIS: The experience versus change issue—they ran a primary on that, and change won. We paid a lot of attention to that. A lot of the way the election was framed, up until that point in time, was an experience versus change election. That's what they wanted. They knew how to win that. The trap that we had to not fall into was playing the experience game, because fifty-two to forty-eight, experience is going to lose to change every single time. This is a point that Bill McInturff made to us very early in the primary after the win. We had a lot of time to get ready, and this was one of the biggest problems we had—the discipline of not falling back on what was the easy argument to make. Frankly, it was the one that the press narrative wanted because they were in the middle of that at the same time with Hillary and Obama.

BILL MCINTURFF: There is a wonderful de Tocqueville quote in *Democracy in America*. He is describing the American character, and he said Americans are the only people in the world who would build a dream house and move in before the roof is finished. My point is that in America, if you have a proven failure and an unknown risk, Americans will take the unknown risk over the proven failure. We were in a situation where the dynamic of this election was that people decided that the Bush era was not working and we needed a very different direction for the country. We had seen in Reagan in 1980 and in other elections that when you have 75 percent wrong track, two-thirds of wrong-track voters vote for the new person. That's 48 percent of the election, and you already lost. When reporters would say, "What do you have to do to win?" I said, "You have to, one, be very different than Bush, two, have your own economic agenda, and three, disqualify Barack Obama." "And what do they have to do?" I said, "They've got to be the change candidate who is acceptable and not risky." They said, "That's real easy and yours is real hard." Yes, that's why if we run the race ten times, they are going to win seven or eight out of ten. The other thing is we tracked a series of dimensions. In July, our candidate was up by twenty-five to twenty-eight points on commander-in-chief and up by thirty points on experience, but we were losing the election by eight or nine points. If people value the commander-in-chief and experience and you have those attributes by twenty-five to thirty points and you are losing by eight, you've got some demonstration that those attributes are not driving the ballot. At that time, in July, the way we framed it was, "We can bring real change to Washington," and we were losing that attribute by thirty-one points. We were getting totally hammered. Almost a majority of Republicans were saying that Barack

Obama will do that, not John McCain. By the time they made the VP pick, we had almost tied the ballot, and we had gone from negative thirty-one in July to about negative twenty-three in late August on "can bring real change to Washington." And then, within a week, we were down fifteen, and fifteen is sustainable. These gentlemen and ladies have talked about, "Why were you playing on our turf?" My point was you can lose the change turf by fifteen to eighteen points and, because of your strength somewhere else, you might be able to cobble a way to win. If you are down thirty points on change in this election, there is no way to win. So you end up being dragged to their turf because you have to be competitive enough on change to get close enough that you have a chance to put something else together.

RICK DAVIS: In that context, the idea was that we really didn't have the luxury of sitting back on the experience argument, and so we had to fight over a period of time—really starting in July, August and September—for the change concept. We knew we were fighting on someone else's turf. It violates all these great rules of politics that you are taught at an early age of "pick your turf that's the most favorable field," but we didn't have that choice. We knew, fundamentally, that there were some ways to do that. We weren't without resources and we had a great candidate. A fundamental thing we haven't really talked much about is when we went into July, and that was at a period of time when the Obama campaign had just won a month earlier. They were out there consolidating his image and fixing problems they had on commander-in-chief. We started a very aggressive effort to try and not only redefine our campaign but redefine theirs. That was the whole Celebrity series—what we did in advertising to try to take their strength and turn it into a weakness. That ran up to the convention. When we are looking at what ideas we want for vice president, it was all in the context of running a two-tiered strategy to reformat the race from our side but also to try and change the dynamic on their side. It was not only that we were running against them but that we were running against the Bush administration that continued to be active in the press. The Obama campaign was very good about controlling the agenda and had relatively good media headwind, following the nomination, historic as it was. At a time when we had to start changing the dynamics—since the election was so late and the conventions were so late—we knew we didn't have much time to spare in September and October—we had to do something then. So as we looked at these lists—the same lists that everybody has debated—who gives you that change? Who can bring back the maverick status? The way we got to change is the history that John McCain had all along in Congress. People had forgotten the fact that he has been sort of everybody's worst enemy in Congress. He fought for change throughout his career—that actually cost him politically. So we thought, "Okay, we've got a narrative here that we can support with history that we remember from 2000 and earlier in our campaign when John was the maverick, he appealed to cross-over Independents and even some Democrats, and we need to get back into that mode." We hadn't been able to shrug that post-Republican primary, so we thought that was the window for us to do that. Mitt Romney is a great guy and turned out to be a huge ally for us. But he doesn't fit that bill. He fits a lot of different bills but not that one. Frankly, a lot of core Republicans aren't going to get into that space.

JEANNE CUMMINGS: What about Governor Pawlenty? Pawlenty could have done some of that.

RICK DAVIS: Some.

JEANNE CUMMINGS: Why was Palin preferable to Pawlenty?

RICK DAVIS: Because she is a maverick. There were a few people walking around, saying, "Pawlenty is a maverick," but she was one. She fought corruption. She fought her own party. When you look at her narrative history—dial yourselves back to pre-August 29—and you examine Palin's record, you see a lot of John McCain in her. You see a woman who fought through a lot of party struggles for her own success. She was immensely popular in her own state and willing to challenge people on issues of corruption in her own party. These are enormously positive attributes in our political time—probably even more important today than they were in August. So, ironically, rather than finding somebody who was different than John McCain, we actually found someone who was very similar to John McCain.

JEANNE CUMMINGS: Tell us about the vetting process because there are lots of questions about that. How many times did McCain meet with her? Who did the vetting on her and how much time was invested?

RICK DAVIS: All that stuff is public record. Those answers have been given. People don't like the answers, but they have been given. [*laughter*] Let me apologize in advance—I will give you exactly the same answers. These campaigns are a reflection of the candidate and every one of them is different. The way that they did the selection process is probably different than the way we did it. Why? Because Barack Obama is a different kind of guy and likes to make decisions in a different way than John McCain does. John McCain's way is probably significantly different than the way Jimmy Carter or Ronald Reagan or George Bush did it. If you are smart, you go to them and you say, "How would you like to make this decision?" Then, they tell you and you do what they tell you to do, and that's really a great way to run a process. The way John McCain makes decisions, and he has been doing it for thirty years in full public view, is that he keeps his own counsel. He gets input from a lot of different sources and then he makes up his mind. He doesn't have to get twenty-five different people to come into a room, and he doesn't read polls. When he makes up his mind, you may or may not know what his mind is but, more times than not, he'll let you know.

BILL MCINTURFF: I do this very simple checklist on the vetting question and I say, "What came out about Sarah Palin that the campaign did not know about in advance?" And the answer is, "Nothing." So was the vetting process successful? Yes. My other point to people is, and I'm sure not going to give the examples here, they went through a vetting process for all these candidates. As a function of that process, I know more about some of the potential downsides and things that aren't particularly well known about all of these potential picks. What we are not talking about is if we had picked so and so, he or she would have had these downsides and there are some things you don't know about them, there are some stories you don't know, there is some baloney that has already been looked at but not looked at in depth. A VP goes through extraordinary scrutiny. So there is one standard—did anything come up about Sarah Palin that this campaign did not know about prior to her being picked? And the answer is no. She was very honest. She disclosed information. They asked the right questions, and they made a determination based on those advantages versus those downsides and the potential downsides of the other picks that were also going to be revealed. For all this talk about vetting, the definition of vetting is were you surprised by something that came out, and the answer is no.

JOEL BENENSON: Let me make a point about the words *maverick* and *change*. Our first moment of worry about the McCain campaign trying to play back on the change territory came about two and a half weeks before Sarah Palin was picked. They put out an ad called the "Original Maverick." McCain gave a stump speech that we looked at, and we said if this is where they are going, this is going to be a tough contest. It was a great stump speech. He went back to taking on Washington in a very clear and crisp way. We were very concerned about that at that point. We tested whether or not people thought McCain was a maverick. We knew from the beginning of the general election campaign that voters did not have this legacy recollection of John McCain as a change agent, even though 2000 was only eight years ago. We came out of the primaries with a much better-defined image than John McCain did, particularly on change attributes. When they started using the word *maverick*, we said, "Do they know something we don't know?" We actually probed it in a couple of focus groups, and then we tested it as a quality in a poll—who is a political maverick? Actually, 19 percent said it applied to Obama and 17 percent to McCain—very low numbers for either one of them—so it was a term we never really worried about. For us, voters had no real attachment to the word. Then they used it a lot after the convention and never got back to that stump speech. For all the talk about being mavericks, that stump speech got put aside. Maybe it was because of the exigencies at the time, but that was kind of a relief to us because we really looked at that speech and said this is where he needed to be.

FRED DAVIS: One thing that I said when we were discussing vice presidents was, it's one thing to keep saying you are a maverick, it's another thing to "do mavericky things," to use the *Saturday Night Live* term. [*laughter*] Rick would not tell me that it was Sarah Palin, and I tried every trick in the book to find out. I remember finding out Friday morning, the same time you did, David, and I'm on the West Coast, so it was really early for me, and there was a brief pause for a moment, and I said, "Well, they solved the mavericky problem." [*laughter*]

JEANNE CUMMINGS: How much debate was there within the campaign over Lieberman?

RICK DAVIS: First of all, we didn't have any debate on anybody. The point I was trying to make is that our process was not a process full of debate and discussion. We had a lot of research done by a very competent lawyer in Washington, A. B. Culverhouse, who operated in perfect anonymity until John McCain announced that he was doing vetting. [*laughter*] Our only leak on the entire process was John bragging in the back of the plane one night—at which point, A. B. informed me that he would just as soon find something else to do until we convinced him that his anonymity would be respected. What I was surprised by is that very few people in the press bothered him. It was like now everybody knew where all the information was, but nobody bothered asking him what was going on. Now, the few that did, he didn't respond very well to.

JOHN KING: That's correct. [*laughter*]

RICK DAVIS: He had a very expansive, very professional operation that did exactly what we asked him to do, and that was to probe every aspect of our candidate's financial, health, business and personal life, and prepare that material for John McCain.

JOHN KING: But there was this narrative that developed that you guys essentially had to go and shake McCain—"You can't pick Lieberman, I know you love him, he is your friend, but we don't have our base with us, the convention would be a disaster. You can't do this, Senator."

RICK DAVIS: That was a narrative made up by the media. There were a lot of people outside of our campaign who lobbied on all of these things. I'm not saying it was an illegitimate narrative by the media, but it wasn't a narrative that was actually realistic inside our campaign. There was never a debate inside our campaign on this issue. There was a very small discussion that went on, on a daily basis, with the senator, but very little inside the campaign. We were in a bit of a trap. You couldn't do an announcement before the Democratic convention because then the one unique thing that you have between now and election day is blown. We expected to be ten points down when we came out of the Democratic convention and ours was that next Monday. You wanted to have some run-up to your own convention. We also realized that because of the unique nature of the speech and the press coverage, the worst possible thing that could ever happen is for it to leak out in advance of Obama's speech, because then it is yesterday's news before it even makes news. We realized, as a campaign that had not been particularly good at keeping secrets—in fact, we were probably the worst political sieve in American history [*laughter*]—we had to try and do things a little bit differently, and we did. When we would read and hear about these big debates going on in our campaign, we knew we were being successful, and our attitude was let those debates go on. Probably 60 percent of the published reports on our process were 100 percent inaccurate, including on

*Sarah Simmons and Trevor Potter remember the challenges
facing the Republican National Convention.*

some of the people we were looking at. We loved it. Everyday somebody who was wrong was in the press was a good day for us because we knew they would then have to go out and commission some research on that person and make sure they had them on the list. It worked. We never complained. I don't think you heard a lot of people arguing with the media about their coverage—it was just not accurate.

• THE CONVENTIONS •

JOHN KING: Let me ask about the conventions. When you are watching each other's convention, was there a theme, a moment, a speech or a person when you said, "Damn, that's good and that's going to be a problem."? Or was there something you saw as a weakness on their part or a mistake and said, "There's an opportunity."?

RICK DAVIS: We knew Thursday night was going to be a great night for them. We think that Barack Obama is probably the great communicator of our lifetime. He can get on TV and give a speech to 100,000 people—which is an incredibly hard thing to do—that looks intimate and connecting. The production effort on that was immense, and we knew that was going to be good. We were surprised about the other three nights because they owned his change label and it was their franchise. And prime-time Monday, Tuesday and Wednesday was the Clintons and the Kennedys—everybody who you already heard from. We really thought there would be something dazzling and unique. In fact, we were hoping on it because that would play to our celebrity theme that we were trying. It disappointed us that they were so traditional in their construct. That was surprising to us because we would sit around thinking, "What's Oprah going to do on Tuesday night? It's going to be so cool. We wish we had Oprah." [*laughter*] Don't think all of this is literal, please, I can't help myself. Then we got the list and it was like, "Wow, this is exactly what you would expect a Democratic nominee for president to do." These are the former presidents. I mean, what do you do with Carter? I thought it was very traditional, except for Thursday night and then, boom, that's the only thing anybody remembers from their convention, which maybe was the construct.

JOHN KING: Anything you particularly loved from their convention?

RICK DAVIS: You had to be disappointed Bush didn't come.[4] [*laughter*]

---

4. Due to concerns about approaching Hurricane Gustav, President Bush and Vice President Cheney canceled their attendance at the Republican National Convention.

JOEL BENENSON: We knew the hurricane was on its way and, given John McCain's penchant for the dramatic, we sensed that no matter what was going to happen, they were going to find a way for Bush not to be at their convention on Monday night. Then that whole night got canceled. The hurricane was a real threat in a part of the country, so I don't think that surprised us. We were anticipating that if they had an opportunity to avoid him, they would. It's not an easy thing to do. Without the hurricane, I think President Bush would have been at the convention. I don't think anything surprised us. Some things tonally surprised us, in some of the speeches, but I don't think anything other than that.

DAVID PLOUFFE: We thought McCain's speech would have had a little bit more separation and a little bit more of, "I'm going to go down and burn down Washington," in it. We were pleased that it didn't. We dial-tested the speech, and it didn't bother us that much. Palin's speech dial-tested pretty well. People received it quite well. But the McCain speech did not test as strongly as we might have anticipated. We were pleased by that. Wednesday night and Thursday were our best fundraising twenty-four hours of the entire campaign, going back to the reverse Palin effect.

JOE ROSPARS: Yes. Specifically, and this was a small thing that I think a lot of people missed and didn't discuss, but both Giuliani and Palin attacking community organizing and our volunteers was something that seemed like a throwaway part of that night for you guys but which got us around twelve million dollars between the time she left the stage and the time he left the stage the next night. We just went to town and said, "They are attacking you, they are attacking this notion that you can be involved in the political process," and that was something that really struck a chord with our supporters.

TREVOR POTTER: I don't think you can really have this discussion without noting the extraordinary circumstances of the Republican convention because when everyone was arriving over that weekend and the McCain senior team was meeting with the convention team, they did something that's never been done in our lifetime. They threw the script out the window and said, "We don't know what we are going to do, we've got a hurricane coming." As the Republican party, we cannot have an opening night of the convention while the hurricane is hitting New Orleans. It wasn't just Bush. Monday night went. At the time, there was no sense about whether Tuesday night went. We had a serious legal discussion about what happens if we don't have a convention. How would the nominee actually get certified if the destruction was so bad, which was possible with the hurricane, that the country didn't want to watch a convention? What would you do?

We went into a situation where the first thing was to cancel Monday and then to say, "We are going to let you know if we are going to do something Tuesday or Wednesday." We talked about moving all these speeches around and maybe we could have the nomination on Wednesday night and the speech on Wednesday. Bill Harris, a political operative who has done these conventions for thirty years, said, "This is unique—I've always come in with briefing books but none of them were from the National Weather Service." [*laughter*] And there is a second hurricane coming at the end of the week, and if we really get this wrong, we'll have a hurricane on Sunday/Monday and another one on Thursday. So the fact that there was a convention and it looked semicoherent on television was something of a miracle in itself.

DAVID PLOUFFE: I remember having a discussion internally. This was hard to do, but we were feeling some sympathy for these guys. [*laughter*] This was obviously a challenging circumstance. But then we said, "You know what? Now Bush isn't going to go there and there is going to be a lot more attention around the convention, so this isn't all negative."

We had a lot of Bush blocking and tackling at our convention, we had to fill in Barack's bio of values, we had to lay out in very specific terms the contrast with McCain. People were a little surprised that Obama's speech was as tough as it was on the contrast. We didn't want to have a lot of razzle-dazzle. We did a lot with real people. The national media didn't cover the real people that were speaking, but we got great coverage back in the battleground states for these people. Generally, I find conventions to be very taxing and archaic. You've got a lot of politics you have to take care of, it's a long time, and the press more and more are covering one speech a night and then talking and analyzing. So I found it to be somewhat of a burden, particularly for a grassroots campaign. Part of it was let's just, through this very archaic process of a convention, try and not lose who we are. We did do as much grassroots stuff as we could. That's why we went outside. The only reason we went outside is we thought it was consistent with who we are. We also thought it would help us win the state of Colorado, and I think it did because it was one of our stronger organizations. But it was a great opportunity. We were always having to reassure people about who Obama was, and that was a great opportunity to do that throughout the week. There wasn't as much razzle-dazzle as people thought, but we thought we just needed to do some basic stuff.

SARAH SIMMONS: The one thing that wasn't mentioned about our convention is we pulled down all of our television advertising. It was Labor Day weekend. We spent most of Sunday rewriting and producing an ad that we were going to put up in response to the hurricane. We were calling TV stations over the three-day weekend, trying to get them to pull down advertising. Our buyers were basically saying, "It's an act of God, you don't want to be the only station in America running negative political ads during the course of massive destruction on the Gulf Coast." It was quite a big task.

JEANNE CUMMINGS: Earlier today, David said that the Roman columns really didn't matter, that they were just small things. Do you all agree with that? You all called a lot of attention to the extravagance of the stage.

RICK DAVIS: It was a one-day news story. We didn't think they mattered anyway, but it was a lot of fun. [*laughter*]

TREVOR POTTER: They looked better on the front page of the newspaper being set up than they did when they were in place.

SARAH SIMMONS: It was at the same time as we were getting a ton of media attention. We had done the celebrity stuff and then we had rolled out a Web video called "The One" that was hilarious. It was capitalizing on this kind of "Barack Obama is a celebrity and is not to be taken terribly seriously." Then he was going to put himself in the middle of this architecture that, frankly, was easy to make fun of.

JOEL BENENSON: One interesting thing about that. You folks really got into our heads. It got much more in our heads than it resonated with voters. We kept going back to voters to see if we were we missing something. Because voters almost had a negative reaction to some of it—thinking that some of these things were too trivial, given the stakes that were out there. What we got back from the Britney Spears ad, when we showed it, was voters said, "This is trivial, we've got a big election here." We still felt you guys were onto something that we were missing. That's why Jim Margolis did go over the night before and start toning down some things on the set. A lot of that stuff was having an effect in our heads.

RICK DAVIS: So it worked. That's excellent. [*laughter*]

JOEL BENENSON: More in our heads than with voters.

DAVID PLOUFFE: I would say this about the celebrity thing. There were some ramifications in terms of our schedule and how we dealt with things, but we did understand that there were some natural antidotes to it coming down the pike. The selection of a vice president, the Democratic nomination speech, and three presidential debates—where just inhabiting those stages, we thought, was going to be an antidote. The fact that our guy did very well in all of those just added to it. So we weren't that concerned about it, but, at some point, we said, "Okay, we can't do these rallies anymore." That was a huge mistake because they had helped us organizationally. And for a while there, you guys had more momentum-looking events than we did.

ALYSSA MASTROMONACO: It's true. You guys had one event in Dayton, Ohio. We were all watching it in our little corner, and I was like, "Oh my God." It was one of the best-looking events I had ever seen.

RICK DAVIS: The day we announced Sarah Palin.

ALYSSA MASTROMONACO: Yes. It was on the front porch, and then they panned out and there had to have been twenty thousand people. Because it was a surprise, we were about twenty miles away doing another event, and we were like, "Oh, my." Coming out of the convention, everyone—especially David Axelrod, who was always very sensitive to our big events—said, "We have to tone it down, we have to show Barack interacting with people and not being a celebrity." So for about two weeks, we did these really small, painful events. Because there was such enthusiasm for Barack, toning down the crowd and limiting the number of people that were coming wasn't helpful to our organizational field efforts. Our state staff was furious. Then Senator McCain is out there with fifteen thousand and twenty thousand people every day. That lasted about two weeks, and then we got back to our rallies.

RICK DAVIS: When we designed, in late June or early July, the whole series, we were getting killed by these big, huge, beautiful events where Obama would stand there with a teleprompter and just look great, sound great, right on message. We knew that we had to throw a monkey wrench into that. The gift to us was the German speech. You couldn't have choreographed that any better for us—that was just perfect. We knew that that would get so much attention that even if this thing didn't work, we would be in the news cycle. We knew that there was going to be twenty miles of coverage and we would fit into five miles of it. It worked out better for us. We actually were surprised that you got off the big events because we thought they worked really well and then, all of a sudden, he was doing town-hallish things and we are like, oh, you are going to hate those things. [*laughter*] We're experts. [*laughter*] And Obama wasn't getting the kind of coverage that he had been getting. That event in Dayton was the first big event. We knew we could get bigger events, but that was never something that we wanted to spend the money on. Even at this point, we were living off the land. We would raise twenty million dollars a month, but we would spend twenty million dollars a month. It was never a situation where there was enough in it for us to want to spend extra money on something like that until we knew that we were going to do a series of these. We did three—Friday, Saturday and Sunday—leading up to the convention. It was fifteen thousand, twenty thousand and twenty-five thousand people, and we thought this is a good way to have momentum. Plus, we wanted to give John the option to pick any one of those three days to roll out his vice president. What was interesting is the press found out about the Friday thing. We weren't trying to hide it. It was on the schedule that we were going to have a big event. But we also had one Saturday and Sunday and never talked about it. It was just assumed that it would be on the first day and that was the best day to do it because it gave us more time to campaign with her. There were many times when we wanted to go back to the small format because that's actually, for John, a better thing. But our field organization didn't want us doing that. They wanted the bigger events. The guys liked turning out, and we had a lot of demand. We would try to do smaller events and it would be oversubscribed by five thousand or ten thousand. It was like, what do you do with these people? You don't want to piss them off when they show up. So we wound up doing exactly what we were trying to get you guys to not do. It was fine—it wasn't a problem for us. It just was more expensive. I quadrupled our advance budget in October because of these events, plus we were doing so many more of them. We never thought we would do them when we designed the budgets. I know budgets aren't very sexy, but they are what actually run campaigns. I think David and I are the only ones who really care about them—everyone else hates them. You design your campaign to spend a certain amount of money on events every week, and you decide how many for your presidential candidate and vice-presidential candidate. Two months out, we designed a vice-presidential schedule all the way out through almost the fifteenth of October. It was mostly a fundraising schedule. We were going to use our vice-presidential nominee to raise money because we wanted McCain off of that. I think we had two events for him in the general election, and we wanted the work horse for fundraising, which we had to have, to be the vice-presidential nominee. It turns out the one that he picked wasn't the best for that. She had sixty thousand people in the small towns, so she shouldn't be doing fundraising. We really had to scramble. We had this staff all put together for smaller events. We thought we'd have a Biden—thousand people a pop, three of those a day, go to a couple of fundraisers, and you call it a day. We had maybe a third of the advance staff that we really needed, and we had to do that the day after the convention. People who were working at the convention got told, "You are getting on that plane, you'll be going to this city. Five of you will be headed there because she is going to be there tomorrow." We had to convert events that were designed for a thousand people into stuff that was designed for twenty thousand people. That chewed up a lot of our cash.

• PUBLIC FINANCING—OR NOT? •

JEANNE CUMMINGS: Speaking of cash, when Obama decided to not go into the public financing system, clearly that decision was probably not a hard one for you all to make. But in addition to making that decision, you had this sort of quasi pledge that he had made that you all had to manage.[5] He had committed to talking to the Republican nominee, and he didn't. When you all made that decision, what was your calculation around making the announcement and dealing with the pledge? I recognize it was Swiss cheese and so you had lots of places to move through it, but at any rate, it was out there. And what was the McCain campaign's reaction inside when you knew he had made this call and then you all had to make a decision for yourselves?

DAVID PLOUFFE: First of all, we made a mistake back in the very beginning of 2007. Because Hillary and Edwards both began raising general election money, we petitioned the Federal Election Commission and said, "Before we do that, we would like to know if you can still have the option to stay in the system." The FEC came back and said, "Yes." We said, "If we are the nominee," which at that point seemed highly unlikely, "we would talk to the Republicans." Trevor will probably dispute the nature of this, but our counsel did have one conversation with him about this. Then we had, as these guys probably did, five hundred questionnaires. They are a pain, and you've got to fill out some of them. We had a staffer fill out a Campaign Finance Institute of Midwest questionnaire who, when asked about public financing, put the word *yes* and added the rest of our rhetoric in there. I never saw it. That was the big problem—it said "yes." Barack Obama never saw it, and I never saw it. It was a mistake at the staff level. He is a reformer, and so this was not as easy a decision as people think. He wrestled with the practical applications of it—the notion of getting out of the system and what that would mean. We did try and shine a spotlight on the fact that John McCain had gotten out of the system in the primary, after taking loans and getting on the ballot in some states, by saying that he was going to be in the public system. We never thought the media paid nearly enough attention to that, and we had very limited success in saying, "Listen, before you crucify

5. In March 2007, the Obama campaign said that if Obama was the nominee, he would "aggressively pursue an agreement with the Republican nominee to preserve a publicly financed general election." Many newspapers interpreted the campaign statement as a commitment to accept public financing in the event of an Obama/McCain race. In a September 2007 Midwest Democracy Network questionnaire asking about participation in the public financing system in the general election, the Obama campaign responded, "Yes. . . . If I am the Democratic nominee, I will aggressively pursue an agreement with the Republican nominee to preserve a publicly financed general election."

us, the reformer, John McCain, who is now throwing darts at us, kept his campaign afloat and got on the ballot in some states by essentially being dishonest about his intentions." But we had very limited ability. There is a lot of focus on the global amount of money we raised. We raised a lot of money. Now, these guys, the Republican National Committee, raised an enormous amount of money in September and October. Yes, there was a disparity, but when you look at all the money, less than some people think. The important thing is we felt good about the way we were raising our money. We had an average contribution of under eighty-five dollars. The reform community's number one goal is to limit the amount of money in politics—no lobbyists, no PACs. We ended up having almost four million contributors. That's the right way to raise money. We weren't going to be lectured about the way we were raising money. We honestly felt proud about that.

It also gave us control of our campaign. These guys were burdened with these horrible hybrid ads or IE ads.[6] IE ads were better, but still you guys couldn't talk to them. David Axelrod and I did the IE work in 2004 at the DNC for Kerry, and it was a terrible thing because we sat around every day and said, "What do they want us to do? Should we answer the Swift Boats or not?[7] They are not buying radio. Does that mean we should buy radio or they don't want us to buy radio?" It's a terrible thing. We spent more money than Kerry did on the air. I didn't think that was any way to run a railroad, so we wanted to control all of our advertising. Most importantly, we did not want to outsource our field organization because so many of those people were volunteering for Obama. They didn't want to volunteer for the Michigan State Democratic Party. They did not want to volunteer for the Democratic National Committee. They wanted to volunteer in the name of Barack Obama. So, from a clinical standpoint, that's why we made the decision, and the control of all aspects of our campaign was more important, in my view, than the overall dollar amount.

TREVOR POTTER: Let me roll it back, because in the end, we weren't at all surprised that you made the decision you did. We were surprised by the manner it came off, and we thought that it gave us some opportunities, which we tried to take, in terms of talking about it with the press. When Senator Obama went to the FEC in 2007 and had that conversation about whether he could raise general funds during the primary and then make a choice about whether to participate in the general public funding, he said,

6. "Hybrid ads" are ads in which the cost is split between the presidential candidate and the party and require that the benefit be shared. IE ads are "independent expenditure ads" that are funded by third parties who cannot coordinate with the campaigns.
7. In the 2004 presidential campaign, Swift Boat Veterans for Truth, a 527 organization, aired a variety of advertisements claiming Senator Kerry had lied about his war record.

at the time, that if the other party nominee participated in the system, he would hope to do so as well. McCain jumped on that because he is McCain and because he believed in it. He said, "They have said that 'if I am the nominee, I agree as well to participate in the public funding system.'" Part of this was, internally, John McCain himself thought there was effectively a deal with Barack Obama. If they were the two nominees, they would be in the public funding system. That's what the reform community thought. Now, it was in the interest of the reform community to think so because you hadn't yet shown all that money, so they thought, "This is one way in which we'll keep the public funding system." Then you fast forward to 2008 and we are the nominees. I don't think there was ever any serious thought of us not being in the public funding system, so it became important to us that Obama keep his pledge and be in it. The record was the FEC comments, the checked-off response to a reform group, and also Senator Obama. On one of the Sunday morning shows in March or April, he was asked, "Are you going to keep your pledge and stay in?" He said, "What I'm going to do if I'm the nominee is sit down and talk with John McCain," who was by then the nominee apparent, "and we'll have a conversation and we're going to see if we can make this work." He left plenty of running room, but he did say he'd have the conversation. We were assuming there would be an overture. The nutshell on my conversation with Bob Bauer,[8] during the week that you all actually got the nomination and Senator Clinton withdrew, was when Bob and I had scheduled a meeting to talk about a joint appearance we were going to have in Rhode Island. I went by his office and we talked about our joint appearance—who was going to go first and what we were going to cover on a variety of campaign finance issues. Then he said, "What are you all thinking on presidential public funding and the general election?" We had a conversation in which I said, "We are assuming you are going to keep your pledge." He said, "Well, you've had the whole spring to raise money and we haven't." And I said, "Well, yeah, but you spent all this money in states that are going to benefit you and you have this huge ground organization, so it's probably even." I went off to lunch, and that was that. I went back to the campaign and I said, "I had this really interesting conversation with Bauer, and I think they are going to make a proposal of some sort." We waited for a proposal and, about ten days later, we opened the morning news cycle to discover that the senator had decided not to participate. The only piece that caused steam to come out of my ears was then Bob was asked a question and responded by saying, "We had negotiations with Trevor Potter," at which stage the entire senior staff of the McCain campaign turned around and said, "You did what?" [*laughter*] I said, "Wait, I told you about that, that was that twenty-minute conversation I had with Bob." From our standpoint, we

8. Bob Bauer served as counsel to Obama for America.

weren't surprised at all, but we were sort of puzzled that there wasn't more of a tactical effort by you all to have a negotiation or a discussion because there were certainly plenty of ways in which you could have said it doesn't work. You could have talked about limiting RNC money, which we practically couldn't have done. What we were unsure of was, why did you miss that step of having the conversation and then saying it wouldn't work?

JEANNE CUMMINGS: Can you answer him?

DAVID PLOUFFE: First of all, I think, in that conversation with Bob, you guys did talk a little bit about RNC money and outside spending. Our sense was this decision had to be made very quickly because we were in June already and we had plans we had to lay down. If we were in the system, we would have probably had maybe not a different map but a less rigorous effort in some of those states to begin with. We knew if we got into a negotiation, we would end up where we were going to end up. Perhaps we would have a more definitive thing to say, "Listen, these guys are full of it, they want to keep raising huge money from the lobbyists and PACs for the RNC, they won't limit that, they are winking at the 527s." We thought we had to make a decision quickly and that we would probably end up at the same place, but we could end up there three or four weeks later, and we didn't think we had that kind of time.

BILL MCINTURFF: We have to recognize what's happened—Senator Obama's decision has destroyed the campaign finance system forever. No Republican will ever be able to run and take even primary money because what they'll say is, given the billion-dollar machine that we'll be facing, that if you do, you'll end up with no money between your primary and the general and you'll be outspent. The public finance system worked pretty well so that George Bush in 1980 and Jimmy Carter, lots of candidates, could get in with a fairly low cost of change, get matching money and run a credible campaign. Those people won't exist anymore. You are going to have to start with the capacity to raise an extraordinary amount of money, and it will change the presidential field. I want you to imagine the outcry by the *New York Times* if George Bush had not taken public money in 2004. As Republicans, it's pretty easy for us to believe that there was a deferential response to Senator Obama's decision that would have never happened had a Republican done it first. The lack of a serious challenge and the lack of the press to have a serious policing of that effort would be extraordinarily difficult had it been done by a Republican. There was a huge difference in the response. This baloney in the U.S. Senate about oh, we'll double the campaign giving limits. I'm sorry. No one will ever do it. It's dead forever. It will have consequences in terms of who is allowed to run in the primary, in both parties, after President-Elect Obama's time is over because it was, in fact, helpful to underdog candidates in the primaries.

SARAH SIMMONS: David talked a little bit about the hybrid nature of the advertising. That can't be underestimated, in terms of what it does tactically to your campaign. Fred and I had many phone conversations about the fact that there's a limited number of things you can say in thirty seconds. Our lawyers were very good at policing us, making sure as soon as that money comes from the RNC, that we are adequately doing something on behalf of the party. Every time we said John McCain's name, we had to say congressional Republicans or congressional liberals as a match. In half of our ads, despite our very talented ad team, it looked like we were running against Senator Harry Reid.

DAVID PLOUFFE: This is a place where we started to have sympathy for you around your convention. We had had conversations and said, "We feel really bad for these guys because the ads were discordant." We exposed voters to these ads and they would say, "I'm not sure what's going on." It was a real burden, particularly in the states you were in. You were advertising in some states where the Republican brand wasn't great, so that was a challenge, and then the content was a challenge.

SARAH SIMMONS: People would say, "Why are you running negative ads?" Because we couldn't run a positive ad where we could say "congressional Republicans." They had a lower job approval. It was very challenging to try to put those ads together, not to mention we had to make sure the pictures we used weren't going to benefit a Democratic candidate by putting one of them in our ads. It was frustrating.

DAVID PLOUFFE: But you didn't really have a choice.

FRED DAVIS: She said there's a limited number of things you can say in thirty seconds—which is none. It's really twelve-and-a-half seconds. Thirty seconds is tough enough. Then some guy named McCain goes out and passes this law that takes away five of your seconds,[9] so you're left with twenty-five. [*laughter*] And then the hybrid comes in and you have twelve-and-a-half seconds to make your point. I will go up against anybody, but that one is a very tough challenge.

---

9. The Bipartisan Campaign Reform Act of 2002, also known as McCain-Feingold, requires every radio and television ad authorized by a political candidate to have an audio disclaimer with the candidate identifying himself or herself and stating that he or she has approved the communication.

RICK DAVIS: I happen to think the disclaimer was what was good about our ads. [*laughter*] The point David made may be actually worse for people like me, which is turning fifty million dollars over to an IE that you cannot talk to, and you're wondering why the hell aren't they on radio? Why aren't they doing this in Pennsylvania? What is that ocean ad?[10] I paid for that ad. [*laughter*] Can I call and at least complain? The only thing worse than a hybrid ad is independent expenditures. It's very easy in hindsight to say, "Wow, not only were we outspent, in many cases two or three to one, in some of these states on TV, but when you look at the ads and the clarity of message and the difficulty we had in trying to project that, it's amazing we were as competitive as we were in some of these places." In a place like the Philadelphia market, if your ads aren't great, you are going to get screwed. That's just how you fight it out there. We would look at our ads and say, "We'll do the best we can with this twelve-and-a-half seconds and see what happens." But, all that being said, it's hard to find examples of specific ads that had a dramatic or material effect on the outcome of this election. In other words, with all the things that occurred that were not on TV, this was not an election that was decided because of the ad wars. There were a lot of things that they did to help and take advantage of, but I don't think it was an advertising victory by Obama.

DAVID PLOUFFE: When we constructed our original budget—it grew because our September and October was bigger than we thought—it took care of the field. We had an ad spending level that was less than you might spend in a Senate or governor's race and we were comfortable with that because we thought in a presidential race, advertising is less important than it is in Senate or governors' races. We raised more money. I agree with Rick. I don't think there was a single ad that really made the difference in the election. What we were able to do is control all this so that in most markets, we had a senior track and a women's track and a positive track. We were able to do the two-minute spots. Mark Putnam, who is here representing Bill Richardson, produced a thirty-minute ad[11] which was very helpful. It locked people in. So we were able to do some things that I do think were helpful. But I agree—that's not what presidential races are, at least anymore. Voters were paying so much attention that the ads were just part of it. They are also seeking out information on their own. They are talking to their neighbors.

---

10. On October 27, 2008, the independent arm of the RNC began airing an ad called "Storm," which showed images of a violent sea and asked, "But what if the storm does get worse with someone who's untested at the helm?"

11. On October 29, 2008, the Obama campaign ran a thirty-minute ad at 8:00 p.m. on CBS, NBC, MSNBC, Fox, BET, TV One and Univision.

SARAH SIMMONS: As somebody who spent a lot of time examining what you were doing, the multitrack stuff was fascinating. That was really difficult for us to respond to because we only had the financing to run one response. Meanwhile, you always had a positive thing, and then you were usually attacking on a variety of issues underneath. For us, it was, we must respond to the health care ad but we are attacking on Ayers[12] this week, so do we pull that down and put this up? It was very difficult.

DAVID PLOUFFE: I thought that you responded to very little we did. Maybe you can argue you should have responded more, but I thought there was a discipline there, just as there was a discipline about waiting to go into Florida. You guys waited to go into Florida until you could afford to do it. We would say, "They are showing very good discipline here." A lot of our attacks—maybe they hurt, maybe they didn't—but you guys had a game plan and a strategy and you stuck to it. We would remark on that. Sometimes we would say, "We don't need to respond to that, they are not responding to our stuff." We would have these discussions like, "Let's not follow every rabbit down a hole." Now, we had the resources where if we decided to respond, it was less arduous because we could still keep our positive up and we could still do our seniors. But I thought you guys showed a lot of discipline about how you dealt with stuff or didn't.

JOEL BENENSON: The fact that we could also run this positive track did give us an advantage. The fact that we had positive stuff on and you couldn't fed, fairly or unfairly, the image that you guys were running a more negative campaign, which really took a toll on Senator McCain in an election when people were tuning out some of the negativity and really wanted to get past it. That's where the volume did help us.

BILL MCINTURFF: Even the most sophisticated reporters keep presuming that somehow we know what an IE is going to do at the RNC and what I keep saying—I just want to repeat again for everybody here—there are now federal criminal penalties and federal criminal penalties means you go to jail, and, as we like to say in our partnership, we won't wear orange jumpsuits for any candidate. [*laughter*]

---

12. Bill Ayers spent ten years as a fugitive in the 1970s when he was part of the Weather Underground, an anti–Vietnam War group that protested U.S. policies by bombing the Pentagon, U.S. Capitol and a string of other government buildings. In the mid-1990s, Ayers hosted a meet-and-greet at his house to introduce Obama to their neighbors during his first run for the Illinois Senate. In 2001, Ayers contributed two hundred dollars to Obama's campaign. Ayers also served alongside Obama on the board of the not-for-profit Woods Fund of Chicago.

Now I'm going to disagree with Rick. I'm not saying an individual ad made a difference. We were tracking every week on "Whose advertising do you recall seeing?" We ended this campaign with 64 percent of voters saying they remember seeing an Obama ad, 12 percent saying McCain. Here's the shocker—we also gave people the categories of both or neither. When sixty-four to twelve they are picking Obama, it's a wave on a chart I've never seen before in a campaign. What would happen is poor Rick would be so excited. He would say, "We're up to seventeen million dollars, we've almost got them, we're almost there at the same volume." Then, the next day, they dropped ten million dollars of two-minute positives. One time, Rick said, "Guess what markets?" I guessed and I went through these markets and he said, "Wow, that's the exact ones." I said, "Yeah, because guess what? Those are the most important markets, that's where these suburban swing voters live." What they are doing is everywhere we are making a little bit of ground, they are filling in a positive—he has a vision. It makes us look negative and it frees them up to spend all that other money with negatives. What it means is they ran more negatives than we did. But, because of an extraordinary candidate on TV, at times in a minute or two-minute spots, people said, "I've seen a lot of positive stuff from that campaign." The first two weeks in October, they spent $105 million. We were teetering on this horrible environment, and somebody drops $105 million on you. So it might not have been one ad, but it was the sheer volume.

RICK DAVIS: Well, four hundred million dollars' worth of ads, so I would say that had an impact. It was very odd. We rarely debated an ad. All that being said, there were billions of dollars' worth of publicity being pummeled into this race without anybody buying an ad. Those things matter, but I still don't think it's what really drove the outcome of the race.

FRED DAVIS: Go back to the middle of the summer real quickly. Birth of Britney. We were sitting in a room, things are miserable, our numbers aren't good. Your candidate, this incredible speaker, isn't even president yet, and you have this incredible trip going on in Europe. We are thinking, "Well, do we go home, Bill? What do we do?" That's when the idea of the Celebrity ad came up. Our numbers actually did increase after that and it really changed the dynamic, at least internally for us. My recollection is it actually changed numbers through August, too.

• 9/11 •

JOHN KING: On September 11, we saw both candidates together—a very respectful day where they went to Ground Zero. This was our second

Joel Benenson and David Plouffe talk about the "up-for-grabs" voters.

presidential election since 9/11. How much different was it in the second presidential election after 9/11 than it was in the first?

JOEL BENENSON: It was dramatically different on a couple of fronts. We had identified in May that the economy was going to be the dominant issue. In particular, it was going to be the dominant issue with a group that David referred to this morning as "up-for-grabs" voters—swing voters. They weren't all undecided, but they were soft or undecided voters. They were very focused on the economy. They were focused on ending the war in Iraq, but they also saw the war in Iraq as an economic issue more than a national security issue. If you go back to 2004 and look at the exit polls, the majority of people voting in 2004 believed that Iraq was the central front in the War on Terror. That was not true in 2008. In fact, now a plurality and a near majority think that Afghanistan is the central front in the War on Terror. So that had receded as an issue. We had always planned through the summer to gear up for a campaign coming out of the convention that would focus on the economy. There are reporters in this room who, when Palin was picked on September 5, before 9/11 and before September 15, would ask me, "Well, how are you going to get these women back?" I said, "Because we are going to talk about the economy and these women voters, who are the swing voters, are focused very much on the economy." This is true of every election. No two elections are about the same thing; dynamics shift. Even sometimes during an election, a dynamic shifts. I think it's fair to say that we had decided early on to make the economy the issue we were going to fight this on and that we were going to use economic issues as values issues to demonstrate whose side each candidate was on.

JOHN KING: But, a forty-seven-year-old guy new to the national stage with very little Washington experience could not have won the first presidential election after 9/11, do you agree with that?

JOEL BENENSON: I don't know. I think the dynamic was different. We were mindful that we had the same kind of numbers Bill had on Senator McCain winning on the commander-in-chief issue. We knew that commander-in-chief was a threshold that we had to clear. We were down the same numbers. We were down around twenty points on commander-in-chief and we were winning the election by five points. But we still knew we had to clear a threshold. We made a decision, that David was more involved in than I was, about wanting the first debate to be on foreign policy. We knew it was perceived as Senator McCain's strength. There were a lot of us in our camp who also believed it was our hidden strength, so we never thought it wasn't a threshold we were going to clear, but it was a different dynamic. You could dial back to 2004 and hypothesize anything you want. You could make an argument that maybe Kerry didn't win because he didn't talk about the economy enough in 2004 because it was already percolating as an issue.

BILL MCINTURFF: Most people in this room live in either New York City, Washington or Boston. Washington was attacked. I didn't know where my children and my wife were—they were over bridges, cell phones didn't work. We were attacked, New York was attacked, and a plane took off from Boston—people knew somebody who knew somebody. What I remind my clients is that if you live very far away, very quickly that emotional resonance in our lives got lost for other people. When I said Americans move in before the dream house roof is finished, that's 2001. 2008 is a universe away. Candidates, if they are going to be president of the United States of America, have to represent those victims and represent what they represented in 9/11. It's perfectly appropriate to stop the campaign and serve in that function as one of our next presidents. But outside of the residents in these three cities, that issue moved on. Pollster Mark Penn has three kind of broad clusters for how people view issues—economic, terrorism and values issues. He was showing what the pie looked like a year before the election, in November of 2007, and those circles were relatively equivalent. Then, by August of 2008, the economic circle was sixteen points bigger and the defense circle had shrunk. He said that that shifting of the electorate, given the Obama and McCain margins in these different segments—if you take an equal pie and

Rick Davis, Bill McInturff, Christian Ferry and Ryan Price stress the importance of volunteers to McCain's campaign.

you add sixteen points on the economic side and you are losing that part by seventy points as the Republican—doesn't bode well. If you said to me, "Bill, the exit polls are going to be 63 percent economy, 10 percent something else, and single digits for every other issue," that is an extraordinary number. I would not have predicted a sixty-three to ten issue cluster, in terms of what the split would be. I found the sixty-three to be perhaps the most extraordinary number in that exit poll.

• THE ECONOMIC COLLAPSE •

JEANNE CUMMINGS: We are going to jump to mid-September when the bailouts began in Washington. The economy, which was already faltering through August and the summer, seemed to have the bottom fall out from underneath it. We had a series of events where we had AIG go and had a bailout for them, we had Lehman go down, and then we had the seven hundred billion dollar bailout proposal—all happen in the course of six days. How did each of you view those events, and how had the campaign itself changed? How had the dialogue changed? What were the implications for your candidate and your message? How did you need to adapt to these things?

BILL MCINTURFF: I just have a quick opening comment on this. When the first African American nominee in history has his announcement speech on the fortieth anniversary of Martin Luther King's "I Have a Dream" speech, our convention is going to have a stage 4 hurricane, and then the markets implode on September 15, we need to all resolve that God has weighed in on the scales of this race and there's now too much evidence that we are fighting forces far beyond human control. [*laughter*] It got to the point when we were preparing for the last weekend and things were getting better—when we were trying to come back—that Steve Schmidt[13] said, "Don't worry, if that ever happened, the campaign bus will hit the CDC carrier with the last bubonic plague and we will release it." [*laughter*] I think it's fair to say, at that point, that you realize that God has weighed in on this campaign and has made a decision—he or she has made a decision.

JEANNE CUMMINGS: Well, if we could get a little closer to earth. [*laughter*] Let's head into the campaign office. Obviously, this changed the dynamics. How did it hit you all in terms of analyzing where you were and where you had to go? Where we are leading to is McCain's decision to suspend his campaign.

JOHN KING: I think she is trying to ask, when did God leave the Republican Party? [*laughter*]

JEANNE CUMMINGS: And did you get an anti-locust thing going on?

RICK DAVIS: I'm afraid of God, so I will not disparage his name. And this goes beyond even God in this case, but we were having a bad week as a campaign. [*laughter*] This was the week that John McCain said the fundamentals of the economy look pretty sound, regardless of Lehman's collapse. We thought Lehman's collapse was good because most of them were contributors to the Obama campaign, so if they were broke, that would help us out a little bit. In campaigns, there are things you can't control. Then there are those things that you try to control, like what the candidate does every day and your surrogates. A couple days after McCain said that about the economy, one of our advisers said that Governor Palin wasn't qualified to run a Fortune 500 company—the country was fine, but not a Fortune 500 company. But that was okay because then, when we sent her back out

---

13. Steve Schmidt was a senior adviser on John McCain's presidential campaign in charge of day-to-day operations.

to clean it up, she threw McCain into that box.[14] [*laughter*] So I knew we were having a rough week without even looking at the markets. By the way, thank you to CNN and the other great news outlets—there was not a speech given for the balance of the campaign without the stock ticker. I've been involved in a lot of presidential campaigns, but the ticker has not. When you are sitting there watching your candidate give a speech and you see the Dow going up, you're thinking okay, okay, okay, stay there, stay there, stay there. [*laughter*] And if it ticks down, you figure, oh boy, the market went down when McCain said *X*. It was really a unique environment. You don't really get that many surprises in a presidential campaign but, that week, with all the things that were both inflicted and self-inflicted on us, it was, wow, this is not good. It was very hard to manage through that because you are trying to put the campaign on a track, and the global financial markets are conspiring against you. And, by the way, they've got a little more assets than we've got. Inside our own campaign, there was a relatively higher-than-normal level of confusion because we've got our own folks out there off message, and that made it much more difficult to blow through.

JOHN KING: Christian and Ryan have been very quiet through this discussion, maybe by choice and for good reason, but I wanted to bring you into the conversation at this point. You guys are talking day by day, minute by minute, to the states, the targeting operations and the political operation. What was the incoming when you think, "We've made up a little ground in Ohio," or "We've had a good week in Florida," leading into this? When that implosion was happening in the economy, was the incoming reinforcing that? It was obvious to everybody it was a bad week, but what was the incoming in terms of the effect in the states where you thought you were picking up traction?

CHRISTIAN FERRY: The incoming was horrible. People were scared about their financial situation. Up until this point, when the actual collapse happened, we were talking about the economy as an issue, and the economy was an issue, but it wasn't something that people felt in their pockets at that moment. They were fearful for the future, but they weren't necessarily feeling it day to day in their wallet. When this happened, they did, and it became very personal to a lot of people. The Republican base and the folks we were talking to—the people who were working our phone banks and going door

---

14. On September 16, 2008, McCain campaign adviser Carly Fiorina, the former head of Hewlett-Packard, was asked in an interview on KTRS Radio in St. Louis whether she thought Governor Palin could run a major company. Fiorina responded, "No, I don't." When asked to elaborate, she said, "I don't think John McCain could run a major corporation."

to door for us—were not only fearful for their economic security, but they were very angry that the government was offering a seven-hundred-billion-dollar bailout. It made it very difficult for our field operation to operate in that atmosphere. And it was a challenge for Senator McCain, being in the middle of this, to keep those folks motivated when they were so upset with everything that was going on.

JEANNE CUMMINGS: What did your field operation encounter?

CHRISTIAN FERRY: Our field program had been on a steady upward swing since the convention and since the announcement of Sarah Palin. We've talked a lot about Sarah Palin—whether she was a positive or a negative. She was a huge positive for our field operation. She generated incredible enthusiasm amongst our volunteers. Folks who probably were going to vote for John McCain on election day were now saying, "I am going to work very hard for John McCain," because of the type of affection they had not just for John McCain but for Sarah Palin. We had been seeing this great uptick in contacts, in phone calls, and in door knocks. With the suspension of the campaign, there was a lot of confusion as to, well, does that mean we actually run a phone bank tonight or does it mean we are not running a phone bank tonight? Our volunteers weren't certain what exactly that meant for them. We had a period of ten days where our volunteer activity went way down. It came back and we had an extremely successful program through election day, but during that period, it was almost like the presidential campaign stopped. It stopped in the news cycle because everyone turned their attention to the financial markets, and it felt that way in our field operation as well.

RYAN PRICE: One thing we mentioned yesterday that we used during the primaries that was very successful is that we took a lot of volunteers from around the country and we shipped them into battleground states. During that ten-day period that Christian just mentioned, that completely dried up. We had this amazing volunteer director who was a volunteer himself on the campaign, and a lot of these people had the means where they could take time off of work for the final two weeks of the campaign to travel and, all of a sudden, they all just disappeared. That's because a lot of them had their net worth decreased by about 25 percent. So that was a noticeable effect. Then, it did pick back up after that period.

JOHN KING: When you say it picked back up, who did you gain in that period? I happened to be in Ashland, Ohio, on a day the Archway Bakery was closed and 240 families lost their jobs. It's a white, rural area. I know you guys think we obsess about this too much, but most of them said that they had been inclined to vote Republican. We found a fair amount of them who said, "Things are so screwed up, I'm willing to think outside the box this time." That's just a snapshot, it's one moment in time, it might not mean anything. You guys did better in that county than John Kerry did four years ago. But did people actually move in that period of time?

JOEL BENENSON: September 15, in our polling, was the last time that the race was really close. It had closed to even between the pick of Palin and September 15. Senator McCain was even up one point one time. That was the last time it was close. The people who moved were the people who we believed drifted away. We never hit a panic button when Governor Palin was picked. We thought we could pull back part of our "up-for-grabs" group—women, rural, independent, middle-class women who were part of our swing voter group that we knew were very economically focused. They were the first group to come back. It was an interesting week. Luck is part of political campaigns, too. There were unanticipated events, like Senator McCain repeating something he had said earlier about the fundamentals of the economy being sound, which we were surprised about because we had already used it and it came out again. As the week unfolded, there were other things that played to our favor. McCain went from that to calling it an economic crisis. He said AIG shouldn't be bailed out, and then he said it should be bailed out. He was suspending his campaign to go back to Washington, canceled his *David Letterman Show* appearance, and then Letterman lampoons him that night for him sitting in the studio with Katie Couric. So at a time when we felt people wanted steady leadership, our candidate, Senator Obama, was on a pretty even keel, and we had McCain kind of going up and down every day. It fed an image that we wanted to contrast a bit that we think played to our favor. We thought the only way we could gain some territory on this commander-in-chief thing was for us to look very steady, and when McCain didn't look steady to capitalize on it. That week, we used the word *erratic*. Some in the press thought it was about age, which it never was. We knew that Senator McCain had a penchant for dramatic events—he liked the drama of situations—and we thought that was a way to say to people, "Wait, when we really need some steady leadership, maybe he is not as steady as you think."

DAVID PLOUFFE: The suspension of the campaign was on Wednesday. The debate was on Friday. Those sixty hours were some of the most interesting—their decision to suspend, our decision not to. The debate was in suspense.[15]

---

15. On September 24, 2008, two days before the first scheduled presidential debate, John McCain called for the debate to be delayed because of the economic crisis. Obama said he would attend the debate, and the University of Mississippi went forward with preparing for it.

Debate prep gets completely torn apart for both of us. We didn't know until Friday at about noon that you guys were coming. It was a remarkable period of time.

RICK DAVIS: We didn't know until Friday at noon. [*laughter*]

DAVID PLOUFFE: It was a high stakes deal all the way throughout.

JEANNE CUMMINGS: How did you find out they were coming?

DAVID PLOUFFE: TV.

JOEL BENENSON: We saw them loading the plane on TV.

JOHN KING: Frank Fahrenkopf, as co-chair of the Commission on Presidential Debates, that must have felt great, right? Were they coming?

FRANK FAHRENKOPF: I was actually in Rome, Italy, packing to come back so that I could be in Mississippi for the debate. I was watching CNN International, and there was McCain announcing what he announced. It was a long trip back.

But seriously, I don't think that the two campaigns and two candidates have really gotten the credit they deserve for the manner in which these debates were handled. I know if Paul Kirk, my co-chair on the commission, was here, he would agree. We have done six cycles now, over the last twenty years—twenty-two presidential and vice-presidential debates. Other than that hiccup, there were really very few problems. We announced in November of 2007 where the debates were going to be, when they were going to be, and what the formats were going to be. On August 5, we announced the moderators with no consultation with the campaigns or the parties. Then, on September 17, we announced that we had extended the invitations. We first heard from Congressman Rahm Emanuel, representing Senator Obama, that they had accepted. Then we heard from Senator Lindsey Graham. There were really only four requests for any modifications or changes. First, they asked to move the first debate from domestic policy to foreign policy. We kicked it around. This was shortly after the Russians had gone into Georgia, so it made sense. We had no problem since both parties agreed. Second, they requested that that first debate be standing with podiums, rather than seated at the table as we had suggested. Again, we had no problem with that. Third, for the vice-presidential debate, the word we got was Senator Biden preferred to stand. There was no problem with that with the McCain campaign. And, fourth, there was some adjustment in the timing. Other than that, it was seamless. Now, there was no White House involved. Over the last twenty years, when you have the White House involved, it sometimes gets a little bit more difficult. But the candidates really did a magnificent job—at least in the way they worked with us.

JEANNE CUMMINGS: Can we go over the suspension period? You all talked a little bit about the decision to suspend, but if you can shed some light on that. When McCain announced the suspension, he set out a couple of goals for himself, and that was to go back to Washington to try to build a bipartisan agreement for a bailout package. When he came back to Washington, had you all mapped out his days, or were you all just going with the flow? Once that decision was made, how much detail had you all laced into this, in terms of where he was going to be? With this spotlight on him, what were the images and messages you all wanted to send?

RICK DAVIS: A lot of campaigns are circumstantial—the decisions come out of things that are happening at the time. We happened to be in New York. We had been building up a series of events trying to turn the page on some of the issues related to the economy. We had scheduled a briefing that morning by a number of our eminent financiers and economists. It was a very similar program as the Obama campaign was going through at the same time. We had always planned to have an announcement of the five principles of what we thought should be included in the bailout package—virtually identical to the speech that Obama later gave. So that was already in the equation. We get there and, to each and every one of their credit, they all said, "People should not underestimate the degree to which this crisis is not only global but deep." There had been an active debate, up to that point in time, in the public on what the problem really was and how hard it was going to be to overcome it. There was actually some enthusiasm, at that point—the fix at Fannie and Freddie was going to work, AIG is now saved, we'll see what happens next. Sure, a lot of banks are worried. But looking back now with what we know today, nobody was predicting this level of gloom and doom—maybe just gloom at that point. These people we met with laid out pretty draconian examples of what would happen to the global economy, our own jobs and finances, and 401(k)s—basically the decimation of liquidity as we know it. This is big stuff. This is not what happens normally in a presidential campaign. You don't become actively engaged in a daily policy issue that has these kinds of ramifications. We had a meeting right after that—a lot of us had happened to be there. I wasn't traveling very much at the time, so just being there was somewhat unusual for us, which I think helped breed the confusion back at headquarters as to what the hell did they do up there? McCain was very worried. He said, "I think running for president is a big deal, but I think global financial meltdown is even bigger, and we've got to do something about this." The information we had was that the legislation that was winding its way through the Senate had no chance of success and that House Republicans were on the warpath. They were very unhappy about the bailout of Freddie, Fannie and AIG. We weren't sure they would support anything else. That's about as much as we knew about it. For a campaign, you could have gotten through with that much information. John's instinct was, "I'm going back, I'm going to roll up my sleeves, I'm going to do what I can with the attention and prestige and power that comes with being basically the leader of my party, and I'm going to try and get something done." We probably should have debated suspending the campaign. I think that became too much of the news story. Not going to the debate became the story. We wanted the story to be "John focuses on the economy," not "we are trying to skip the debates." We like debates. We wanted to do more debates—earlier, more often. But, nonetheless, that sort of gummed up some of the news story when, for us, it was just a throwaway thing. Plus, we thought that the media would then put pressure on Washington to get something done because they would want this to happen—they would want a debate, they would want the campaign to continue. What happened was, instead, the pressure came on us—why the hell are they going to skip the debate? Global financial meltdown—that's a little bit more important than a debate. But we got caught in a process story, and it surprised us because we thought this is so much more important than this process story, so they are bound to report that. They didn't. Then, by the time we got to Washington, there was a whole series of events that conspired to put us in a room with George Bush.

BILL MCINTURFF: Let me get back a second. I want to do one other thing that happened that Wednesday morning and I want to compare notes with Joel. Joel was talking about their tracking. He said that on September 15, which was a Monday, he might have had McCain up plus one, which is the last time he had McCain ahead in their tracking. Now, we are talking about Wednesday morning. On Wednesday morning, which is two nights' more tracking—Monday and Wednesday—what's your rough recollection, in terms of where you had the ballot in the battleground states?

JOEL BENENSON: Three.

BILL MCINTURFF: We had three and he had three. The ABC News/ *Washington Post* poll had him negative nine, so the banner headline above the fold Wednesday morning was "McCain down nine." So, the other thing we need to talk about here is that there was a press filter that said this had nothing to do with John's concern about the country and the world economy and his role as a Republican leader. It was just a campaign stunt. It was based on the fact that the *Washington Post* had a headline above the fold that said John McCain drops nine points down. That happens to be six points different than I had and six points different than Joel had. John McCain was down, but negative nine is a huge number—not that we didn't see it lots by two weeks later. But on that day, it was not a negative nine campaign. What happened was when you were doing pushback with the press, they would say, come on, you guys are nine points down, you are doing this for the campaign, and you would say, we're not nine points down, that's bullshit. Polls are polls, but when things got better, it was always a small little headline and some other lead. The bad news for McCain in the *Washington Post* was always a huge story but, that day, that coincidental timing of that poll, that number, that type of coverage in the *Post* combined with this decision was a really consequential thing that changed the filter of how that event and that decision was recorded.

JEANNE CUMMINGS: Since Rick Davis had to leave, Bill, if you can carry us through the tactical part of the return to Washington—in terms of the poll and some of the language you all chose at the time. Your initial announcement we received in a way you didn't fully intend it to be received. Then, when you got to Washington, you had those sets of circumstances thrown in your lap. Did you all plan his days in Washington, in terms of trying to send particular messages or to set a certain image during this critical period when the spotlight was so bright?

BILL MCINTURFF: I want to speak well of the Democratic caucus because when they went to the White House on Thursday, they made a decision to have Senator Obama take the lead. We feel strongly that there was never a deal. When they leaked there's a deal and John screwed it up, the Democratic party and its leadership did a very good job protecting their nominee's interests. Our party and our House leadership didn't serve our nominee in the same way. Ron Brownstein of the *Los Angeles Times* wrote this incredibly interesting article in August of 1994 talking about game theory. He was talking about how each individual Democratic House member was casting votes and doing so because they thought those votes were better. They didn't recognize that in the entire caucus, nothing was getting done, and that their individual vote was going to get swamped by the entire caucus. Republicans don't like having seven hundred billion dollars spent on buying banks and having the U.S. government own things. This is very hard. But we had a lot of individual House members who thought they were making the safe, better vote for them. Their individual vote was safe, without looking at the consequence of what happened when that bailout didn't go through. What was the consequence? One consequence was it had an impact on "how can John McCain be the leader of the party if he can't deliver the House?" That was bad. Two, and the most demolishing thing, is it kept this story alive for eight more days. Our candidate was acting as he always does. On Iraq—I'll lose my candidacy, we're not going to lose the war in America. On immigration—I'm not going to lose, I'm not going to be [former California Governor] Pete Wilson. We are going to be a different party. This is the core and the future of the Republican party, so I don't care what happens to my race. When you get to these big things, he steps away from the day-to-day political calculations. That's not our job in the campaign and so, in the day-to-day political calculation, what we said was, one, Senators Obama and McCain need to end up in the same place—we don't want there to be a distinction. And, two, Treasury Secretary Paulson was calling Senator Obama and us and saying, "Please, God, do not submarine this deal because if either one of you oppose this, this whole thing will collapse." Since these two men are the future president of the United States of America, we end up with three of the same guidelines for the bailout.

We are collapsing, this economy is collapsing, and this campaign is collapsing. We have one shot and that shot is to get this vote over with before anybody in America understands the whole horrible scope of what's happening. We have the vote, hope to God it stops, and we can get back to three weeks of the real campaign. If this goes on and becomes protracted, there is no way for the nominee of the same political party to survive what's going to happen, and now we are drifting towards 90 percent wrong track. We know many of the House members who shifted their votes because when they voted no, they were stunned because the small business community, their donors and others started calling them and saying, "Are you out of your mind? Don't you understand what it means when I can't borrow money from the bank and I can't get a bank loan?" The Democrats used to joke that they are Democrats, they are not part of an official organized party. But the job that they did to protect their nominee during those days was a very sophisticated political operation where the leadership for the House and Senate and the leadership of their party defended their nominee's interest. Our nominee was not as well served. We were told, and everyone was hoping, that if you do the bailout, things get better. Then, after the bailout, we drop another thousand points in the market. We had been winning white, college-educated men by a fairly traditional margin. Then we end up with the bailout and the thousand-point drop after the bailout, and we are down to single digits. In a Republican campaign, when you are only winning white, college-educated men by single digits, you are in a heap of trouble. One of the stunners in our exit poll is that we only won white, college-educated men by single digits, and I can tell you the day they hit the road—they hit the road the day after the bailout, which they didn't like anyway, when we dropped a thousand more points in the market. They said, "That's it, I'm trying something new."

JOHN KING: We had that remarkable moment where you had George W. Bush in the middle of the cabinet room with the two nominees for president at the table. It was certainly a picture you did not want at that point in the campaign, but it was such an unprecedented and remarkable moment. I'm wondering if they came out of that meeting and said anything—just a little bit of inside information, a little color, a little anecdote—about what it was like to be sitting at that table at that moment in time.

DAVID PLOUFFE: That it was a mess. It was not a confidence-inspiring session. Things are falling apart and it was not great. I got called by White House Chief of Staff Josh Bolten, who said, "We are going to have this meeting." They blamed it on the McCain campaign. They said McCain asked for it, so we have to do it. I said, "You guys are inserting yourselves in a presidential campaign." I wasn't suggesting whether this would be a positive or negative thing, but we were in the middle of debate prep, so we had to fly back to Washington. It was an interesting period. At the meeting, clearly things were falling apart a little bit and I don't think it sends a great message to the American people that the city is collapsing and those with some responsibility are not stepping up to the plate. So that was the takeaway—and that our party was much more unified—there is no doubt about that. We had a game plan going into the meeting, it was carefully orchestrated with our leadership, and everybody in the room was a unit. On the Republican side, people were storming out of the meeting. I think it was Senator Shelby who went out. It was not a good scene.

BILL MCINTURFF: I'm not here to speak for what John said. Candidates ought to be allowed the privacy of their confidences in the campaign, so this is not John McCain's inference. I think on the Republican side, talking to other people in the room, they were surprised by Senator Obama's tenor in his opening remarks. Some of our House members came out and said, "We couldn't carry the vote because Nancy Pelosi gave a partisan speech."[16] There was a feeling that, given the stakes, the average American voter was not going to be worried about the tenor of the speaker's remarks. But I think on the Republican side—again, I'm not speaking for John McCain—there was a sense of surprise about the tenor of Senator Obama's remarks. In a very

---

16. On September 29, 2008, after the House voted to defeat a seven-hundred-billion-dollar financial rescue package, House Republican leader John Boehner accused House Speaker Nancy Pelosi of delivering a partisan pre-vote speech that caused some Republicans to refuse to back the proposal. Pelosi had delivered a tough attack on Bush economic policies, calling it a "right-wing ideology of anything goes, no supervision, no discipline, no regulation" of financial markets.

difficult situation, they felt that that tenor made that situation a little more tenuous and difficult to deal with.

JEANNE CUMMINGS: When they announced they were suspending, what went on in your shop?

DAVID PLOUFFE: The two principals talked, and I called Rick Davis. They had discussed putting out a joint statement that says, "Here's the principles we agree on." I think they both had the same view of this—this can't collapse, we've got to get something done. They felt if the two nominees say we think this should pass and here are the principles, that that would be a helpful thing—Senator McCain and Senator Obama discussed that. I called Rick and Rick says, "Maybe we'll do a statement, but we are going to announce we're suspending our campaign and we're not going to attend the debate and McCain is on his way out to tell the press." We huddled. We were all together because we were prepping for the debate. It was a very quick discussion. It was, are we going to suspend the campaign? No. We thought the debate, and Senator Obama thought the debate, was more important than ever. People were very unsettled, and they needed to hear from their next president. You have to do more than one thing at a time. Our press conference was one of his strongest performances of the campaign. We certainly didn't take a poll. We didn't have more than a few minutes to decide. I'm always struck by sometimes less time is better. I think you can make crisper decisions, and that's what we did. It was a high-stakes two or three days, but I thought he handled himself well throughout that period, and I thought we made good decisions.

TREVOR POTTER: In answer to your earlier question about what was the plan when McCain came back to Washington, and was it scheduled in terms of optics and so forth, the answer really is that McCain had said this is not a campaign moment, this is a come together to solve a national problem moment, and it should be non–campaign related. So, to some extent, the campaign stepped back. McCain was in Washington, and he was in official meetings. We weren't in the middle of scheduling those and being involved with them. He was back in his role as a senator, he has a Senate staff, and so, rightly or wrongly, the campaign stepped back, consistent with having said we are suspending the campaign and this is not a political event. We were much less involved for what was about twenty-six hours. The campaign really felt this was the senator's and his official staff's to deal with.

FRED DAVIS: Steve Schmidt called me and said something during this time that gives a little clue as to the thinking on our side. It was, "Fred, if the terrorists had nuked Kansas City today, would we go forward with the debate?" The answer is obviously no, and our side felt that this failing of free market was equally as important. That's where it came from.

• THE DEBATES •

JOHN KING: Heading into the first debate, there was a lot of discussion about how important it would be because of the contrast between the two candidates. I spent a lot of time talking to Peter Hart, the pollster doing the NBC/*Wall Street Journal* stuff, who likened it repeatedly to 1980, saying that the mood in the country was for change and the only question was, like it was for Ronald Reagan back then, was this Barack Obama guy too risky? Was he too new? Was he too inexperienced? If he could get over the credibility and the safety threshold in the debates, principally in the first debate, that might close the door. David, did you view it that way going into the first debate? Did you guys have the same impression?

DAVID PLOUFFE: Yes, we did. We thought these debates were going to be enormously important. We did want the first debate to be about foreign policy because we thought the expectation from the media and from the public would be that that would be McCain's home field. We thought it was a secret strength for Obama. We thought Obama was very comfortable in this arena. Obviously, the stakes were raised by what was going on economically and the turmoil about whether there was going to be a debate or not. A lot of the press reaction, as the debate was going on, was somewhat mixed—McCain is doing pretty well, Obama is doing pretty well. But our sense was a couple of things. One, we thought that was a win for us because it was foreign policy. Two, we were dial-testing and we really liked what we were seeing. We saw what you guys were doing in the media, and our sense was we had just scored a big victory with voters. That was confirmed in some of the research afterwards. Those were a long five weeks after that, and filled with peril—we had Joe the Plumber[17] and two more debates and any number of things. But I do think that, at that point, it made it harder for them to dig out of the hole. What we saw then was people began to lock in. At some point, we stopped paying much attention to undecided voters and paid a lot more attention to the people who recently converted to Obama because in many states, they were the key to the election. We had gotten to forty-nine, fifty, fifty-one, and we held onto what we had. We had researched this, and

---

17. Joe Wurzelbacher, an Ohio man looking to buy a plumbing business, was videotaped questioning Barack Obama about his small business tax policy during a campaign stop in Toledo, Ohio. In the presidential debate on October 15, 2008, John McCain cited that exchange, calling him "Joe the Plumber," when asked to explain why his economic plan was better than his opponent's.

those people were sticking. Once they crossed the line, they were there. The "up-for-grabs" voters would respond to Ayers and other things a little bit differently than the people who had converted to Obama. They were locked in, and not much was going to pull them off. After the debate was when movement started. We would pay a lot more attention to individual states than to our national battleground tracker and, in some of these states, we hit the win number. In Colorado, Nevada and Virginia, we were where we needed to be.

BILL MCINTURFF: I think it was Sunday, September 29. The bad day. [*laughter*] That Sunday, we were shifting from the phone bank that we owned to the phone bank we kind of owned, and so we took our multistate tracker from the new center. They called me first at 4:00 in the morning with the number, and that number was horrible across the battleground states. Horrible, vomitous horrible. [*laughter*] As a skilled pollster, even at 4:00 in the morning, my instincts were sharp. I said, "We changed the phone center. I'm not going to panic until we get the other six state numbers from my own phone center." At 4:15 in the morning, they called me with the numbers on the six states from the phone center we owned. Those were worse. [*laughter*] When you are in a campaign and wrong tracks move to ninety, what you are waiting for is an implosion. You are waiting for things to collapse. We were negative seven to negative fourteen across every state on that one Sunday. Then you say, "Oh my God, this is it." Then we had another day like that two weeks later. Then we had the Monday after Colin Powell's endorsement.[18] So we had three days where the campaign just collapsed. What happened was that on all three occasions, including that week after Powell's endorsement, things got better—not enough to get over the top, but they definitely got better. So I think it's fair to say that when David Plouffe and David Axelrod say the campaign ended up being won between September 15 and September 29, I got the message on the twenty-ninth. It was kind of a psychiatric moment in my life history. [*laughter*] When I talk about the fifteenth, I say here's what happened. Number one, we were starting a campaign against Obama on the fifteenth. We started with the Chicago ad.[19] We weren't saying Obama is like that, but we were starting a campaign that had been laid out to walk people through this different narrative about who this guy is. To do that ad the day Lehman collapsed, instead of there being

---

18. On October 19, 2008, on NBC's *Meet the Press*, former Secretary of State, Ret. Joint Chiefs Chairman Colin Powell, endorsed Barack Obama for president.
19. On September 22, 2008, John McCain's campaign unveiled a campaign ad called "Chicago Machine," which the McCain campaign said "highlights the Chicago friends that surround Barack Obama, including a lobbyist, a convicted felon, a political godfather and a governor with a legacy of investigation."

four days of a discussion of essentially the second wave of "Celebrity," it just died. Number two, wrong track goes to ninety. Number three, your campaign implodes. There is no campaign anymore. There is only the economic collapse in America, and what do you want to say about that? Number four, what happened is we got stuck in that, and the Obama campaign had $105 million in the next two weeks. So they had enough money to rise above that, and we did not. I think the twenty-ninth was not determinative. I think it was their taking $105 million and then dropping it over the next two weeks in October.

SARAH SIMMONS: That was when the spending was the most dramatically out of sync. We were being outspent by about thirty million dollars. We had a big chart that had every media market, our daily tracking numbers from each of our polls and the spending in each of the places. There was this huge chart that we looked at every morning, and I just remember the column being red—every number was in the red in terms of spending by big digits, seven-digit numbers.

JOHN KING: When David says that was when they realized they didn't have to worry as much about the undecideds anymore, talk about how you change what you do in terms of whose doors you are knocking on, who you are calling on, how the candidate changes his message and how your ad mix might change.

DAVID PLOUFFE: We loaded up in the beginning of October and, proportionately, a little bit later. First, because of early vote—that was a good way to lock in people because we could get them to vote. Second, just to stay in front of people. They had made a decision and we wanted to keep a lot of positive information in front of them. We did two-minute ads throughout that whole period, which were a huge help to us because, one, it was positive when there was a lot of negative on the air, and, two, people responded very well to him and he was able to get into some detail. Around the economic crisis, we put on the two-minute ad of Obama talking directly to people about the economy and what he would do—it was enormously impactful in those markets. You keep communicating to the recent converts, but you turn more to conversion about getting them to vote. We put a huge priority on getting people who converted early to vote early, if the state allowed that. It was a huge priority for people who were more sporadic voters, but it was also a consistent finding. We would do focus groups on Ayers—we would show their ads and we would make our own ads about it. We would do an undecided voter group and a recent Obama convert group and, time and time again, the Obama people would say, "I'm not worried about it. I've made my decision." It was a source of great comfort for us because it was clear—not in all the states, but in most of the states—we were about at our win number. The spending was geared towards that a little bit. We thought early October was when most people were going to make up their minds, and so we wanted to pour it on then.

JOEL BENENSON: In that period, from September 15 to September 29, something that was also a very big factor on the numbers was Sarah Palin's interviews with Katie Couric, which transpired in that period. She went from having, in our poll, the highest favorable/unfavorable ratio to the worst of the four principals. By the time she got to the vice-presidential debate, in our polling, her negatives were almost as high as her positives—her unfavorable almost as high. This dynamic had a clear impact, particularly at a time when I would characterize Senator McCain as erratic—I'm only using the word *erratic* because it's the word we used in the campaign. The way he was jumping around at that point, coupled with her performance, multiplied the concern that voters had at that point. I think that those factors are what led up to the numbers on the twenty-ninth, plus a very strong performance by Obama in the first debate. The first couple of weeks of October solidified it. The vice-presidential debate on October 2 also helped because the threshold and the bar for Governor Palin in that debate was actually raised. She didn't just have to give a good performance, which she did—she gave a very good performance. She was now being held to having to pass a threshold test on being ready to be vice president and president. None of the data that we got back indicated that she won that metric. She wasn't even close to Senator Biden on that metric after that debate.

SARAH SIMMONS: I want to address Palin coming out of the convention. We went into the convention trailing dramatically with women and knowing that was the demographic where we had to make up ground. When we came out, we had a giant leap among some of the groups that David talked about earlier—suburban women and swing women that we knew we had to appeal to. We were saying the next thing they are going to do is attack her on abortion. And then, sure enough, within days, they were on the air—in the Philly market, in the Denver markets—saying she is going to repeal the right to choose. There was basically a three-pronged attack on her—it was abortion, it was experience, and there was an underlying debate about whether or not it was possible for a woman to raise a family and be a vice president, which I thought was shocking. I think the very direct and, frankly, visceral debate against her speaks to the importance of women as a voting bloc in terms of Democratic core coalitions. It was something that we were trying to respond to, but it was very dramatic in terms of the numbers.

JEANNE CUMMINGS: In the second presidential debate, McCain unveiled the housing package.[20] Can you talk a little bit about the strategy behind that? That evening when the fact sheet came out on it—and the fact sheet changed by morning—it raised questions about why you did it and how did that happen.

BILL MCINTURFF: I think it's fair to say the first two debates did not move the campaign forward. So there was a discussion about whether there was a way, heading into the third debate, to create some other additional way to talk about something positive that John McCain would do in the economy. This was an interesting campaign because when Sarah and I would look at our dials and our work the night of the debates, we could also read [Democratic pollster] Stan Greenberg's stuff and we could read CNN. So those mornings you were looking at all the other published polls, and our internal stuff was not very different than Greenberg's stuff and CNN. You might argue that if you took African American voters out of the equation and you looked at whites, Hispanics, Asians, maybe the first debates scored as a break even. But I don't think break even was pushing and helping moving our campaign forward. In the second debate, the numbers were weaker for the senator. So going into the third debate, there was a discussion about can there be an additional narrative? Can we have something else on the table so that, in addition to the debate, we have some other way to talk about something positive about Senator McCain? That was at least part of the rationale. It also fit into a broader discussion. As a Republican, how is it that we would help real people? It was a way to move away from hundreds of billions of dollars and from we are all going to buy these investment banks to no, the attempt we are going to make is to help real people with their homes. From a policy dimension, remembering that we have Joe the Plumber, it was going to be a focus on who is going to do what for real folks. Christian has given you a preview of how our donors, volunteers and others are feeling about the bailout vote and the bailout in general. Part of that anger was, "Let me get this right, they get hundreds of billions of dollars and I'm having these kind of troubles? Who is going to bail me out?"

SARAH SIMMONS: And, "I've lost my kid's college fund. I have no ability to get credit for my small business." The visceral anger is something that you see when you spend a lot of time talking to voters or a lot of time watch-

---

20. On October 7, 2008, in the second presidential debate, John McCain proposed a new three-hundred-billion dollar federal program to buy failing mortgages directly from homeowners and mortgage providers and replace them with government-backed fixed-rate mortgages.

ing focus groups and something that we really had to contend with. I think they were effective, coming out of the first debate, saying that not once did John McCain mention the middle class. One of our financial advisers was a former Wall Street guy, and I would constantly make him come in my office and explain it to me—explain it to me that I'm not going to be able to get a loan to buy a house, explain it to me, who doesn't make any money. That's the part where you try to communicate that visceral anger, and we were trying to draw that connection to the middle class.

JEANNE CUMMINGS: When McCain threw out that housing program, David, what was your response? In many ways, you all turned it to your advantage?

DAVID PLOUFFE: I'm trying to recollect. It sounded similar to something he had already said. I think our response that night was that it wasn't terribly new. Then, we saw that they had made an adjustment in the morning, and we just pounced on that, and it wasn't hard to get the press to focus on it. I think that's something that worked to our benefit. I think we said it's erratic and we tried to put things in that frame.

JOHN KING: I heard two or three times now the mention of Joe the Plumber. You are at the win point, as you put it, in so many states, and they seize on Joe the Plumber. It seems a little odd. Maybe in today's media world, it's normal and this will happen from now on out. When they seized on that, the first glance is what, no big deal? One-day story?

DAVID PLOUFFE: We just knew things were going to tighten at the end. We ended up winning by a larger national margin than we thought was possible, so we weren't going to win this by ten points. We immediately exposed voters to Joe the Plumber, and they weren't terribly interested in Joe the Plumber. It provided some energy to the base, and it gave McCain an ability to talk about the economy, but I think voters didn't see the connection to him. What does he really have to do with me? I think they were getting a little tired of how exposed he was, and that would come up in our focus groups—this election is not about Joe the Plumber. We checked on it almost every day, and it just wasn't a source of real concern in terms of what we were seeing.

JOEL BENENSON: It actually even came up in our first night's dial groups, during the course of the debate. I don't know how many times Senator McCain brought up Joe the Plumber. It was some very high number. By the end of the dial groups, each time he mentioned Joe the Plumber, the dials went down. Then we did a focus group session afterwards with people, and they said to us, "What does Joe the Plumber's life have to do with me?" It just wasn't connecting with them. We did continue to watch it because we didn't know if that was aberrational. I don't think we ever saw it have a big impact after that. Maybe it did help with the base, and it did gin up some of their supporters and keep them in there. But we never saw it working with the "up-for-grabs" voters and our recent converts.

TREVOR POTTER: On Joe the Plumber, there were two messages the campaign was intending to focus on there. One was Senator McCain's connection with working-class Americans and the backbone of the country. The other was the fact that what Joe the Plumber, in the original video discussion with Senator Obama, had been talking about was redistribution of wealth and Senator Obama's economic plan. The goal—which I think we were unsuccessful at—was to have a discussion about just exactly what do we know about Senator Obama's economic plan, and where does he want to take us as a country? Joe the Plumber was, in that sense, shorthand for a broader economic discussion, and I think we didn't get to that broader discussion.

JOEL BENENSON: If I could ask Bill a question in relation to that. It's pretty late in the campaign here to change an image that had been cultivated during the course of the campaign. We, at that point, were already dominating on who would be more likely to cut your taxes and, oddly enough, we were winning among middle- and working-class voters who were thinking that we would cut their taxes and not the Republican candidate. I don't know if you had that at that point but, if you did, it's pretty hard to change that image.

TREVOR POTTER: We thought that was odd, too.

JOEL BENENSON: It's hard to change that image from October 15 to November 4.

SARAH SIMMONS: Right, but it was our one opportunity to do that because we had Barack Obama on camera saying, "I am going to raise your taxes," to a regular guy who he encountered on the street. I would take issue with Joe the Plumber being something that didn't work. I actually think it gave our campaign a tremendous amount of energy. We ran ads on it that were some of the best-recalled ads that we did. We had people coming into our headquarters saying, "I am Donna the Dancer," and all sorts of people coming in with these iterations of how they were Joe the Plumber. People did get it. The other backlash part was that we exposed the public to who Joe the Plumber really was. Joe the Plumber was the guy in his front yard who encountered Barack Obama and suddenly there are investigations going on into whether or not he was paying child support and all sorts of other nefarious things that you were trying to dig up about this regular guy, who we didn't expose. We didn't go out and say, "Wow, Joe the Plumber, you are going to be a public figure." We did try to exploit on that opportunity, but I don't think we went out and found this guy and said, "Okay, we are going to hold him up as somebody we vetted." He was held, frankly, to the same standard as Sarah Palin was. I think it ended up not working out so badly for him. But I think at first it kind of sucked for him. [*laughter*]

JOEL BENENSON: Keep in mind you had a guy who was a plumber who was giving network interviews. How often does that happen? I mean he was capitalizing on it himself, Sarah. [*laughter*]

BILL MCINTURFF: We had a campaign we were going to start against Senator Obama on September 15. That Chicago ad was the first of what was going to be a sequence of advertising to have a narrative against Senator Obama. That narrative never happened. We never had the background, and we never filled in the blank. So there were only two things left, and two things left that had some salience, because what people can't dispute is that he said it. There were two ads that had some impact, and one ad was where he actually said this, and what does that mean? When you are a Republican candidate and you are starting to get squished on who will cut your taxes, you are in big trouble. The fact that we could get some of that back and, you have to remember by the way, we were losing during some of this period by eight to twelve points. When you are losing by eight to twelve points, losing by four or five is a better day. So your first job is to get a campaign back in contact—to put yourself at a prayer of winning. We were winning white, college-educated men by seven. If we were winning by twenty, this would be a four-point race. The other ad was the Senator Biden ad that we did with his quote about, "Sure, this president is going to be challenged."[21] Here's how and why I felt happy—they finally had to run an ad responding to our ad. I said, "We haven't thought about this, but it has probably been five weeks since those guys have had to do a single thing in response to our campaign." In a presidential campaign, if you said to me, "Let me get this right, your opponent has not had to respond to anything you've done in

---

21. On October 19, 2008, at a fundraiser in Seattle, Biden said, "Mark my words. It will not be six months before the world tests Barack Obama like they did John Kennedy. The world is looking. We're about to elect a brilliant forty-seven-year-old senator president of the United States of America. Remember I said it standing here, if you don't remember anything else I said. Watch, we're going to have an international crisis, a generated crisis, to test the mettle of this guy. I promise you it will occur. As a student of history and having served with seven presidents, I guarantee you it's going happen. I can give you at least four or five scenarios from where it might originate."

five weeks?" that doesn't bode well. I was so thrilled. Real people said, "Say what you want, it's his VP and he is saying things are going to be riskier." The point that I'm suggesting is that because we did not fill in September 15 through October 15 with the campaign that should have been run—when you've lost those three or four weeks of background—you are left with, what would people be willing to believe? The only thing that we tried that they were willing to believe is what they would say themselves. Going from where we were the day after the Colin Powell endorsement, which was another very difficult day, we were negative eleven or twelve on our stuff. Negative eleven or twelve on October 19 and October 20, you've got a very short time left, and you had better get very focused at how at least do we get back to something that puts us in the contact or range that keeps a pulse in this campaign. On October 19, it was very possible for people to have a discussion on the campaign, saying, "Is this it? Do we have a pulse or—with this kind of number after this kind of endorsement and with everything else over the last four-plus weeks—is this it?" It's a credit to Senator McCain, with how volatile this race was and what happened internally, that we found one more way to try to get this campaign back into contact.

• THE RACE QUESTION •

JOHN KING: I want to stop for a few minutes and spend a little time on this issue because anyone who reads this book years down the road will think that we are idiots if we don't bring it up and discuss it—the race question. From a campaign's strategic and tactical question, is there anything on McCain's side that you did specifically because you were running against an African American? Or anything in your ads, in your message, anywhere, that you could not do that you might have been able to do? Language? Pictures? Anything? Imagery?

FRED DAVIS: Start with language. Almost any word, pick a word, king. We went through this filter of, "Will they be able to call that racist? Will the press call that racist?" Sarah and I oftentimes talked about how many hands we had tied behind our back in this race, and that was one of the big ones. It was nothing that you guys did to cause that. It was just something that we had to be so incredibly overly sensitive on. Some words that to this day— *risky*—I'm from California, but I don't see the connection between risky and racist. There were a lot of words like that. We have a long list of them.

SARAH SIMMONS: The first person who called Barack Obama "the one" was Oprah. We have footage of Oprah, in our very first version of "The One" video, and we looked at it again and we said, "No, we can't do that." There was an extra layer of scrutiny by the people who were involved in the television and radio advertising and our direct mail. All of those people are veterans of a lot of campaigns, so nobody is naive about the power of images or language. But there was an extra level of scrutiny.

FRED DAVIS: It kind of went over the top, I thought. We had to be so careful that you were left with about five words. Now you have twelve-and-a-half seconds and five words you can say. [*laughter*]

SARAH SIMMONS: Maybe we were overly sensitive to it, but when Barack Obama said, "They are going to say I don't look like other presidents on the dollar bill," I think that the reality was there is a human factor to all of these campaigns. None of us wanted John McCain to be in a position where he was being called racist. There was a very public profile that the campaign leadership was in, from being featured in a million dollars' worth of advertising, and I didn't want my friend Steve Schmidt to be called a racist on national television or my friend Rick Davis to be called a racist on national television—that's not a cool position to put the human beings that are involved in the campaign in. So there was a high degree of sensitivity because that wasn't going to be good for us. It's not good to get into a racial debate when the people that you are challenged with are young people. Any voter that was going to not vote for Barack Obama because he was black, they decided that when they found out Barack Obama was African American. So there was no benefit to us strategically to go that route, and I don't think it's a place where any of us were comfortable.

BILL MCINTURFF: Our candidate instinctively did not want to run a race that ruptured any racial flow in this country because you are going to be one of two people who is going to be president of the United States of America. Given John McCain's career and everything he has done—essentially imploding his own race over immigration—I felt there was a little unfair standard. We are trying to make sure we don't rupture the standard, and they've got an ad on the air in Spanish where they had Rush Limbaugh calling Latino folks stupid and lazy and saying, "That's John McCain's friend." Jim Margolis was very gracious. He said, "Hey, we did that for the press, we all made a lot of ads, you guys went overboard, we went overboard." But I think it's very important—and this is where we should feel proud of our country—that our country had this powerful thing happen. We were going to elect either the first woman president, the first African American president, or the first woman vice president. We were guaranteed something historic was going to happen.

We privately recorded the race and gender of all of our interviewers and then all the people interviewed. We have thousands of interviews. We have African Americans interviewing whites, African Americans interviewing African

Americans. We looked at all those numbers and there was no difference in the ballot. Despite the race and gender of these interviewers, whoever they were talking to, they were getting the same numbers. When the campaign said, "Is there in fact some secret vote? Is there a Bradley effect?" what I said is, "If there were, we would be picking it up through thousands of interviews, and I think what's going to happen is that Barack's going to get what he gets in the tracking." Unfortunately, he got fifty-two, which is what he got in the tracking. I didn't think any of those undecided voters were going to vote for this guy, and my argument was very simple. If you spend four hundred million dollars and he is ahead by this much, and people have been told for weeks and weeks and weeks that he is going to be the next president, if you wanted to vote for him, you would have done so by now. I think there is zero evidence of anybody in the last minute voting against him because of race. I'm not saying race is not a huge issue in America. I'm not saying there aren't people who made that decision, but they weren't the people who were the undecided voters.

Here's the other thing. When these guys would say, correctly, the African American vote is going to go from ninety-two to eight or from ninety-seven to three and it's going to go up by two or three points, that shifts states. North Carolina is in play because of this. Georgia is possible. The other thing that was happening in states was that margins were shifting because of this incredibly unique coalition that Senator Obama put together. You add on top of that a forty-, thirty-five-, thirty-eight-point margin with Latinos, and my point to my party is really clear. All this crap about whether McCain ran a good campaign—John McCain's campaign performed and got the same percentage of the white vote as George Bush did in 2000. What happened is in eight years, our party and our country has moved to be more Latino and more African American. So instead of being tied, you are down six and a half or seven points. That is a powerful, huge story. John McCain, with everything that we've talked about here for two days, given the national environment, performed at the same level as George Bush in 2000 with white voters, and he went from tied to minus six and a half. That is an extraordinary story about his coalition, his unique appeal, and the demographic change in this country. It says powerful things about my party. Our party had better get the memo very quickly about what's at stake in terms of the Latino community and people of color in this country, or we are not going to win elections.

JEANNE CUMMINGS: Can we just reverse that question? David, was there anything you didn't do because your candidate was an African American or did do because of it? They've explained what they didn't do.

DAVID PLOUFFE: We talked about this at some length throughout the course of the campaign. It really was not the factor people think it was. First of all, it was what it was. He was an African American candidate when he ran. Our assumption, or at least our hope, was that he would be able to appeal to folks and race would not be a big factor. We had a lot of experience in the primaries and the caucuses—there was no Bradley effect. There was a question of whether the Bradley effect actually existed twenty-six years ago, but it certainly doesn't exist now. We were able to appeal to white voters. Coming out of the primary, it was we are not going to do well with white, blue-collar voters or older women or Hispanics. Our fundamental belief was it may take a while, but all that was going to correct itself. There was a twenty-seven point swing in Florida with Hispanics between 2004 and 2008, which is why we won the state of Florida, so a lot of that was a misnomer. Were there some people who didn't vote for him because of his race? Sure, but I think it was pretty minimal. I do think there were positive effects with younger voters of all races and with African American turnout that can't be overstated. We went into states like Indiana, where it's not a huge population but enough that we thought we could win Indiana by a point or two. In North Carolina. In Virginia. We were always bullish on Florida because we thought there were a lot of African Americans who did not vote in 2004 who we could get out and register. We ran a lot of advertisements that talked about his values and his culture and where he came from. Honestly, that was less about race. It was just that we knew they were going to try to paint him as a liberal Democrat and someone out of the mainstream—who is Barack Obama? Maybe race was a small part of that, but less so than just that we really had to ground him.

• THE ELECTORAL MAP •

JOHN KING: Someone else will write the book about the government that will begin in a few short weeks, but when you've closed the book on the campaign, is this Barack Obama's map, electorally, or is it a new Democratic map? Meaning that when Barack Obama fades from the stage, what do he and his party have to do to make it a Democratic map, or is it not one? Then, lastly, a very simple question—is there anything you think should be in this discussion that you have not been asked at any of the sessions that you want to say before we all say thank you?

DAVID PLOUFFE: We talked a little bit about the role technology played in this campaign. It was a remarkable thing. In four years from now, I don't think we really know what's going to change, but a lot will. I think that's important. Our grassroots campaign, our ability to raise money, the use of technology—we had great people like Joe Rospars who put that together and helped strategize—was a focal point of our campaign the whole time.

But you can have the machinery and if you don't have the magic, it's not go-ing to matter. He inspired people. He brought new people in. I think there's going to be a lot of people, sadly, who will try and replicate what we did in 2010, and I think they are going to find some difficulty doing that.

On the map, there are some structural changes going on out there that are pretty powerful. I do think Indiana and North Carolina are probably Obama states more so than a huge change. I do think the West is chang-ing. I think Arizona is going to be a big battleground in 2012. I think Montana will remain in play. I think Virginia has changed in fundamental ways. In Virginia, I think maybe another Democrat could have won it—we won by six points—but there is no doubt that our appeal to the suburban Northern Virginia voters, what we did in the African American community, and younger voters, of which there is a lot of growth there, was somewhat unique to Obama. There are some changes going on there that are good for our party, although that can change. This is a dynamic process and four years from now, we'll see if we are where we are now with Hispanic vot-ers and younger voters. If we are, it's going to be hard for the Republican party to win. We spent a lot of time on this in the campaign, but less than I would have liked, on how voters made their decisions and got information. It's changing very rapidly. We all need to understand that a little bit more because the TV ads and the news media, at least in a presidential campaign, became a little less important. It was a much more dynamic process. People are having a lot more conversations in their lives, they are e-mailing a lot more people, they are on the Web a lot—there's a lot going on out there, particularly with people under forty. We were mindful of that, but I don't think we understand it as well as we need to.

JOEL BENENSON: The only point I would make on the map, since I'm a pollster, is I might push North Carolina a little bit. If you look at the book that Rudy Teixeira and John Judis wrote on the emerging Democratic ma-jority back in 2000—and it looked like it was obsolete when the Democrats didn't win in 2000—the two states that they called out and focused on were Virginia and North Carolina because of certain dynamics. In Virginia, we've seen two Democratic governors and two Democratic United States senators elected. In North Carolina, we won, barely, a Democrat in the Senate. I would watch that state. I agree with David that the Southwest is changing and it does pose some problems for the Republican party.

BILL MCINTURFF: We have already seen in Georgia and Louisiana that it's going to be hard to maintain the level of composition of African Americans without Senator Obama on the ballot. I think that will continue. But my party has to understand this Latino issue, Independents, younger voters and moder-ates. This is not one cycle that it was bad. This is two cycles. So this baloney debate about whether we are a center, right-center or left country—here is a very simple premise. It doesn't matter which direction you are on the opposite end because we've lost the center two cycles in a row. You've got to look at the hard, cold facts. There is a composition in the American electorate that is critical for winning elections, and we got smoked twice. There are elements that are unique to the president-elect's, in terms of composition, but the basic structure is not just the cycle. I think we have to deal with that. Why am I a Republican? I believe in markets. The Democrats went through the eighties saying, "It's just Ronald Reagan, he had a unique appeal." They said, "Wait until we get to George Bush." Then, in 1988, the guy creamed. And then, guess what? A candidate came along and said, "We are going to be a new Democratic party because we've gotten smoked three cycles in a row." It can take political parties a long time, but there is a certain element of market force, which is if you keep losing, sooner or later people say it's time to change. I know Sarah and I and Senator McCain and others would be devoted to making sure that we don't go one more cycle or two more cycles through another presidential before we get the message that change is coming. It certainly has to come to our party and its candidate and what we run on.

SARAH SIMMONS: As a veteran of a 2006 election that was successful with Arnold Schwarzenegger, one of his lines that was hilarious that he always used was, sometimes the Republican ideas aren't doing so well at the box office. That market force that Bill talks about is something that our party has to address. 2006 was something of a wake-up call. There were a lot of other factors involved at the end of the election that people wanted to blame things on, but I think there's a lot of work to be done. It is young voters and it is Latino voters. We have all the Internet tools—maybe not every last gadget that you guys have, but we are aware of those things and we are using those things—but the fact of the matter is we were losing voters under forty by dramatic margins. Did we have as much of a Facebook presence? Well, we had a Facebook presence, but the voters that were on Facebook weren't our core supporters. So I don't think it's so much about the tools and tactics as it is about global messaging.

FRED DAVIS: To take nothing away, these guys did a spectacular job. We had the same tools, they had the same tools, and somehow they used those tools a bit better. They had one of the great candidates that I've ever run against in my life. The answer to your question for me, John, would be both. It's Democrat a bit but, boy, did they have somebody that brought the bacon home. I look at our party right now and I don't know who that's going to be next time around.

BILL MCINTURFF: Tell me if you find one. [*laughter*] In terms of what I'd like noted is, when you said what did we miss? There was that raft of

The Obama team analyzes the long-term impact of Obama's
win on the electoral map.

articles in early October about why is John McCain's campaign such a terrible campaign? [Campaign strategist] Mark McKinnon said, "Barack Obama is Secretariat and he is running against Seabiscuit—these are two fabulous candidates and one of them has got a little bit of a handicap." So, my only notation would be, in my secret dream, in a secret world, I would just say, "God, couldn't you just collapse the American economy in December?" I would have liked to run this campaign where we collapse the American economy on December 15 instead of September 15, and I would have liked to run with close to equal money. I have been working with John McCain since 1991. He is an extraordinarily gifted candidate. He is an American hero, and I believe that he, uniquely out of any Republican, dragged this campaign and dragged himself farther, and I acknowledge and appreciate all that they did for that margin. I believe that John McCain is an underrecognized asset still and deserves extraordinary credit for finding a way to win the nomination and keeping himself in play as long as he did. It is a credit to what a uniquely gifted candidate he is because I don't think any single person in this party, other than John McCain, could have accomplished what he accomplished. That's what I would like to note.

DAVID PLOUFFE: We agree with that.

BILL PURCELL: On behalf of everyone here, I want to thank these campaign managers and campaign teams.

2008 Campaign Timeline

• 2005 •

February 7   Vice President Dick Cheney says he will not run for president.

• 2006 •

April 17   Mike Gravel states his intention to run for president.

October 12   Governor Mark Warner states that he will not run for president.

October 22   Senator Barack Obama tells NBC's Tim Russert that he has considered the possibility of running for president.

October 30   Congressman Duncan Hunter becomes the first Republican to announce his intention to form a presidential exploratory committee.

November 9   Governor Tom Vilsack files papers with the FEC announcing that he's a candidate for the Democratic nomination.

November 13   Mayor Rudolph Giuliani forms a presidential exploratory committee.

November 15   Governor Tommy Thompson announces he will form a presidential exploratory committee.

November 16   Senator John McCain forms a presidential exploratory committee.

November 29   Senator Bill Frist states he will not run for president.

December 3   Senator Evan Bayh announces the formation of a presidential exploratory committee.

December 3   Senator Tom Daschle withdraws his name from the presidential race.

December 4	Senator Sam Brownback forms a presidential exploratory committee.
December 11	Congressman Dennis Kucinich announces his plans to run for president.
December 15	Senator Bayh withdraws from the race.
December 28	Senator John Edwards officially kicks off his campaign in New Orleans.

• 2007 •

January 3	Governor Mitt Romney files papers to form a presidential exploratory committee.
January 8	Governor Romney raises $6.5 million in one day of fund-raising.
January 9	Governor Jim Gilmore files papers to form a presidential exploratory committee.
January 11	Senator Christopher Dodd announces his candidacy and files papers for a campaign committee.
January 11	Congressman Ron Paul forms a presidential exploratory committee.
January 12	Congressman Hunter forms a presidential exploratory committee.
January 15	Congressman Tom Tancredo announces he will file papers to form a presidential exploratory committee.
January 16	In a Web video, Senator Obama announces he has filed papers to form a presidential exploratory committee.
January 20	Senator Brownback formally announces his candidacy for president.
January 20	Senator Hillary Clinton announces her candidacy via an Internet video.
January 21	Governor Bill Richardson announces the formation of a presidential exploratory committee.
January 24	Senator John Kerry says he won't run for president.
January 25	Congressman Hunter officially enters the Republican presidential race.
January 29	Governor Mike Huckabee files papers to form a presidential exploratory committee.
January 31	Senator Joe Biden formally becomes a presidential candidate.
February 5	Mayor Giuliani files papers with the FEC declaring his candidacy.
February 10	Senator Obama formally announces his candidacy.

February 13	Governor Romney officially announces his candidacy.
February 21	Democratic candidates participate in a presidential forum in Carson City, Nevada.
February 23	Governor Vilsack withdraws from the presidential race.
March 11	Senator Fred Thompson announces that he is considering a bid for the presidency.
March 12	Congressman Paul officially announces his candidacy for president.
March 22	Senator Edwards's wife, Elizabeth, announces that her cancer has returned but her husband's campaign will go on.
April 1	Governor Thompson announces that he is a candidate for president.
April 2	Congressman Tancredo announces that he is a candidate for president.
April 23–25	Senator McCain kicks off his presidential campaign with stops in New Hampshire, South Carolina, Iowa and Arizona.
April 26	Democratic candidates participate in a debate in Orangeburg, South Carolina.
May 3	Republican candidates participate in a debate in Simi Valley, California.
May 15	Republican candidates participate in a debate in Columbia, South Carolina.
May 21	New Mexico Governor Bill Richardson formally enters the race.
May 23	An internal campaign memo urging Senator Clinton to skip the Iowa caucuses is leaked.
June 3	Democratic candidates participate in a debate in Manchester, New Hampshire.
June 5	Republican candidates participate in a debate in Manchester, New Hampshire.
June 28	Democratic candidates participate in a debate at Howard University.
July 10	McCain campaign manager Terry Nelson and chief strategist John Weaver announce their resignations from the McCain campaign.
July 14	Jim Gilmore withdraws from the presidential race.
July 23	Democratic candidates participate in the CNN/YouTube Presidential Debate at The Citadel in Charleston, South Carolina.
August 4	Clinton, Edwards, Obama, and Richardson participate in the progressive bloggers' conference Yearly Kos.

August 5	Republican candidates participate in a debate in Des Moines, Iowa.
August 9	Democratic candidates participate in a forum on LGBT issues hosted by Human Rights Campaign and Logo TV in Los Angeles, California.
August 12	Governor Thompson withdraws from the race.
August 19	Democratic candidates participate in a debate in Des Moines, Iowa.
September 5	Republican candidates participate in a debate in Durham, New Hampshire.
September 6	Senator Thompson announces his candidacy for president.
September 9	Democratic candidates participate in a debate in Coral Gables, Florida.
September 10	Nebraska Senator Chuck Hagel announces he will not run for president.
September 26	Democratic candidates participate in a debate in Hanover, New Hampshire.
September 27	Republican candidates participate in a debate in Baltimore, Maryland.
September 29	After months of speculation about a potential run for president, Newt Gingrich declares he will not run.
October 9	Republican candidates participate in a debate in Dearborn, Michigan.
October 12	Governor Thompson endorses Rudy Giuliani.
October 19	Senator Brownback withdraws from the presidential race.
October 23	TV star Chuck Norris endorses Mike Huckabee.
October 30	Democratic candidates participate in a debate in Philadelphia, Pennsylvania.
November 7	Senator Brownback endorses John McCain.
November 15	Democratic candidates participate in a debate in Las Vegas, Nevada.
November 28	Republican candidates participate in a CNN/YouTube debate in St. Petersburg, Florida.
December 6	Mitt Romney delivers a major speech on religion at George H. W. Bush's Presidential Library.
December 8	Oprah Winfrey joins Senator Obama on the campaign trail for a series of rallies in Iowa and South Carolina.
December 9	Republican candidates participate in a debate in Coral Gables, Florida.
December 12	Republican candidates participate in a debate in Johnston, Iowa.
December 13	Democratic candidates participate in a debate in Johnston, Iowa.

December 15	The *Des Moines Register* endorses Hillary Clinton.
December 16	Senator Joe Lieberman endorses John McCain.
December 17	Ron Paul raises six million dollars in one day.
December 20	Congressman Tancredo drops out of the Republican presidential race.
December 21	The *Boston Herald* endorses John McCain.
December 29	The *Concord Monitor* endorses Hillary Clinton.

• 2008 •

January 3	Obama wins the Democratic Iowa caucuses and Governor Huckabee wins the Republican Iowa caucuses.
January 3	Senator Dodd and Senator Biden drop out of the Democratic race.
January 5	Republican and Democratic candidates participate in back-to-back debates in Manchester, New Hampshire.
January 6	Governor Mitt Romney wins the Wyoming caucuses.
January 8	Senator Hillary Clinton wins the New Hampshire primary.
January 8	Senator John McCain wins the New Hampshire primary.
January 10	Republican candidates participate in a debate in Myrtle Beach, South Carolina.
January 10	Governor Richardson drops out of the race.
January 15	Governor Romney and Senator Clinton win the Michigan primary.
January 19	Governor Romney wins the Nevada caucuses.
January 19	Congressman Hunter drops out of the race.
January 19	Clinton wins more votes in Nevada caucuses, but Obama wins more delegates.
January 21	Democratic candidates participate in a debate in Myrtle Beach, South Carolina.
January 22	Senator Thompson drops out of the race.
January 23	Congressman Hunter endorses Mike Huckabee.
January 24	Republican candidates participate in a debate in Boca Raton, Florida.
January 24	Congressman Kucinich drops out of the Democratic race.
January 25	Florida Senator Mel Martinez endorses John McCain.
January 26	Senator Obama wins the South Carolina primary.
January 26	Florida Governor Charlie Crist endorses John McCain.
January 27	Senator Ted Kennedy and Caroline Kennedy endorse Barack Obama.
January 29	Senator McCain and Senator Clinton win the Florida primaries.

January 30	Senator Edwards drops out of the race.
January 30	Mayor Giuliani withdraws from the race and endorses John McCain.
January 30	Republican candidates debate at the Reagan Presidential Library in Simi Valley, California.
February 5	Twenty-four primary contests are held on Super Tuesday.
February 6	Senator Clinton's campaign announces that she loaned her campaign five million dollars.
February 7	Governor Romney withdraws from the race.
February 9	Congressman Paul rules out a third-party bid and begins to scale back his campaign.
February 10	Clinton campaign manager Patti Solis Doyle resigns and is replaced by longtime Clinton aide Maggie Williams.
February 12	Senator McCain rejects FEC matching funds.
February 12	Senator Obama and Senator McCain win the Maryland, Virginia and District of Columbia primaries.
February 14	Governor Romney endorses John McCain.
February 15	Senator McCain challenges Senator Obama to use public financing if he wins the Democratic nomination.
February 21	Democratic candidates participate in a debate in Austin, Texas.
February 26	Democratic candidates participate in a debate in Cleveland, Ohio.
February 27	Congressman John Lewis switches his endorsement from Hillary Clinton to Barack Obama.
February 28	Mayor Michael Bloomberg officially rejects speculation of a possible run for the presidency as an Independent.
March 4	Senator McCain wins Texas, Ohio, Rhode Island and Vermont and passes the 1,191-delegate mark.
March 4	Governor Huckabee withdraws from the GOP presidential race.
March 4	Senator Clinton wins primaries in Ohio and Texas.
March 5	President George W. Bush endorses John McCain.
March 18	Senator Obama gives a speech on race relations in America.
March 21	Governor Richardson endorses Barack Obama.
March 26	Senator Gravel ends his run for the Democratic nomination and announces his intentions to run for the nomination of the Libertarian Party.
March 28	Senator McCain launches his first general election television ad.
April 11	Senator Clinton loans her campaign five million dollars.

April 16	Democratic candidates participate in a debate in Philadelphia, Pennsylvania.
April 22	Senator Clinton wins the Pennsylvania primary.
May 6	Senator Obama wins the North Carolina primary, and Senator Clinton wins the Indiana primary. NBC's Tim Russert says, "We now know who the Democratic nominee will be."
May 13	Senator Clinton wins the West Virginia primary.
May 14	Senator Edwards endorses Barack Obama.
May 31	The Democratic National Committee's Rules and Bylaws Committee decides to give half-votes to delegates from Michigan and Florida.
June 3	Senator Clinton wins the South Dakota primary, and Senator Obama wins the Montana primary.
June 7	Senator Clinton suspends her candidacy.
June 12	Congressman Paul announces that he is suspending his GOP presidential bid.
June 19	Senator Obama announces that he will reject public financing.
July 30	The McCain campaign launches "Celeb" television ad.
August 16	Senator McCain and Senator Obama make a joint appearance at Pastor Rick Warren's Saddleback Church in California.
August 27	Senator Obama is officially nominated for president by the Democratic Party.
August 29	Governor Sarah Palin is selected by McCain as his choice for the Republican vice-presidential candidate.
September 3	Senator McCain is officially nominated for president by the Republican Party.
September 11	Senator McCain and Senator Obama make a joint visit to Ground Zero.
September 24	Senator McCain announces that he is suspending his campaign.
September 25	Senator McCain and Senator Obama participate in a meeting at the White House with President Bush and congressional leaders on the economic crisis.
September 26	The first presidential debate is held at the University of Mississippi in Oxford.
October 2	The vice-presidential debate is held at Washington University in St Louis, Missouri.
October 7	The second presidential debate is held at Belmont University in Nashville, Tennessee.

October 13	Bill and Hillary Clinton make their first joint campaign stop for Obama.
October 15	The third presidential debate is held at Hofstra University in Hempstead, New York.
October 19	Ret. Gen. Colin Powell endorses Barack Obama on *Meet the Press.*
October 23	Senator Obama stops campaigning for forty-eight hours to visit his ailing grandmother in Hawaii.
October 23	*The New York Times* endorses Barack Obama.
October 29	Senator Obama runs a thirty-minute prime-time ad.
October 30	Al Gore campaigns in Florida for Obama.
November 3	Senator McCain visits seven cities in seven states for the last push before election day, and Senator Obama finishes his campaign in Virginia.
November 4	Senator Obama is elected the forty-fourth president of the United States.

INDEX